Conflicts in the Knowledge Society

In *Conflicts in the Knowledge Society*, Sebastian Haunss demonstrates how conflicts related to the international system of intellectual property have resulted in new cleavages in the knowledge society. He argues that new collective actors have emerged from these conflicts with the ability to contest the existing dominant order. With a focus on political opportunity structures, collective action networks and framing strategies, he combines a theoretical discussion of social change in the knowledge society with empirical analyses of four recent developments: software patents in Europe, access to medicines, Creative Commons licensing and Pirate Parties.

SEBASTIAN HAUNSS is a senior researcher in political science at the University of Bremen, where his research interests are social conflicts and political mobilizations in the knowledge society, changes in political and economic legitimacy, social networks and social movements.

Cambridge Intellectual Property and Information Law

As its economic potential has rapidly expanded, intellectual property has become a subject of front-rank legal importance. *Cambridge Intellectual Property and Information Law* is a series of monograph studies of major current issues in intellectual property. Each volume contains a mix of international, European, comparative and national law, making this a highly significant series for practitioners, judges and academic researchers in many countries.

Series editors
Lionel Bently
Herchel Smith Professor of Intellectual Property Law, University of Cambridge

William R. Cornish
Emeritus Herchel Smith Professor of Intellectual Property Law, University of Cambridge

Advisory editors
François Dessemontet, *Professor of Law, University of Lausanne*
Paul Goldstein, *Professor of Law, Stanford University*
The Rt Hon. Sir Robin Jacob, *Hugh Laddie Professor of Intellectual Property, University College, London*

A list of books in the series can be found at the end of this volume.

Conflicts in the Knowledge Society

The Contentious Politics of
Intellectual Property

Sebastian Haunss

CAMBRIDGE
UNIVERSITY PRESS

CAMBRIDGE UNIVERSITY PRESS
Cambridge, New York, Melbourne, Madrid, Cape Town,
Singapore, São Paulo, Delhi, Mexico City

Cambridge University Press
The Edinburgh Building, Cambridge CB2 8RU, UK

Published in the United States of America by Cambridge University Press,
New York

www.cambridge.org
Information on this title: www.cambridge.org/9781107036420

First published 2013

Printed and bound in the United Kingdom by the MPG Books Group

A catalogue record for this publication is available from the British Library

Library of Congress Cataloguing in Publication data
Haunss, Sebastian.
  Conflicts in the knowledge society : the contentious politics of intellectual
  property / Sebastian Haunss.
    pages   cm. – (Cambridge intellectual property and information
  law ; 20)
  Includes bibliographical references and index.
  ISBN 978-1-107-03642-0 (hardback)
  1. Intellectual property–Political aspects.   I. Title.
  K1401.H38 2013
  346.04'8–dc23
  2012044895

ISBN 978-1-107-03642-0 Hardback

Contents

Figures

Tables

Acknowledgements

The plan to write this book grew out of a puzzle: being aware of the relative rarity of coordinated political protest at the European level (Imig and Tarrow 2001), I was wondering how, of all things, software patents were able to galvanize a truly European protest mobilization and to create a political conflict of surprising scale. How was it possible that an issue that seemed to be the prototype of arcane was able to mobilize hundreds of thousands on the internet and thousands, in more traditional forms of protest, on the streets of Brussels, Strasbourg and other European cities?

When I started to take a closer look, first at the software patents conflict, and then at a broader range of conflicts which were developing around issues of intellectual property rights, only a handful of social scientists had begun to explore the politics of intellectual property, and their main focus was the inclusion of these rights into international trade agreements. But it turned out that a growing number of junior and some senior scholars with a variety of disciplinary backgrounds had also become aware of the growing politicization of intellectual property, and the ongoing exchange with them in a series of conferences and workshops sponsored by the European Consortium for Political Research (ECPR), the American Political Science Association (APSA) and others, provided the intellectual stimulation to proceed with my project. Some of them have read and discussed single chapters or even large parts of this book's manuscript in its various stages of production. For this, I'm most grateful to (in alphabetical order) Jan Biesenbender, Thomas Eimer, Jeanette Hofmann, Katharina Holzinger, Kai Huter, Lars Kohlmorgen, Ingrid Schneider, Volker Schneider, Susan Sell and Peter Yu. Their feedback and critical comments have been invaluable to iron out a number of mistakes and to unentangle my argumentation.

Writing this book would have been much harder, if not impossible, without the legwork and help of my student assistants Kamil Kolata, Susanne Münn, Jonte Plambeck, Fabian Reichert and Anna Schwarz who dug through endless amounts of information in newspaper archives and websites and coded, sorted and processed this data, allowing me to work with it in meaningful ways. I'm also grateful to my interview partners who openly shared their knowledge and their views about the conflicts this book is about, and who provided me with background information that only longtime participants in these conflicts have. A special thank you goes to Sigrid Quack and Leonard Dobusch for sharing – in a truly open access spirit – their interview transcripts with core activists of the Creative Commons project.

Beyond intellectual support I'm most grateful to Katharina Holzinger for hiring me as a PostDoc researcher and for supporting my research for many years. Financial support was also provided in the form of research grants from the Fritz Thyssen Foundation, the Hans Böckler Foundation, and the University of Konstanz's Young Scholar Fund. Without these grants this book would never have seen the light of day.

Abbreviations

A2K	Access to knowledge
ACT UP	AIDS Coalition to Unleash Power
ACTA	Anti-Counterfeiting Trade Agreement
ACTN	Advisory Committee for Trade Negotiations
AEL	Association Electronique Libre
AFUL	Association Francophone des Utilisateurs de Linux et des Logiciels Libres
AIDS	Acquired immune deficiency syndrome
AIPPI	International Association for the Protection of Intellectual Property
ALDE	Alliance of Liberals and Democrats for Europe
ANVISA	Agência Nacional de Vigilância Sanitária
ARV	Antiretroviral
ASCAP	American Society of Composers, Authors and Publishers
BDI	Bundesverband der Deutschen Industrie
BGH	Bundesgerichtshof
BITKOM	Bundesverband Informationswirtschaft, Telekommunikation und neue Medien
BKA	Bundeskriminalamt
BMGF	Bill and Melinda Gates Foundation
BMS	Bristol-Myers Squibb
BSA	Business Software Alliance
BUKO	Bundeskoordination Internationalismus
CAFC	Court of Appeals for the Federal Circuit
CC	Creative Commons
CCC	Chaos Computer Club
CCTV	Closed circuit television
CEA-PME	Confédération Européenne des Associations de Petites et Moyennes Entreprises
CEEC	Central and Eastern European countries

CII	Computer-implemented inventions
CIPIH	Commission on Intellectual Property Rights, Innovation and Public Health
CompTIA	Computing Technology Industry Association
COREPER	Committee of Permanent Representatives
CPTech	Consumer Project on Technology
CSIR	Council of Scientific and Industrial Research
CSO	Civil society organization
CULT	European Parliament Committee on Culture and Education
ddI	Didanosine (2′,3′-dideoxyinosine)
DDOS	Distributed denial of service
DG	Directorate General
DRM	Digital rights management
EC	European Commission
EDRi	European Digital Rights
EEA	European Economic Area
EEUPC	European and EU Patents Court
EFA	European Free Alliance
EFF	Electronic Frontier Foundation
EFPIA	European Federation of Pharmaceutical Industries and Associations
EGA	European Generic Medicines Association
EICTA	European Information and Communications Technology Industry Association
ENA	École Nationale d'Administration
EP	European Parliament
EPC	European Patent Convention
EPO	European Patent Office
EPP-ED	European People's Party-European Democrats
ESC	Economic and Social Council
EU	European Union
FFII	Foundation for a Free Information Infrastructure
FIAR	Forum for Interamerican Research
F/OSS	Free/Open source software
FSFE	Free Software Foundation Europe
FTA	Free trade agreement
GATT	General Agreement on Tariffs and Trade
GDP	Gross domestic product
GFDL	GNU Free Documentation License
GNU	GNU's Not Unix

GphA	Generic Pharmaceutical Association
GPL	General Public License
GPO	Government Pharmaceutical Organization
GUE/NGL	Confederal Group of the European United Left/ Nordic Green Left
HAART	Highly active antiretroviral therapy
HAI	Health Action International
Health GAP	Health Global Access Project
HIV	Human immunodeficiency virus
ICTSD	International Centre for Trade and Sustainable Development
IFPI	International Federation of the Phonographic Industry
IFPMA	International Federation of Pharmaceutical Manufacturers & Associations
IGWG	Intergovernmental Working Group on Public Health, Innovation and Intellectual Property
IIPA	International Intellectual Property Alliance
INGO	International non-governmental organization
INPI	Instituto Nacional da Propriedade Industrial
IPC	Intellectual Property Committee
IPR	Intellectual property right
ISP	Internet service provider
ITRE	Committee on Industry, Research and Energy
JURI	Committee on Legal Affairs
KEI	Knowledge Ecology International
MEP	Member of the European Parliament
MIT	Massachusetts Institute of Technology
MSF	Médecins Sans Frontières
NGO	Non-governmental organization
NHSO	National Health Security Office
NIH	National Institutes of Health
OECD	Organisation for Economic Co-operation and Development
PCT	Patent Cooperation Treaty
PhRMA	Pharmaceutical Research and Manufacturers of America
PLWHA	People living with HIV/AIDS
PMA	South African Pharmaceutical Manufacturers' Association
PPI	Pirate Parties International
PSE	Party of European Socialists

QUNO	Quaker United Nations Office
R&D	Research and development
RIAA	Recording Industry Association of America
SME	Small and medium-sized enterprises
SMO	Social movement organization
SPLT	Substantive Patent Law Treaty
SUS	Sistema Único de Saúde
TAC	Treatment Action Campaign
TPN+	Thai Network for People living with HIV/AIDS
TRIPS	Agreement on Trade-Related Aspects of Intellectual Property Rights
TWN	Third World Network
UEAPME	Union Européenne de l'Artisanat et des Petites et Moyennes Entreprises
UK-PTO	UK Patent and Trademark Office
UN	United Nations
UNAIDS	Joint United Nations Programme on HIV/AIDS
UNCTAD	United Nations Conference on Trade and Development
UNICE	Union of Industrial and Employers' Confederations of Europe
UNITAID	International facility for the purchase of drugs against HIV/AIDS, malaria and tuberculosis
USTR	United States Trade Representative
VCR	Videocassette recorder
WHA	World Health Assembly
WHO	World Health Organization
WIPO	World Intellectual Property Organization
WTO	World Trade Organization
ZVEI	Zentralverband Elektrotechnik- und Elektronikindustrie

1   Introduction

On 22 December 1999, about 100 people protested in front of the Thai Ministry of Public Health building demanding that the authorities grant a compulsory licence for ddI, a widely used antiretroviral HIV/AIDS drug (Limpananont et al. 2009: 146). This was the beginning of a campaign that seven years later mobilized 10,000 people during protests against the US-Thailand Free Trade Area in which the question of compulsory licences and access to medicines played an important role, and which became part of a global mobilization for access to essential medicines (Krikorian 2009). A couple of months earlier, on 11 February 1999, eleven people met in a backroom of the restaurant Rhaetenhaus in Munich to found FFII, the Federation for a Free Information Infrastructure (FFII 1999). This NGO – created with minimal resources and maximal commitment – grew in the next ten years to 850 members and 100,000 supporters, has chapters in twenty European countries and spearheaded the campaign that in 2005 stopped the introduction of software patents in Europe (Eckl 2005; Eimer 2007; Haunss and Kohlmorgen 2009, 2010). Also at about the same time a small group of lawyers from US Ivy League law schools started to think about alternatives to the current copyright regime, leading to the establishment of the Creative Commons project in 2001 (Dobusch and Quack 2008).

What do these seemingly unrelated stories have in common? They are examples of mobilizations that question the current regimes governing intellectual property (IP). The Thai AIDS activists had realized that the existence of a seemingly distant international treaty on 'Trade-Related Aspects of Intellectual Property Rights' (TRIPS) was hindering their access to the medication needed to keep the infection at bay, at prices they could afford. The software programmers, entrepreneurs, computer geeks and civil liberties activists had realized that the seemingly arcane matter of software patents was affecting the viability of their business models and the ability to create free and open software like Linux that today drives major parts of the internet infrastructure.

1

And the university-based lawyers had realized that the current copyright regime was effectively closing access to ever larger parts of the knowledge produced inside and outside academia.

The first two cases are examples of IP mobilizations from below. Groups and individuals without formal education in patent or copyright law started to join the game that was until then almost exclusively played by specialized lawyers and officials working in the relevant IP bureaucracies (patent, copyright, trademark offices and the like). In the third case IP specialists developed a project to establish an alternative to the existing copyright framework that quickly reverberated far beyond the legal community, and now involves individuals with various professional backgrounds from many parts of the globe.

The cases are just three examples in a series of similar mobilizations. The struggles against 'biopiracy', i.e. the private appropriation of traditional (indigenous) knowledge (Wullweber 2004), the conflicts about file-sharing in peer-to-peer networks (Krömer and Sen 2006), the coming-together of the access to knowledge (A2K) movement (Krikorian and Kapczynski 2010) and the advent of Pirate Parties in various European countries (Demker 2011) address similar and related issues. Obviously in the past fifteen years a number of conflicts have developed which challenge the normative and institutional frameworks that regulate how knowledge is produced, appropriated and used.

1.1.   Why now?

The institutions that govern intellectual property are not particularly new. The Berne Convention for the Protection of Literary and Artistic Works, which governs copyrights and related rights, came into existence in 1886 and was last revised in 1971; the Paris Convention for the Protection of Industrial Property, which governs patents, trademarks and designs, dates back to 1883; and even the Agreement on Trade-Related Aspects of Intellectual Property Rights, which is often seen as the most important recent change in IP governance, was signed back in 1994. Intellectual property rights are obviously not a new political issue. They have been around internationally for more than a century and for much longer periods in national legislations.

But despite this long history, conflicts like the ones mentioned above are relatively new. Obviously there was no timeless consensus about the merits of strong IP rights among states, within national administrations, or in the scholarly community. The tension between strong patent rights and anti-trust legislation, for example, led to several shifts in US IP policies in the twentieth century. The US Supreme Court decision in

Henry v. *A.B. Dick Co.* in 1912 marked the heyday of strong patent rights at the beginning of the twentieth century. In their decision the judges ruled that A.B. Dick Co. were allowed to sell their patented 'Rotary Mimeograph' a stencil-duplicating machine with a licence restriction, 'that it may be used only with the stencil paper, ink, and other supplies made by A.B. Dick Company, Chicago, U.S.A.' (*Henry* v. *A.B. Dick Co.* 1912), even though these supplies were not patented themselves. But this over-inclusive position that effectively expanded patent protection far beyond the patented invention did not prevail. For most of the twentieth century strong anti-trust policies in the name of free competition de facto invalidated many patent rights in the USA. Only in the 1980s was this development once more reversed, when the Supreme Court – in light of the growing economic importance of immaterial goods – revalued intellectual property rights as high as or even higher than free competition (Sell and May 2001: 486 ff.). Nevertheless, these ups and downs in the breadth and scope of intellectual property rights have not been accompanied by political mobilizations that involved actors other than the immediate economic stakeholders. They were of interest mostly to the potential rights-holders and their competitors, but there are no accounts of mobilizations resembling the ones mentioned above that predate the late 1990s.

1.2.   Politicization of IP

To understand why IP has become a contentious issue it is necessary to take into account several parallel processes:

(1) the growing economic importance of knowledge-based industries,
(2) the growing internationalization of IP issues, exemplified in the increasing number and reach of international treaties and trade agreements that centrally address IP,
(3) the growing attention IP issues receive in non-specialist and high-level political fora,
(4) and the trend to personalize IP rules.

These processes will be discussed in Chapter 2. Taken together these macro and micro processes have facilitated the politicization of IP. Politicization means that, on the one hand, more, and more diverse actors are getting involved in IP issues. Industry, legal specialists, national administrations, patent and trademark offices and specialist courts are being joined by academics, farmers, indigenous people, consumers, political activists and NGOs. On the other hand, the range of issues is expanding and the forms of action are getting more diverse. The issues that are being raised range from biopiracy, to health, access to medicines, fair use, access to knowledge and the limits of patentability. Conflicts are carried out in various arenas, ranging from international organizations, national parliaments and courts to the public sphere, where actors try to influence the policy process by exerting political and economic power, by lobbying and petitioning decision-makers, and by organizing street demonstrations, boycotts and other tactics from the repertoire of contentious politics.

The politicization of IP – and this is the main argument of the book – is embedded in more wide-ranging processes of social change associated with the transformation of industrial societies into knowledge societies. The current conflicts about intellectual property rights are harbingers of a new class of conflicts addressing new cleavages. They reveal a number of underlying conflict lines specific to the type of society that authors have variously labelled the information society (Lyon 1988), network society (Castells 2010a [1996]), post-industrial society (Bell 1999 [1973]), knowledge society (Stehr 1994a), risk society (Beck 1986) or programmed society (Touraine 1972). The one thing that unites these various descriptions of current societies is that their social and economic structures are organized around the creation, valorization and use of knowledge – the term *knowledge society* is thus the most generic term, capturing the central element that distinguishes these societies from earlier forms.

All processes of large-scale social change alter the overall structures of social conflicts in a society. New cleavages emerge that potentially lead to new conflict constellations in which new collective actors challenge the dominant order of society. The aim of this book is to show how the current conflicts about the international system of intellectual property address key new cleavages of the knowledge society, and to analyse to what degree in these concrete conflicts new collective actors emerge with the ability to contest the dominant order of current knowledge societies.

1.3.   The organization of this book

To grasp the scope and the meaning of current conflicts about intellectual property rights it is necessary to understand how the international system of intellectual property rights has historically developed, how it is governed and how it is legitimized. Chapter 2 will thus start with an analysis of the reasons for the current politicization of IP, present an overview of the current and historical institutional frameworks in which intellectual property rights are governed, and discuss legitimizing narratives on which the IP system rests.

The current state of the international IP system is the product of historical developments in which government innovation policies, private interests, market dynamics and other factors have interacted in sometimes more and sometimes less consistent, and sometimes even contradictory ways. The fact that the politics of intellectual property has become an issue so important that it appears on the 2011 G8 meeting's agenda before nuclear safety, climate change, development and peace, is a result of the transformation of our current societies into knowledge societies. To understand this social transformation and the new social conflicts that accompany it I will review in Chapter 3 the most influential theories of the post-industrial (Bell 1999 [1973]), network (Castells 2010a [1996]) and knowledge societies (Stehr 1994a). The focus of this discussion will be on possible cleavages that these authors of theories of the knowledge society identify, and it will be embedded in a more general evaluation of the theoretical literature about the relationship between conflicts and social change. Based on these discussions a preliminary model of the relationship between social conflicts and social change emerges that enables a more systematic assessment of the general conflict lines that the empirical struggles about IP policies address.

Equipped with this theoretical knowledge it is possible to gain insights beyond the level of the concrete policy issues that current empirical conflicts about intellectual property rights and the governance of knowledge address. An empirical analysis, guided by a theory of conflicts and change in the knowledge society, forms the main part of this book. Chapters 4, 5 and 6 present analyses of the four most important conflictual mobilizations about the rules, norms and institutional arrangements that govern the production, use and valorization of knowledge: the conflict about *software patents in Europe* (Chapter 4), the transnational mobilization for *access to medicines* (Chapter 5), the emergence of *Pirate Parties* and the establishment of an alternative bundle of licences to foster access to knowledge, under the label of *Creative Commons* (both Chapter 6).

These cases have not been selected in a classical comparative perspective to facilitate comparison along a limited set of factors. Instead the four cases represent – maybe not the whole universe, but – the largest, most visible and thus most important contentious mobilizations around issues of intellectual property of the last two decades. Other conflicts such as the more recent ones about the Anti-Counterfeiting Trade Agreement (ACTA), copyright exceptions for blind people or the mobilization against the European Intellectual Property Rights Enforcement Directive never reached a comparable breadth or remained confined to expert committees of the transnational institutions concerned with intellectual property rights.

The conflict about *software patents in Europe* developed into one of the most contentious issues in the recent history of the European Parliament. It involved more than a thousand committed actors and a support network of several hundred thousand, actively engaged in the contentious interaction. In the course of the conflict new actors established themselves in the field of IP politics and some surprising coalitions were formed. The *access to medicines* conflict is a prime example of a truly international mobilization, involving several hundred core activists, supported by tens of thousands engaged in local mobilizations. As in the software patents case, here too new actors have stepped onto the stage of international IP politics and a remarkable coalition of NGOs and government actors from developing countries has been formed. The *Pirate Parties* stand for the integration of some of the conflicts of the knowledge society into the electoral process, and thus for the arrival of these conflicts at the centre of the parliamentary system. *Creative Commons* is the smallest mobilization in terms of immediately involved activists. But the adoption of its alternative rule-set by millions of users willing to share their works freely on the internet makes it another crucial case to understand the structure and dynamics of current conflicts in the knowledge society.

Together these four cases are paradigmatic cases (Flyvbjerg 2006) for collective mobilizations that address conflicts of the knowledge society. Their analysis follows a common structure which is a consequence of my general assumption of the relationship of conflicts and change in the knowledge society. If changes in important parts of the social structure may lead to the emergence of new cleavages bringing about new kinds of conflicts and new collective actors, then the analysis of each case has to address three questions:

(1) What is the wider social and institutional context of the conflict?
(2) Which actors are involved in the conflict and in what relationship do they stand to each other?
(3) What are the conflict lines addressed in the conflict?

The first question concerns the aspect that changing social structures influence the emergence and persistence of collective actors which in turn attempt to change the social structures they are confronted with. Both co-evolve interdependently. To understand this interplay it is necessary to analyse the *context* in which the conflicts take place. In which institutional, political, economic and cultural frameworks are the conflicts embedded? What are the relevant social structures that limit the field of opportunities and constraints, and how do these contexts change over time?

Contexts and configurations in which collective action takes place have been the core focus of political process theories. The main idea of this approach (for an overview see Kriesi 2004) is that an analysis of political conflicts should account for the structures, configurations and interaction contexts. Structures encompass the institutional settings that determine channels and ease of access, openness or closure of political institutions, strength and weakness of the executive and other relatively stable aspects like cleavage structures and international contexts that influence the chances of oppositional actors being heard and influence decision-making processes. The institutional structures have often been conceptualized as 'political opportunity structures' (Eisinger 1973). They are complemented by 'discursive opportunity structures' (Koopmans and Statham 1999a: 228) that influence chances to find resonance for one's claims in the public sphere.

The context of collective action also entails the alliance structures and the relationships between protagonists, antagonists and bystanders (Hunt, Benford and Snow 1994). There is thus no strict separation between contexts and actors, since third parties can be part of the action context in which the main protagonists act. Alliance structures may be persistent but are usually less stable than social and institutional structures, and can change more quickly over time and usually differ significantly between policy fields. They have been analysed as policy networks (Adam and Kriesi 2007; Schneider et al. 2009) or advocacy coalitions (Sabatier and Weible 2007) and comprise institutional as well as non-institutional actors that have stakes in a certain policy field. Interaction contexts link structures and configurations to agency and action (Kriesi 2004: 77). Authors have focused here on the strategies of social movements and on a more abstract level on mechanisms that explain how collective actors influence and change policy outcomes (McAdam, Tarrow and Tilly 2001).

The second question is the most central as it concerns the collective actors themselves. Collective actors are the agents of social change, and to understand social conflicts it is necessary to know who mobilizes and who gets mobilized. Who are the actors that address the grievances of the knowledge society? What is their social base? Who are their adversaries and allies? This entails on a material level the network of individuals and organizations involved in conflicts, and on an analytical level the emergence and development of collective actors. How do individuals begin to act together, how do they define common goals and adversaries, and construct a collective identity?

Collective mobilization processes have been researched from many perspectives, with a focus on material resources (McCarthy and Zald 1977), moral convictions (Jasper 1997), organizations (Curtis and Zurcher 1973) or overarching movement dynamics (Koopmans 1993). The most systematic approach to analysing the interplay of various actors in collective action networks has been developed within a social networks perspective (Diani 2000, 2003; Diani and McAdam 2003; McAdam 2003; Saunders 2007). But before collective actors can be observed as empirical actors they have to be constituted. This entails the creation of a collective identity, which is the precondition for a collective actor to be able to establish itself as a collective, as a 'we' that is discernible from other collective actors in a society (Haunss 2001, 2004, 2011). Beyond the level of empirically observable collective actor networks the construction of collective actors is a process that is located mainly on the cognitive level. Melucci has emphasized this aspect in his theory of collective action and has drawn attention to the processes of collective identity through which movement participants define the meaning of their action and the field of opportunities and constraints of this action (Melucci 1995, 1996).

The third question finally addresses the fact that, while empirical conflicts are often about very concrete policy goals, these goals are often pursued for much more general reasons. A concrete policy conflict may thus on an underlying level address a much more fundamental social conflict. For example, a conflict about the right to be served at a lunch counter can be at the same time a conflict about fundamental human rights and racist segregation in a society. A conflict about a nuclear power plant can also be a conflict about the general value of an ecological perspective or about citizen participation in a democracy. The extent to which these more abstract levels are also present in concrete conflicts depends largely on how the participants frame this conflict. It is thus necessary to ask, which frames are used to construct the conflict? How do the challengers identify themselves as collective actors? How do they interpret the situation, which aims do they formulate, which opponents and strategies do they name?

The literature that addresses this discursive level of conflicts (Snow et al. 1986; Gamson 1992; Benford and Snow 2000; Snow 2004) defines frame, in adaption of Goffman (1974), as an 'interpretive [schema] that simplifies and condenses the "world out there" by selectively punctuating and encoding objects, situations, events, experiences, and sequences of actions within one's present or past environment' (Snow and Benford 1992: 137). In the simplest form, frames are the interpretations that underpin an actor's argumentation. In a more complex perspective, frames provide overarching interpretations of the world, and can constitute meaning for actions beyond their immediate context. In political conflicts framing can be differentiated depending on its function in the mobilization process. Snow and Benford identify three core framing tasks, diagnostic, prognostic and motivational framing, on which successful mobilizations depend (Snow and Benford 1988). Diagnostic frames define the problem and often name those that are its source or held responsible for it. Prognostic frames present a solution for the problem and outline tactics and strategies to come to this solution. Motivational frames give reasons for action beyond the simple problem definition. They can offer emotional, personal or situational reasons why it is necessary to act now.

These three general questions concerning the contexts, actors and frames of the conflicts will be addressed in each of the case studies. They all start with a 'thick description' (Geertz 1973) of the conflict that introduces the core actors and informs about some aspects of the institutional and social context of each conflict. From there on each case study follows a slightly different path. Because the four cases each help to understand different aspects of the complex constellation of conflicts and social change in the knowledge society, the analysis will follow to some extent the idiosyncrasies of the individual cases.

The first two cases, which involved large numbers of actors in protracted contentious interactions, will be analysed in more detail than the latter cases, which involved a much smaller group of core actors. Moreover, I will vary the concrete methodological tools used to analyse the contexts, actors and frames of the four conflicts. For example, in the cases of the access to medicines campaign, the Pirate Parties and Creative Commons, where sets of core documents exist in which the main participating actors have stated their positions, I will trace their framing activities using interpretive text-analytical methods. In the software patent case, where such documents are missing for some core actors, but where reliable newspaper reports about much of the claims-making activities are available, I can use a more sophisticated discourse network-analytical tool (Leifeld and Haunss 2012). The specific methodological tools that have been used to analyse the contexts, actors and frames will therefore be introduced in the respective chapters.

After these case studies the final chapter (Chapter 7) summarizes the more general findings of the analysis of the four cases and relates these findings to the theoretical discussions of the first part of this book. What are the general contours of conflict and change in the knowledge society embedded in the empirical conflict? Which similarities and differences exist between the four mobilizations, and what do they tell us about the cleavage structure of the knowledge society and the collective actors that challenge this structure? Based on the empirical knowledge about the contentious mobilizations it will be possible to give the abstract model of conflict and change in the knowledge society a more substantial form.

The mobilizations that originate in the struggles for access to HIV/AIDS drugs in Thailand, that bring a handful of software programmers to confront the phalanx of transnational IP companies, patent attorneys and EU Commission bureaucrats, that incite medical doctors to raise their voice in the World Trade Organization (WTO) and the World Intellectual Property Organization (WIPO), that make US law professors vanguards of a social movement against intellectual property; these mobilizations address – beyond their concrete policy goals – a set of underlying conflicts of the knowledge society, no longer rooted in the cleavages of the industrial era. In these conflicts new collective actors emerge who challenge the current order of the knowledge society and who try to establish an alternative version of a knowledge society based on democratized access to knowledge and far-reaching limits to the propertization of ideas, knowledge and cultural goods. How this unfolds will be shown in the following pages.

2   The politicization of intellectual property

Controlling access to knowledge is probably one of the oldest technologies of power. Literacy is often seen as one important precondition
for the development of the early Greek democracies (Goody and Watt
1963), and the Roman Catholic Church – well aware of the destabilizing
potential of universal access to knowledge – tried hard with its attempts
to prohibit the distribution and use of bible translations to secure its
exclusive interpretive power (Reusch 1883). Traditional knowledge
about crafts and medicines was and is usually protected through secrecy
and handed down through the generations to select individuals. Access
to modern technical and theoretical knowledge is still to some degree
protected by secrecy, but the prime mechanism is a state-backed system
of exclusive rights. Today these privileges of – temporary – exclusive use
usually take the form of intellectual property rights.

Intellectual property has been called 'the oil of the 21st century'
('Blood and Oil' 2000). The famous quote by Mark Getty, chairman
of stock images company Getty Images, expresses the notion that intellectual property rights would fuel the knowledge economy just as oil is
fuelling the industrial economy. Whether this implies that we may soon
be facing an intellectual property crisis like the oil crisis of the 1970s,
or whether we will see a transition to a post-carbon, post-IP economy in
the course of the twenty-first century, remains to be seen. What is certainly clear is that intellectual property rights have become sites of conflicts with a global reach. No longer are intellectual property rights the
preserve of specialist lawyers and a select group of business interests.

In this chapter I will show where and how intellectual property rights
have become focal points of social conflicts involving various kinds of
actors from all regions of the world. I will show how the politics of intellectual property (Haunss and Shadlen 2009) have started to involve
new groups of actors which brought new conflict lines to the legal and
political frameworks that regulate the production, valorization, use and
distribution of knowledge in the past two decades. To do this, I will
describe the ascent of IP to a high-profile political issue and analyse the

parallel processes that have led to a politicization of IP. This politicization changes a system that has developed in a non-linear process over several hundred years. To enable readers not familiar with the rules and institutions of the international regulatory framework of intellectual property rights to judge the scope of the current conflicts, I will present in the second and third parts of this chapter a brief overview of the historical development of intellectual property rights and of the institutional framework that governs these rights. I will then address the legitimatory narratives that have been developed to justify historical and current IP regimes and discuss how these narratives are challenged in the scientific literature and in current political conflicts. This chapter closes with a brief discussion of current developments that point to increasing contention about issues of intellectual property and the regulation of knowledge.

2.1.   How IP has become political

The protests in Thailand about compulsory licences for HIV/AIDS drugs, which are part of a worldwide campaign for access to medicines, the political mobilization around software patents in Europe, the electoral success of Pirate Parties, and the explosive growth in the number of Creative Commons licensed works on the internet, resulting in the de facto establishment of an alternative copyright regime; these contentious processes are directly connected to fundamental changes in the worldwide intellectual property regime. Four broad processes of change alter the scope of actors involved in IP politics and the constellations between those actors:

(1) the growing economic importance of knowledge-based industries,
(2) the growing internationalization of IP issues, exemplified in the increasing number and reach of international treaties and trade agreements that centrally address IP,
(3) the growing attention IP issues receive in non-specialist and high-level political fora,
(4) and the trend to personalize IP rules.

2.1.1.   The growing economic importance of IP

On the macro level the most important process is the growing economic importance of immaterial goods in some core highly developed countries, above all in the USA. In the twentieth century the structure of the world economies has fundamentally changed. In the industrialized

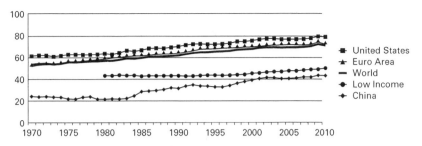

Figure 2.1 Share of service sector (per cent of GDP 1970–2010).

Source: World Bank, World Development Indicators (http://datbank. worldbank.org).

global North the service sector has surpassed the industrial sector both in terms of the number of employees and in terms of its share in the overall production of added value. This observation led Daniel Bell in 1973 to predict the coming of post-industrial society in the next thirty to fifty years (Bell 1999: x). The trend that he observed in the early 1970s has since continued. The available data clearly shows a robust and constant growth of the service sector's share in overall GDP in the industrialized countries between 1970 and 2010 (see Figure 2.1). During the last decade the growth rate may have been declining (the data is somewhat inconclusive in this respect) but the service sector is still growing steadily in relative as well as in absolute terms. In the USA the proportion grew from 61 to 79 per cent, in Europe from 52 to 72 per cent. In the more recently industrializing China the relative economic value of the service sector grew from 24 to 43 per cent. This means it grew even more strongly than the industrial sector, which grew an astonishing 6,218 per cent in absolute terms while the share of the industrial sector in overall GDP remained almost constant.[1] This picture is still radically different in low-income countries where the industrial sector is slowly growing at the expense of the agricultural sector while the service sector remains constant at about 43 to 45 per cent of the GDP.

Several authors have argued that a portrayal of these seemingly linear trends as in Figure 2.1 may actually obscure more than it reveals (Kumar 2005; Webster 2006; Castells 2010a). The service sector is essentially a residual category into which everything that is not agriculture and manufacturing is thrown. The service sector in Canada may therefore mean something completely different from the service

---

[1] In comparison, the industrial sector in the USA grew 'only' 188 per cent in constant 2000 US$ in the same period between 1970 and 2009.

sector in the Pacific island state of Kiribati, one of the world's poorest countries with exactly the same service sector share in its GDP as Canada. Nevertheless, what the data shows is that almost four decades after Bell's writing the trend that the manufacturing sector is gradually losing its leading position is still unbroken.

More interesting would be data that would represent the role of those industries that heavily depend on the processing of theoretical knowledge. But unfortunately such data is not available, not least because the value added by knowledge in complex production processes is almost impossible to estimate. In general it is assumed that within the service sector the so-called IP industries, that is industries whose revenues depend heavily on the sale of IP protected goods or services, have been gaining much greater economic importance from the 1980s onwards.

Unfortunately, no detailed and reliable statistics on the economic share of IP industries exist. This is due to the fact that on the one hand even in core copyright industries[2] only a part of the added value directly stems from IP. The profit of a print shop, for example, may only be weakly connected to the strength or weakness of copyright laws in a given country. The same will be true for theatrical productions that produce copyrighted art based to a significant extent on works that have long entered the public domain. On the other hand intellectual property rights clearly contribute to the added value in many industries where, for example, patents allow firms to request monopoly prices for their goods. But here again the exact share of IP is almost impossible to determine. With similar patent protection the same package of the HIV/AIDS drug Norvir costs €400 in Sweden, €600 in Germany and €2,200 in the USA. In none of the countries are generic versions available, so obviously other factors than IP determine the price of this drug.

In spite of these imponderabilities the volume of international trade in royalties and licence fees may nevertheless serve as a relatively reliable indicator for the much larger market of IP protected immaterial goods. Figure 2.2 shows the dramatic rise in the economic value of these goods in the past thirty years. According to OECD statistics, for the USA, the volume in trade in royalties and licence fees increased by a factor of 12 between 1986 and 2009, a growth rate that is more than two times higher than that of the overall service sector, which grew in

---

[2] Following the WIPO definition, core copyright industries are press and literature, music, theatrical productions and operas, motion picture and video, radio and television, photography, software and databases, visual and graphic arts, advertising services, and copyright collective management societies (WIPO 2003a: 28).

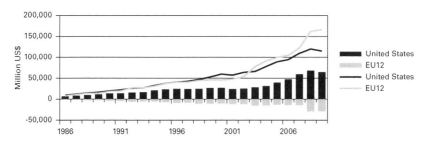

Figure 2.2 Trade in royalties and licence fees, 1986–2009, USA and EU12.

Note: Bars represent trade balance, lines represent trade volume.
Source: OECD Statistics on International Trade and Services, 1970– 2006, 2011 Edition.

the same time by a factor of 5.4. By 2009 US industry received about US$90 billion in revenues for royalty fees and licences. Using other data sources the IP interest group International Intellectual Property Alliance (IIPA) estimates that the US core copyright industries have been responsible for 8.64 per cent (US$110 billion) of the country's revenues from foreign sales and/or exports (Siwek 2006). In the EU12 trade in royalty fees and licences grew even more strongly than in the USA, by a factor of 21 between 1986 and 2009.

But while the overall volume of the trade in the USA and Europe is comparable, the USA is over the whole period a net exporter whereas the EU countries are on an aggregated level net importers of IP goods. Among the EU12 countries only the UK was for most of the time an IP net exporter. More recently also Denmark, France and the Netherlands had a positive trade balance whereas Germany, Greece, Ireland, Italy, Portugal and Spain have always had negative trade balances, with Ireland being responsible for the lion's share of the EU12's overall negative trade balance.

These figures do not preclude the possibility that European countries might nevertheless profit overall from strong IP rights, since for example the volume of trade in pharmaceuticals – an industry in which patent protection plays a very important role – still exceeded the volume of trade in royalties and licence fees in 2006 by a factor of 1.2, with Europe being a net exporter of pharmaceuticals. But the available trade statistics clearly show that the USA, and to a lesser degree also the EU, are the only significant net exporters of IP goods, a fact that has been noted repeatedly in the literature (Drahos and Braithwaite 2003: 11). No wonder that in all international fora the US administration and US industry representatives and, again to a lesser degree, the European Commission and European industry advocates, are constantly pushing for stronger IP rights and tighter regulation with the effect that '[w]hatever limited space the TRIPS Agreement retained, that space has been further enclosed by the aggressive push by developed countries for TRIPS-plus bilateral and regional trade and investment agreements' (Yu 2007: 11 f.).

2.1.2. A growing number of international treaties

The growing economic importance of IP industries goes along with intellectual property rights becoming a high-profile issue in international politics. Certainly the 1994 Agreement on Trade-Related Aspects of Intellectual Property Rights (TRIPS) was a pivotal event as it substantially changed the international framework of IP regulation. It requires all WTO member states to establish a set of substantive minimum standards of IP protection that goes far beyond what most developing countries would have liked to provide and even exceeds the standards of many developed countries at that time (Deere 2009: 1). Several in-depth studies have analysed the process by which the agreement was reached and its consequences for developed and developing countries (Correa 2000; Maskus 2000a, 2000b; May 2000; Sell 2003; Drahos 2005; May and Sell 2006; Deere 2009). Susan Sell has convincingly argued that the steady push for stronger rights by IP advocates constitutes a 'global IP upward ratchet' (Sell 2008) characterized by constant forum-shifting from WIPO to WTO, back to WIPO, to bilateral and regional agreements, or to exclusive deliberations. Today a multitude of international treaties govern intellectual property rights, and IP issues are implicated in almost every ongoing international trade negotiation. Significant resources are invested to influence the frameworks that govern ownership of and access to these immaterial goods.

It should be noted, though, that after TRIPS these negotiations have been usually far from consensual. One important reason why the Doha round of WTO trade talks has not been progressing since 1999 is disagreement over IP issues between countries of the global North and newly industrializing countries, Brazil, India and China in particular (Yu 2008). Negotiations on a Substantive Patent Law Treaty (SPLT) under the auspices of WIPO that would ensure patent protection beyond what has been agreed in TRIPS have also stalled. And the latest push to expand intellectual property rights in the negotiations to the Anti-Counterfeiting Trade Agreement (ACTA) among a select group of core OECD and newly industrializing countries (Geist 2009) has been met with increasing resistance. The secretive nature of the negotiations, manifested in the unwillingness to make the draft documents publicly available, has provoked criticism from several members of national legislative bodies and finally led to the rejection of the treaty by the European Parliament, with the consequence that ACTA will most likely not come into force.

2.1.3. *IP as a high-profile political issue*

But aside from IP issues being on the agenda of every trade negotiation they have also stepped into the limelight at much more prominent political meetings. In the concluding statement of the 2007 G8 meeting in Heiligendamm, Germany, intellectual property rights occupy a prominent position. They have been addressed as the fourth topic after global growth and stability, financial markets and freedom of investment, and before climate change, responsibility for raw materials, corruption and trade. Under the heading 'Promoting Innovation – Protecting Innovation' it is claimed that 'innovation needs to be protected worldwide. Intellectual Property Rights (IPRs) are a critical precondition for innovation. The protection of IPRs is of core interest for consumers in all countries, particularly in developing countries' (G8 2007) – which adds an interesting twist to the hitherto framing of IPRs as trade issues.

In the following years, climate change and the global financial crisis have displaced IP issues from the top of the agenda, but they nevertheless have remained firmly established through a special G8 Intellectual Property Experts' Group that has met and delivered reports at the 2008 and 2009 summits with an increasing number of more concrete policy recommendations (G8 2008, 2009), calling for TRIPS plus IP protection in the form of an international Substantive Patent Law Treaty (SPLT) and a multilateral agreement to strengthen enforcement measures within the framework of an Anti-Counterfeiting Trade Agreement (ACTA). And in 2011 IP issues were, again, a top priority at the G8 meeting. In the G8 declaration prepared by the French presidency IP issues are addressed before nuclear safety, climate change, development and peace, with a clear statement in support of 'business friendly, robust and efficient national intellectual property systems' (French Presidency of the G8 2011: para. 29).

Before 2007 IP issues were far less prominent in the official summit documents. In the 2006 St Petersburg Chair's Summary, IP was mentioned as one of several 'other issues' towards the end of the document, with a focus on piracy and counterfeiting (G8 2006). In earlier summit documents IP issues appeared even less prominent, usually only in sub-ordinate clauses or as one among many bullet points in a long list, and before 1996 they disappear altogether from the list of issues that merit the attention of the world leaders.

While the G8 summits may have less tangible impact than many of the trade negotiations, the summit documents are excellent indicators about the symbolic order of politics. The issues that are touched upon in the official documents reflect on a symbolic level the political prior-ities of international politics. The ascent of intellectual property from the sidelines to the centre in the past decade reflects the changing per-ception of IP, shifting from a technical specialist issue to a general pol-itical issue of great importance.

These three parallel and interwoven processes at the macro level, the growing economic importance of IP, the strengthening and deepening of international legal frameworks and the recognition of IP as a priority issue at the highest levels of international politics, reflect the changing role of IP in current societies: the move from the periphery to the core of politics. These macro processes are accompanied by a micro process that also reflects the changing role of IP in society.

2.1.4. IP becomes personal

At the micro level intellectual property rights have always affected indi-vidual citizens – mainly through the price mechanism. Since intellec-tual property rights are (temporary) monopoly rights, producers are able to ask for monopoly prices for those goods that are protected by copyrights, patents, trademarks or other intellectual property rights. Monopoly prices are in general set on the market and depend primarily on demand elasticity (Lerner 1934). The higher the demand elasticity, that is the bigger the leeway potential buyers have to decide whether or not they will buy a certain good, the lower the monopoly premium a producer can successfully ask for.

Patented technologies in consumer products thus usually lead to higher prices – sometimes for a single product, sometimes for whole product segments when key technologies are patented and have to be licensed by competitors. But customers are often able to choose a patent-free alternative or refrain from purchasing a good, thus limit-ing the premium that can be charged. The situation is different when it comes to goods that are critically needed, goods for which there is little or no elasticity of demand. This is the case for essential medi-cines, where IP monopoly premiums can therefore be especially high. It is important to note, though, that health insurance systems have in many developed countries significantly mitigated the effect of pharmaceutical monopoly prices for individual customers. High prices for patent-protected medicines only really became a political issue in the course of the AIDS/HIV crisis in the mid 1990s when it became clear that many countries of the South that were severely hit by the epidemic could not afford the new antiretroviral drugs. In these countries comprehensive health insurance often does not exist and/or available funds are too low to cover the costs of patented drugs, leaving patients in the developing world without medication that is available for patients in the countries of the global North.

In these and other cases individuals have long been affected by intellectual property rights, but the main role in which they have been affected was as customers. Competitors in the market have been sued with copyright or patent infringement if they violated IP laws. They may have been pushed out of the market if they were unable to license a core technology, or they may have been unable to enter a market that was fenced in by tight IP protection. But overall the consequences of intellectual property rights have been limited to economic actors, and had little or no effect on individuals apart from monopoly prices. Buying a bootleg record in a record store or a flea market, buying a pirated edition of a book from a hawker in a pub, or buying a fake brand accessory on a street market usually did not have any consequences for the buyer. The seller may have been charged with infringement but for the buyer the most serious consequence of acquiring infringed goods may have been inferior product quality.

IP protection – in other words – was a system that mainly regulated relationships among producers and to a lesser degree among producers and sellers. It affected most individuals only indirectly. Workers in IP industries may have profited from higher wages, consumers were confronted with higher prices, but neither workers nor consumers played a significant role when it came to IP litigation. This has changed significantly since the 1990s. End-users have come more and more into the focus of laws governing intellectual property. In April 2006 Jammie Thomas-Rasset was brought to court by the Recording Industry Association of America (RIAA) for illegally sharing songs through the peer-to-peer file-sharing network Kazaa. In June 2009 after a series of trials she was sentenced to statutory damages of US$1.92 million for wilful infringement of the copyright of twenty-four songs (US$80,000 per song), an amount that was in January 2010 reduced to US$54,000.[3]

---

[3] See http://news.cnet.com/8301-31001_3-10439636-261.html (accessed 1 March 2010).

According to the NGO Electronic Frontier Foundation (EFF), up to the end of 2008 in the USA alone, 'the recording industry has filed, settled or threatened legal actions against at least 30,000 individuals' (EFF 2008). In Germany a whole litigation industry has developed where law firms are mass mailing cease-and-desist letters to file-sharers, requesting them to pay between €300 and €600 per song or face a lawsuit. No reliable data is available on the exact scope of this industry but estimates range between tens of thousands and more than four hundred thousand cease-and-desist-letters that have been sent annually in 2008 and 2009 (Bleich 2010). In France in 2009 the so-called Hadopi[4] or three-strikes law was passed that envisions for internet users accused of repeatedly infringing copyrights two warning letters and, after that, suspension of their internet access, up to three years imprisonment and fines of up to €300,000 (Giradeau 2009). Similar 'three-strikes' laws are being discussed in New Zealand and the UK.

All these cases represent significant changes in the scope and function of intellectual property rights. IP laws traditionally regulated relationships between industrial market actors, and even though copyright and patent laws protect individual authors and innovators, the legal measures these laws provided to combat infringement were mainly aimed at firms, corporate actors or at least entrepreneurs. At their core they regulated the industrial production of knowledge and information. James Boyle has aptly noted that 'it used to be relatively *hard* to violate an intellectual property right' (Boyle 2003: 40). But with the proliferation of the internet this has changed fundamentally.

Digital technology has blurred the line between using, storing, transmitting and copying the products that are available online. IP laws have been expanded to cover all of these activities, and they increasingly target individual citizens who do not profit economically from their incriminated activities. Unlike pirated DVDs, fake fashion items or counterfeit electronic devices, music, videos and software that are made available in peer-to-peer networks are not offered for profit but are made available for free for everyone. Even if those who are making their collections available may profit indirectly by being able to download songs, programs or movies in return, profit-seeking is usually not the driving force behind the use of peer-to-peer networks.

The economics of material counterfeit goods or generic copies are quite simple: they are produced to grab a market share from the original manufacturer by offering seemingly – and sometimes even

---

[4] Named after the newly established 'Haute autorité pour la diffusion des oeuvres et la protection des droits sur internet' that is responsible for administering the legal measures.

actually – similar goods for a fraction of the original price. The economics of immaterial counterfeit goods are much more complicated and until now far from understood. While the music and software industry annually offers ballooning numbers about the economic damage of music and software piracy, solid scientific evidence about the actual losses is scarce or points even in the opposite direction (Towse, Handke and Stepan 2008). In a report for the Dutch Ministries of Education, Culture and Science, Economic Affairs and Justice, Huygen and her collaborators conclude: 'Taking all the empirical data into consideration, the conclusion to be drawn from the international scientific literature is that a negative effect of file sharing on the purchase of CDs can be neither ruled out nor indisputably confirmed' (Huygen et al. 2009: 98). The authors even see a net welfare effect of file-sharing and report a rapidly growing market for entertainment goods in which losses in one sector are more than offset by gains in other sectors. Apparently file-sharers overall do not spend less money for entertainment goods but change their spending patterns by buying for example fewer CDs but more computer games.

Taken together these macro and micro processes have led to a politicization of IP. More, and more diverse actors are becoming involved in IP issues. Industry, legal specialists, national administrations, patent and trademark offices and specialist courts are being joined by academics, farmers, indigenous people, consumers, political activists and NGOs. The issues that are being raised range from biopiracy, to health, access to medicines, fair use, access to knowledge and the limits of patentability. Conflicts are carried out in international organizations, national parliaments, specialist and general public spheres, and in courts and the tactics employed span the whole spectrum of (contentious) politics.

This is all upsetting a complex international institutional framework. In the following pages I will give a very brief overview of these institutions that today govern intellectual property rights. I will start with a glimpse into the history, then describe the current legal and institutional framework for the protection of intellectual property rights, discuss the core legitimizing narratives on which these institutions are built, and close the chapter with a brief discussion of some problems and shortcomings of the current system.

2.2.   The history of intellectual property rights

Today's intellectual property rights still bear the traces of their long history. Over the course of several hundred years they have been changed and adapted many times to suit varying goals. Their substance changed along with the narratives in which they were embedded. Their history in not one of simple linear expansion, but follows a more complex historical path. Copyright, for example, was in the beginning sometimes a perpetual right granted to the printers of a book. Today's time-limited protection is a more restricted right, even though the term of protection has been continuously expanded over the past three hundred years from twenty-eight – under the Statute of Anne – to life of the author plus seventy years – under current EU and US legislation. Several exceptions of fair use or specific limitation clauses have been added, removed and modified over the years to partially countervail the stronger protection. The scope of works covered by intellectual property rights has changed, too. Because the legal process has often been one of incremental change and adaption the resulting rights are not always fully consistent and reflect the historical development as much as the current goals.

The history of intellectual property goes back to the Mediterranean city states of the High and Late Middle Ages, where in Venice the world's first formal patent statute was established in 1474 (Machlup 1958: 2; David 1993: 59). The decree stated that 'whoever makes in this city any new and ingenious device, not previously made within our jurisdiction, is bound to register it at the office of the *Provveditori di Comun* as soon as it has been perfected, so that it will be possible to use and apply it. It will be prohibited to anyone else within any of our territories to make any other device in the form or likeness of that one without the author's consent or license, for the term of ten years' (cited in Phillips 1982: 76; see also May and Sell 2006: 59). While it was an established practice to grant privileges for the exclusive use of technologies, the 1474 Venice statute marked an important point because it established general rules for the granting of such privileges and detached them from the arbitrariness of individual rulers' decisions.

One should note that the decree already contains the requirement of novelty, which is a central part of all current patent systems, but that a device only had to be new within the state of Venice's jurisdiction. It was thus possible to receive exclusive rights for a tool or technology in Venice even if the technology was already established elsewhere – and commentators agree that attracting foreign artisans was, indeed, one core objective of this decree (David 1993: 44; May and Sell 2006: 65). Whether this objective was reached remains unclear, since despite the decree privileges in Venice continued to be granted for reasons and in forms that did not conform to the wording of the decree (Phillips 1982: 76, fn. 37). What is certain is that the idea that patents could be used to attract foreign experts, and thus be a tool to stimulate knowledge imports, remained an important objective in the granting of similar privileges during the Renaissance in many European countries. Paul

David has pointed out that the typical patent term in England at that time was seven years, which coincided with the duration of an apprenticeship. The aim was clearly to grant foreign artisans exclusive rights for the use of their knowledge for the time it took them to teach their craft to an apprentice, who would then be able to use the knowledge without restriction (David 1993: 45). But like every government favour patents not only served the noble goal of furthering innovation and attracting foreign experts. In the sixteenth century the Elizabethan court 'often issued patents to either support courtiers in financial difficulty by enabling them to profit from monopolies or to reward favorites' (May and Sell 2006: 81). And it was not before the seventeenth century that patents in England started to be granted for inventions and not as a means of technology transfer or as a personal favour.

In a similar way the creation of copyrights was also mainly driven by economic considerations. The Venetians were again vanguards when the Venetian Council of Ten established in 1544–5 what is said to be the world's first copyright law 'that prohibited the printing of any work unless written permission from the author or his immediate heirs had been submitted to the Commissioners of the University of Padua' (David 1993: 52). It should be noted, though, that while the decree makes the permission to print dependent on the author's consent, authors and their interests were not at the centre of this legislation. It was essentially a rule to regulate the growing book trade.

Lyman Ray Patterson underlines this point in his study of the history of the Anglo-Saxon copyright. He argues that '[c]opyright began in the 16th century as a device for maintaining order among members of the book trade organized as the Stationers' Company' (Patterson 1968: 223). It was first and foremost a right to govern the development of an economic sector with growing importance, and in the second place was used to censor what was deemed inappropriate to be printed. Authors' rights were not considered to be an issue before the eighteenth century when authors' rights were formalized in the 1709 Statute of Anne – named after Queen Anne of Great Britain (1665–1714). The legislation that was enacted by the British Parliament is generally seen as the precursor of modern copyright. It prohibited the printing and reprinting of a book without the consent of the author, established a general copyright term of fourteen years (twenty-one years for books that were already covered by existing copyright) that fell back to the author – if he or she was still alive – and that could be extended once for another fourteen years. But, again, its main purpose was not the creation of authors' rights but the regulation of the book market, through the establishment of publishers' rights. Authors' rights appeared mainly to restrict the earlier perpetual stationers' copyrights. Patterson argues that the purpose of the Statute of Anne was 'to provide a copyright that would function primarily as a trade regulation device – acting in the interest of society by preventing monopoly, and in the interest of the publisher by protecting published works from piracy' (Patterson 1968: 14), and that to fulfil this end the law was constructed around an author's right. Ironically the stronger position of the author was advanced by the printers and booksellers who in subsequent lawsuits used the argument of 'natural' authors' rights to perpetuate their monopoly – since authors usually signed over their rights to the booksellers and printers, they were the ones who profited from enhanced authors' rights.

The patent and copyright laws of the seventeenth and early eighteenth centuries still lacked the notion of 'property'. Patents and copyrights protected the exclusive use of certain technologies or granted the right to exclusively print a certain book for a limited time. The granted rights were more akin to a lease and in the laws no references were yet made to the concept of property. The analogy that is so prevalent today was not created before the late eighteenth and early nineteenth centuries when lawyers and journalists transferred the notion of individual property to the area of inventions and literary works (Fisher 1999: 286; Siegrist 2006a: 69). Their argumentation was based on Locke's labour-desert theory of property in which he argued that an individual would have a natural right to own the fruits of his labour. I will discuss this theory in more detail below (section 2.4) in connection with the other legitimatory narratives of intellectual property rights.

This propertization of knowledge has been interpreted as a parallel process to the development that is known as the English enclosure movement: the transformation of previously collectively used land into individual property that started in the fifteenth and culminated in the nineteenth century (Boyle 2003; Siegrist 2006b). But even after the property metaphor was established the notion prevailed that – apart from literary production – the important aspect of the new form of immaterial property was its value for the industrial production process, and thus the common term used when referring to patents, trademarks and copyrights was not 'intellectual property' but 'industrial property' (David 2000: 17). Figure 2.3 shows that only in the late 1970s do we see a dramatic increase in the use of the term intellectual property that around 1980 quickly surpasses the previously common term 'industrial property'.[5]

---

[5] For a detailed description of the dataset see Michel et al. (2011). The graph can be reproduced at http://ngrams.googlelabs.com/graph?content=intellectual+property%2Cindustrial+property&year_start=1800&year_end=2008&corpus=0&smoothing=3.

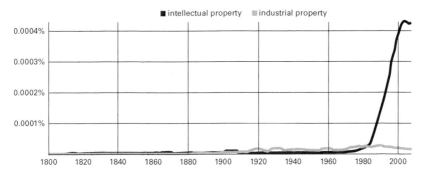

Figure 2.3 Frequency of 'industrial property' and 'intellectual property' (1800–2008).

Note: The graph plots the occurrence of the two terms 'intellectual property' and 'industrial property' in the corpus of more than 5 million books digitized in the course of the Google books project, representing about 4 per cent of all books ever published. The graph shows the relative frequency of the two 2-grams 'intellectual property' and 'industrial property' as a proportion of all 2-grams found in the full text of the literature published in the respective year, where 2-grams are all possible combinations of two words.

In the nineteenth century intellectual property rights were consolidated in the industrialized countries – a development that culminated in the establishment of the two international treaties that cover industrial (Paris Convention 1883) and artistic (Berne Convention 1886) property rights. But this consolidation was accompanied by intense controversies about the merits of intellectual property rights in general and the justifications of the patent system in particular. In his economic review of the patent system Fritz Machlup (1958) discussed the arguments and counterarguments of the patent controversy of the nineteenth century (1850–73) in some detail, and his conclusion that many of the problems addressed in this controversy remain unresolved is still valid today.

I will come back to these controversies when I discuss the main legitimizing narratives of the current IP system in section 2.4. For here it is enough to bear in mind that this brief glimpse into the history of the two most important intellectual property rights – patents and copyright – illustrates that at the origin of these rights stood economic considerations: regulating domestic markets and trade, controlling the development of monopolies and competition, acquiring knowledge from abroad and supporting economically interesting innovation. Authors' rights were a relatively late addition and remain even today essentially publishers' rights. The generation of knowledge as such was never the purpose of these rights, but rather the regulation of the valorization of economically useful knowledge. The development of knowledge, ideas, innovation and creativity without the prospect of immediate economic profits had and has to rely on other mechanisms like state-funded university systems, subsidized cultural institutions or private philanthropy.

2.3.   The current legal and institutional system

While the distinct legal and political-institutional traditions are still reflected in the respective national laws, the past fifty years brought a high degree of harmonization. There are two main mechanisms that have driven harmonization: colonialism and international treaties. The first falls clearly in Holzinger and Knill's (Holzinger and Knill 2005) category of imposition-mechanisms, where harmonization follows from one-sided pressure. The second mechanism, harmonization through international, bi- and multilateral treaties, is formally different, but as I will argue, was de facto based on much the same economic and political power differences.

The first mechanism, the colonial imposition of IP laws in the colonies, often left the countries, even after independence, with intellectual property rights systems that show strong resemblance to the laws of the former European colonial powers (Okediji 2003; Mgbeoji 2008). Ruth Okediji has argued that colonial IP laws were strategic tools in the commercial competition between colonial powers. They were the results of the European countries' attempts to secure their national interests within the colonies and against their European competitors, and thus a 'central technique in the commercial superiority sought by European powers in their interactions *with each other* in regions beyond Europe' (Okediji 2003: 324). Few countries – among them India – made changing their intellectual property rights system a priority when they gained independence, and thus the colonial roots are still present in many national IP laws.

The second mechanism responsible for the high degree of congruence in relation to protection terms and substance covered by IP laws is the international harmonization through international and bilateral treaties, notably the Berne Convention for the Protection of Literary and Artistic Works from 1886 that governs copyrights and related rights, the 1952 Universal Copyright Convention that was intended to offer an alternative to the Berne Convention, the Paris Convention for the Protection of Industrial Property that governs patents, trademarks and designs and dates back to 1883, and the TRIPS agreement that came into effect in 1995. The latter is the international treaty with the most far-reaching consequences as it contains minimal protection terms for copyrights and patents, and thus in the field of patents goes clearly beyond the Paris Convention. In the area of copyrights TRIPS incorporates the relevant articles of the Berne Convention (with the exception of Article 6bis that secures the author's moral rights, a provision that is not present in the US copyright law). Because WTO members automatically have to subscribe to the TRIPS agreement as well, it dramatically expanded the reach of the Berne Convention's provision.

Because of the high degree of congruence between national IP laws it suffices to present the core elements of the international legal system to describe the general structure of the institutional system of IP protection. This does not deny the existence of important and sometimes principal differences – the difference between the continental European *droit d'auteur* tradition that assigns the author of a literary or visual work an inalienable moral right against mutilation or modification of his or her work, and the Anglo-Saxon copyright tradition in which no such right exists; or the difference between the US first-to-invent patent system and the European first-to-file principle (Eimer 2008). But the principal difference between national systems has often only a limited practical relevance, because the systems provide mostly very similar scopes of protection.

The three pillars on which the international IP system rests are patents, copyrights and trademarks. Trademarks differ from the other two as they do not protect innovation, but rather are essentially a mechanism to secure trust between buyers and sellers. They predate by far the other forms of intellectual property rights and can be traced back to the Roman Empire (May and Sell 2006: 10). Other intellectual property rights that cover industrial designs, microprocessor layouts (masks), databases, plant varieties or geographical indications are in essence special cases of the three core rights. Mask and database rights are special cases of copyrights, plant variety or breeders' rights a special class of patents, geographical indicators can be seen as a special class of trademarks, and industrial designs fall in between trademarks and copyrights. A separate mechanism that is usually mentioned in the literature is trade secrets. But while there are laws and treaties that impose sanctions for the unauthorized acquisition of trade secrets, this mechanism is in its essence not a legal mechanism, but relies on individual non-disclosure of information.

Clearly the two most important rights are patents and copyrights, because they tap into the innovation processes which lie at the core of modern economies. Trademarks are an important substitute for trust in anonymous market interactions where trust cannot be based on repeated interpersonal interaction. They provide important information to judge the value of a good, regardless of whether such trust is based on image or material quality. The brand name suggests that the consumer can expect certain qualities of the branded good, and geographical indicators generalize this concept to goods from a specific region. But while a trademark may often exceed the value of any given patent, copyrights and patents are nevertheless the more important intellectual property rights, as they occupy structurally important positions that allow them to function as regulatory mechanisms for the core processes of generating, commercializing and accessing knowledge in current societies.

2.3.1.   Patents

Patents are exclusionary rights that grant the patent holder the right to prevent others from producing, using, selling, distributing and importing the patented product, or using the patented process without his or her consent. A patent offers the possibility for a time-limited monopoly and secures the effective exclusion of others. At the international level patents are governed by the Paris Convention and the TRIPS agreement. Article 27 of the TRIPS agreement states that 'patents shall be available for any inventions, whether products or processes, in all fields of technology'. Exceptions can be made if the technologies are used in diagnostic, therapeutic and surgical methods for the treatment of humans or animals, or if the 'inventions' are plants and animals other than micro-organisms – but TRIPS then requires a *sui generis* system of protection of plant varieties. To be eligible for a patent an invention has to be new (novelty), has to involve an inventive step (non-obviousness) and has to be capable of industrial application (or in a weaker version of the US patent law: has to be useful). All three conditions have to be fulfilled, but the precise meaning of each element is contested, or as Ikechi Mgbeoji writes: 'None of the key elements of patentability, especially the concepts of "novelty" and "invention," has any globally accepted definition' (Mgbeoji 2001: 175).

The case of US patent No. 5401504 for the use of turmeric powder as a wound healing agent gives an idea about the scope of the problem. In this case a US patent was granted in 1995 to the University of Mississippi Medical Center for the use of turmeric powder for wound healing. It was revoked two years later after the Indian Council of Scientific and Industrial Research (CSIR) challenged the patent on the grounds that turmeric had been used for precisely this application in traditional Indian medicine for ages, and the patented use would thus not fulfil the novelty criterion (Dutfield 2001: 248). But despite this ruling patents continue to be granted for herbal drugs or drugs based on the chemical compounds of herbs used in traditional medicines. The underlying problem is that novelty can only be falsified if a written proof of prior use exists, and in the area of traditional knowledge, which is often orally transmitted, such a written proof often does not exist. Moreover, the case also points to an intrinsic problem with the non-obviousness criterion. An inventive step is deemed non-obvious if 'a person skilled in the art' would not immediately come to the same conclusion. But the question then is: who would be the appropriate expert to judge the non-obviousness of the inventive step? In the turmeric case, for a US medical student the use of turmeric powder for wound healing might not have been an obvious idea, but for an Indian villager the same practice might have been quite natural. Thus, both the novelty and the non-obviousness criteria are ultimately relative criteria which depend on the knowledge that is used as reference and the selection of experts. The industrial applicability or usefulness criterion is interpreted very differently in various legislations. In the USA this is interpreted to the effect that an intervention shall produce a 'concrete, useful and tangible' result. In Europe patent offices generally require an invention to produce a 'technical effect' – thus excluding, for example, business methods from patentability (Bakels and Hugenholtz 2002: 13).

While international treaties form increasingly important frameworks, actual patents are still granted at the national level. The international Patent Cooperation Treaty (PCT), which was enacted in 1970, offers the possibility to simultaneously apply for a patent in all its signatory states, and lets one patent office conduct an international search for prior art that then can be used by the national patent offices in the countries in which the final patent application is made. But the decision about the application remains with the national patent offices, who are free to use the results of the international search if they want to. Attempts to further harmonize the national granting procedures through a proposed 'Substantive Patent Law Treaty' (SPLT) have effectively stalled since 2005 on the grounds of a fundamental disagreement between developing and developed countries about the scope of harmonization. While developed countries are pushing for harmonization of the criteria for novelty, non-obviousness, utility and industrial application, developing countries insist that any substantial patent harmonization should also include provisions for technology transfer, anti-competitive practices, safeguards for flexibilities and disclosure of origin for bio-patents (New 2005).

An exception to the exclusive national administrative sovereignty over the granting of patents is the European Patent Convention (EPC), which offers applicants the possibility to apply at one single institution, the European Patent Office, for a European patent that is effectively a bundle of national patents valid in the member states of the EPC (for a detailed discussion see Schneider 2010).

While patents are granted by patent offices, the scope of patent protection is ultimately determined through litigation. This is true for countries with a civil law tradition such as Germany as well as for countries with a common law tradition such as the UK or the USA in which legal development in general is strongly driven by case law. As a consequence specialized courts that are in some countries responsible for patent litigation gain a strong influence on the scale and scope of patent protection that is available in various fields of industry. Commentators generally see for example the establishment of the US Court of Appeals for the Federal Circuit (CAFC) in 1982, with its exclusive jurisdiction over patent appeal cases in the USA, as a strategic move that has significantly strengthened the position of patent holders (Drahos and Braithwaite 2003: 162; Sell 2003: 67 ff.; Jaffe and Lerner 2004: 10).

Recent developments are: a growing focus on implementation and enforcement; a tendency to shift further reform attempts from the international to the bi- and multilateral level and some attempts to countervail the strong position of the IP industries by a group of developing countries; and some tentative attempts to sidestep the restrictive current system through the use of voluntary licensing schemes. These will be discussed in more detail below.

2.3.2.   Copyrights

In contrast to patents that have to be registered before becoming effective, copyrights come into existence with the creation of the literary or artistic work. As mentioned above, this has not always been the case. Early copyrights usually required registration and many countries – among them the USA – did not recognize the copyrights of foreign authors until late into the nineteenth century (Halbert 1997: 59).[6] Copyrights in general give longer protection than patents, but the scope

---

[6] In the United States copyrights of foreign authors have only been protected since the 1891 Chace Act that established the recognition of copyrights regardless of the nationality of the author.

of protection is more limited. Copyright protects the concrete expression of an idea in a literary text, a photo, drawing or painting, a musical score or recording, a film, a sculpture, architecture, or in a computer program. It does not protect the idea as such. So if Shakespeare were to write Romeo and Juliet today, his work would be protected until at least fifty years after his death, but this would not curtail the options of other writers to write a play on the theme of a tragic love story that involves the children of two feuding families and that ends with the death of the two lovers. Unlike patents, thus, copyright does not require novelty, but only originality of the work. In the twentieth century copyrights have been constantly expanded to cover more kinds of works and to protect them for ever longer periods.

As with patents, no single international copyright law exists. The various national laws differ with regard to scope, subject matter and length of protection and with regard to the types of non-infringing uses of copyrighted materials that are allowed. But while national idiosyncrasies are substantial, the similarities that result from international legal frameworks outweigh the differences. The most important international treaty that governs copyrights is the Berne Convention, which has been reinforced though its incorporation into the TRIPS agreement. The Berne Convention guarantees a minimum protection term of fifty years after the death of the author (fifty years after production for cinematographic works and twenty-five years after production for photographic works). It allows member states to exempt certain expressions – for example public speeches or lectures – from copyright, and offers contracting states the possibility to allow the limited free use of copyrighted works for quotations, for teaching and for reporting, provided that a reference to the author of the work is given. In common law systems these exceptions usually have the form of 'fair dealing' or 'fair use' (USA) exceptions. In civil law systems they are codified as limitations and exceptions for specific uses.

While no international unified copyright exists, the harmonization in the field of copyright is more extensive than in the field of patents, because all 164 Berne member states fully recognize the copyright of a work regardless of its geographical origin. Where patents have to be granted separately in each country, a novel or a scientific paper published in one of the Berne contracting states automatically enjoys copyright protection in all other states. This protection may vary in time and some works may not be eligible for copyright protection in all countries, but in principle copyrights have a universal validity.

Current technical developments question some of the foundations of the existing copyright system: the fact that in the digital world transmission can no longer be separated from copying is subverting the differentiation between the various forms of use defined in the copyright laws. To display an ebook on a computer monitor it is necessary to copy the digital information from the storage media to the computer memory. Is this already copying? And what happens if the ebook is displayed simultaneously on more than one computer terminal? Usually copyright laws have not been adapted in ways that would take advantage of and promote the new technical possibilities but in ways that force digital media to emulate the characteristics of paper-based publications. The German copyright law (Urheberrechtsgesetz, UrhG), for example, allows in general the creation of temporary copies within a computer system in order to display or transfer a digitized copyrighted work (§ 44a UrhG), but it allows libraries, museums and archives to only display as many versions of a digitized work concurrently as there are copies of the work in the possession of the institution (§ 52b UrhG). A library which has digitized a book in its collection thus is only allowed to show it to one user at a time if it owns only one copy of the original book. And the library is only allowed to do this on specialized terminals within the library (Ensthaler 2009).

In other areas new rights have been created. The European database directive,[7] for example, created – with doubtful results (Maurer, Hugenholtz and Onsrud 2001) – a copyright-like *sui generis* protection for databases with a protection term of fifteen years.

The virtualization of the copyrighted goods furthermore goes along with a growing tendency to replace traditional copyright with adapted licensing contracts (Lessig 2006), which confer even fewer rights to the user of a copyrighted work. A typical licence, for example for an mp3 music track or a digital video, does not allow the user to re-sell the digital good that he or she has bought, whereas a reader of a paper-based book, a vinyl LP, a music CD or a video DVD is able to re-sell the good after having read, heard or seen it.

On the other hand, the technical advances are also offering opportunities for developments that go in the opposite direction. Based on the option to waive some or all of the granted copyrights in private contracts, the free and open source software (F/OSS) community has established an alternative copyright licence for computer software, the GNU General Public License (GPL), that secures public access instead of exclusive use of licensed works. In a similar way Creative Commons has established a licence for granting maximum access to other digital

---

[7] Directive 96/9/EC, *Official Journal* L 077, 27 March 1996, pp. 20–8.

creative works. These developments will be discussed in more detail in later parts of this book (section 6.4).

2.4.   Legitimatory narratives

The legal frameworks that regulate intellectual property rights build on two broad groups of legitimizing narratives. The first group of legitimizing narratives locates the source of intellectual property in an individual's personal labour that is invested in the creation of a work and in his or her personal rights. The second group of narratives relies on a utilitarian argument that intellectual property rights would be the most effective way to spur the creation of (useful) knowledge. Both narratives can be combined and often are combined in arguments for strong intellectual property rights. But analytically they can be separated because they rely on different underlying assumptions and emphasize in the first case the contribution of the creator, inventor or author, and in the second case general assumptions about welfare and efficiency effects of intellectual property rights.

2.4.1.   Natural and personal rights

The natural and personal rights-based narratives draw on John Locke's and Georg Wilhelm Friedrich Hegel's property theories. Locke develops his *natural rights-based labour theory of property* in his *Second Treatise of Government*, where he starts from the assumption that 'God, who hath given the world to men in common, hath also given them reason to make use of it to the best advantage of life, and convenience' (Locke 1690: § 26). The earth and all natural resources thus belong to humankind in common, and this extends also to each person, so that 'every man has property in his own person' (§ 26). Building on this assumption Locke argues that the labour also belongs to the person that carries it out, and that if this labour involves the work on commonly owned natural resources, they then become the property of the labourer (§ 27). The examples Locke uses to illustrate his general reasoning are taken from the physical realm, they refer to the cultivation of land or the processing of natural resources. He does not develop a theory of intellectual property or adapt his reasoning to the realm of immaterial goods – the idea of intellectual property was still absent at the time of Locke's writing. Only subsequently has it been argued that this theory would be especially apt for the field of immaterial goods, which do not possess any intrinsic material value, where the stock of knowledge can be seen as being commonly owned, and where the value is created by investing intellectual labour (for a detailed discussion see Hughes 1988; for a critical evaluation see e.g. Fisher 2001).

Hegel's idealist philosophy builds in many aspects on the notion of natural rights but abandons the idea of God-given common property and instead starts from the idea that the constitutive element of the ego is the free will. Things do not possess this free will, and thus, Hegel argues, a 'person has the right to direct his will upon any object, as his real and positive end. The object thus becomes his ... Mankind has the absolute right to appropriate all that is a thing' (Hegel 2001 [1820]: § 44). Property rights are thus an immediate consequence of an individual's free will and do not necessarily require the investment of labour (Hughes 1988). In his *Philosophy of Right* Hegel explicitly addresses the issue of intellectual property. He argues that '[s]ome goods, or rather substantive phases of life are inalienable' (§ 66) and among those are mental endowments, science, art, religious sermons, masses, prayers and blessings, and inventions (§ 43). They can be sold in their material embodiment as books or machines, but the idea on which they are based cannot be alienated. On this argumentation the *narrative of moral rights* – original and inalienable author's rights – builds (Hughes 1988: 337 f.; May and Sell 2006: 21). In the French and German and some other continental European legislations these author's rights remain untouched even after a creator has sold or otherwise relinquished his or her rights to a publisher or producer. They are separate from the commercial rights which can be transferred through a licensing contract.

Both philosophical justifications have been extensively criticized. A classic example is Robert Nozick's general critique of Locke's assumption that investing labour into something should generate ownership, or as Nozick in his flowery prose writes: 'Why does mixing one's labor with something make one the owner of it? ... If I own a can of tomato juice and spill it in the sea so that its molecules (made radioactive, so that I can check this) mingle evenly throughout the sea, do I thereby come to own the sea, or have I foolishly dissipated my tomato juice?' (Nozick 1974: 174–5; cited after Feser 2005: 64). William Fisher summarizes these and other problems of the transfer of Locke's labour-desert theory to immaterial goods and concludes that '[w]hether Locke's theory provides support for any intellectual-property rights is thus uncertain' (Fisher 2001: 185), because the intellectual equivalent of physical labour remains unclear, and the notion of an intellectual commons that is not yet the result of human activity and untouched, like the virgin land in Locke's example, is highly problematic.

The last argument is related to a line of criticism that focuses on the *myth of the author*, and that undermines both philosophical legitimations.

Boyle (2008) for example argues that both the Anglo-Saxon copyright and the continental European *droit d'auteur* assume a romantic notion of the author, who creates a piece of art only from his or her mind, as does the inventor who conjures up an idea out of thin air. But in reality literary, scientific or artistic production is often a collective process involving a highly specialized division of labour. The production of a movie for example often involves many hundreds or even thousands of persons who contribute on various levels to the final copyrighted product. In US law the problem of attributing the relevant part of the copyright to the participating artists is usually solved by declaring the movie as a 'work for hire' for which the copyright belongs to the employer, which usually is the film-production company. Notwithstanding the problems with the natural rights-based legitimatory narratives mentioned above, it is extremely hard to argue that for a corporation moral rights analogous to a human individual should exist.

A different angle is addressed by criticism that focuses on the issue of *incrementality*. Like the myth of the author, the argument is based on a consideration of the empirical reality of current cultural and scientific production. The core of the argument here is that creation of literary or artistic works is usually a process that builds heavily on existing knowledge and cultural material (May 2000; Lessig 2004). Musicians are inspired by existing tunes, authors of literary works draw on the stock of existing books, plots and styles, the notion of movie genres means nothing else than that films that belong to one genre have copied certain elements from each other. This does not deny the authors their genuine creativity, but claims that this creativity would not have been possible without the prior existing art.

Critics of the current regime usually do not want to abolish the system completely, but argue for drastically shorter protection periods and more extensive exceptions and limitations. Their aim is to find a better balance between exclusive rights and public interests to enable public access to the results of creative, scientific and innovative works.

2.4.2. *Utilitarian legitimations*

The second strand of legitimatory narratives builds on various utilitarian arguments. In his seminal economic review of the patent system Fritz Machlup identified three utilitarian narratives that are used to legitimate intellectual property rights (1958: 21):

(1) The *reward by monopoly narrative* argues that useful inventions should be rewarded in proportion to their social value, and that

society should intervene if the market alone does not generate the appropriate reward.

(2) The *monopoly-profit-incentive narrative* builds on the assumption that inventions, due to their public good character, will be under-provided by market mechanisms alone, and thus additional incentives (in the form of patents or prices) have to be created to secure sufficient generation of inventions.

(3) The *exchange-for-secrets narrative* assumes that innovators have a strong incentive to keep their knowledge to themselves in order to prevent others from acquiring this knowledge. But since society has an interest in the speedy dissemination of new knowledge in order to speed up overall innovation the state may offer intellectual property rights in exchange for disclosure.

More recently two additional utilitarian narratives have surfaced, addressing the role of innovation in the world system.

(4) The *trade narrative* is an extension of the monopoly-profit-incentive narrative. The argument here is that a producer will have no, or only a limited, incentive to export a product, for which he or she has intellectual property rights protection in the domestic market, to a foreign market, where no such protection exists. To increase international trade thus an intellectual property rights system should provide similar levels of rights in all countries. The development of a coherent trade narrative is usually attributed to Jacques Gorlin, an economist who worked for the Intellectual Property Committee (IPC) – the industry lobbying coalition that was pushing for the TRIPS agreement (Gorlin 1985; for a more detailed analysis of Gorlin's role see Sell 2002a, 2003).

(5) The *development narrative* is an international version of the exchange-for-secrets and the reward by monopoly narratives and argues that international technology transfer will only occur if intellectual property rights guarantee that the transferred technology will not be used to compete with the provider of the technology on its home market. The strongest proponent of the development narrative is WIPO, which – as a UN organization – has an obligation to include development concerns in its policies. From one of its earliest statements in which WIPO declared that its goals are to assist 'developing countries in promoting their industrialization, their commerce and their cultural, scientific and technological development through the modernization of their industrial property and copyright systems' (WIPO 1975: 13, cited in May 2007: 27), to more current publications in which IP is lauded as a '"power tool"

for economic development that is not yet being used to optimal effect in all countries, particularly in the developing world' (WIPO 2003b: 4), WIPO has consistently argued for more and stronger IP protection. The development narrative is also present in several recent G8 statements, in which an argument is developed that 'IPRs is of core interest for consumers in all countries, particularly in developing countries' (G8 2007: 2).

More recently the general thrust of the development narrative has been somewhat displaced by a developing countries' coalition pushing for a 'WIPO Development Agenda' in which development is equated with more balanced and more flexible IP protection (Yu 2009a). I will address this development in more detail at the end of this chapter.

All utilitarian argumentations draw on the assumption that in an unregulated market public goods will be under-provided. The basic reasoning was developed by Jeremy Bentham, who argued strongly for a patent system, because '[w]ithout the assistance of the laws, the inventor would almost always be driven out of the market by his rival, who finding himself, without any expense, in possession of a discovery which has cost the inventor much time and expense, would be able to deprive him of all his deserved advantages, by selling at a lower price. An exclusive privilege is of all rewards the best proportioned, the most natural, and the least burdensome. It produces an infinite effect, and it costs nothing' (Bentham 1843: III, § 23). Neoclassical economists have more systematically developed the idea of market under-provision of public goods (e.g. Pigou 1932), and Paul Samuelson has later elaborated and formalized the argument in his seminal article on welfare economics (Samuelson 1954), in which he claims that rational actors will have no incentive to provide, what he calls, collective consumption goods as long as these goods can be freely accessed by everyone, because every actor is individually better off, if he or she abstains from investing in the creation of these goods and instead uses the freely available goods that have been provided by others. If every actor behaves like this, no (or at least not enough) public goods will be created. The market will only provide an optimal supply of goods if there are only private and no public goods (for a detailed discussion see Holzinger 2008). The difference between private and public goods is that the latter can be used or consumed without restricting the use and availability to others. Vincent and Elinor Ostrom (1977) have elaborated the goods taxonomy and developed a four-field matrix (Table 2.1) dividing goods along the two axes subtractability and exclusion. A public good is then a good characterized by low subtractability and difficult exclusion – it is hard

Table 2.1 *Types of goods*

		Subtractability	
		Low	*High*
Exclusion	*Difficult*	Public goods	Common-pool resources
	Easy	Club goods	Private goods

Source: Hess and Ostrom (2003: 120).

to exclude others from seeing a sunset, the prototypical public good, and my enjoyment of the sunset does not diminish its value for others. Private goods, in contrast, are goods where others can be relatively easy excluded from using them, and where its use by one actor diminishes its use for others.

Knowledge and information are intrinsically public goods. They are even a very special case of public goods where their use does not only not diminish their usefulness for others but might even enhance it – they exhibit what economists call network effects. If knowledge and information can in principle be seen as public goods, the argument about market under-provision of public goods in general can be translated to them. This perspective is most clearly expressed by Kenneth Arrow when he states 'we expect a free enterprise economy to underinvest in invention and research (as compared with an ideal) because it is risky, because the product can be appropriated only to a limited extent, and because of increasing returns in use' (Arrow 1962: 619).

Intellectual property rights are offered as a solution to this under-provision of inventions because they offer incentives to invest in research and development (R&D) by privatizing the otherwise public good and thus offering the inventor the possibility to extract gains from the application of the invention that exceed the costs of the research. In his often cited study William Nordhaus has argued that especially for small inventions patents would provide an almost ideal mechanism to maximize welfare gains while minimizing the deadweight loss that results from raising the marginal cost of information above zero (Nordhaus 1969).[8]

---

[8] Because information can be replicated without loss the cost of producing another unit of (the same) information – the marginal cost – is ideally zero. In real life copying information generates minimal costs for transferring the information on a blank medium or through a computer network. But these costs can usually be neglected if they are very small compared to the worth of the information.

The utilitarian IP narrative has been extensively criticized. The counterarguments fall roughly into four groups, which address the myth of under-provision, the myth of innovation, the problem of (partial) system failure, and the problem of the wrong kind of innovation.

(1) The *myth of under-provision* argument is the most fundamental as it questions the core assumption on which the utilitarian legitimatory narrative of intellectual property rights systems is built. This argument comes in a variety of forms. On the most abstract level James Boyle (2003) questions the assumption that only monetary self-interest would drive the creation of knowledge. In reality persons and firms have all kinds of different reasons for creating artistic, literary, scientific and technical knowledge. 'Assume a random distribution of incentive structures in different people, a global network: transmission, information sharing and copying costs that approach zero, and a modular creation process. With these assumptions, it just does not matter why they do it. In lots of cases, they will do it' (Boyle 2003: 46).

In a similar vein Yochai Benkler argues that, instead of only one incentive structure, three ideal information production strategies exist: a rights-based exclusion strategy, a non-exclusion-market strategy, and a non-exclusion-non-market strategy (Benkler 2006: 43). The first is followed by authors and artists who are selling their rights to publishers, by publishing houses, music and movie production companies, and by firms who rely heavily on the added monopoly profit of their IP protected goods. The second strategy is followed by firms that invest in knowledge production primarily to optimize production and reduce production costs, network firms that share information in inter-company networks, or bands who freely distribute their songs to increase their fan-base and thus the number of people coming to concerts. The third strategy finally is followed by people who provide content on the internet for free – be it in blogs, in Wikipedia articles or in other forms, by academics who publish for fame and recognition, or by government and non-government think-tanks and service units who provide in-house expertise.

This reasoning is supported by scholars who have researched how public goods or common-pool resources are empirically managed. Charlotte Hess and Elinor Ostrom argue that the growing empirical evidence of successful and sustainable models of common-pool resource management in the absence of intellectual property rights 'does not challenge the empirical validity of the conventional theory *where it is relevant*, but rather questions its presumed, universal generalizability' (Hess and Ostrom 2003: 118). They see the growing universe of open access repositories for scholarly articles as a clear counter-example that disproves the universal validity of the assumption that under the condition of universal availability no one will have an incentive to produce the relevant good. Furthermore, they argue, there is neither a theoretical nor an empirical foundation to assume a necessary connection between the nature of a good and the appropriate property regime. Private goods can be managed in open access systems as can public goods be managed in private property regimes. Ronald Herring shows in a similar vein that commons often do not deteriorate in the absence of privatization and that privatization has often not solved the assumed under-provision or overuse problems (Herring 1990).

In addition, several historical studies have questioned the premise that strong intellectual property rights would positively correlate with enhanced innovation or creative activities. In his review of the patent system Fritz Machlup (1958) came to the conclusion that '[n]one of the empirical evidence at our disposal and none of the theoretical arguments presented either confirms or confutes the belief that the patent system has promoted the progress of the technical arts and the productivity of the economy' (1958: 79), a position reiterated half a century later by Reinier Bakels and Bernt Hugenholtz when they conclude in their assessment of the state of the art of the literature on intellectual property rights: 'The abundance of opinions, promises, theories, fears and concerns expressed about the patent system in the course of literally centuries is by no means matched by factual data' (Bakels and Hugenholtz 2002: 18 f.).

In his voluminous historical comparison of the British and the German book market in the eighteenth and nineteenth centuries, Eckhard Höffner even comes to a much more sceptical judgement. He argues that the German book market and intellectual life flourished between 1770 and 1837 precisely because at that time no copyright existed that would prohibit unauthorized reprinting of books. At the same time Great Britain most likely lost its leading role in knowledge-based industries because of the detrimental consequences of the copyright (Höffner 2010: vol. 2, 389). In Germany more new books were published than in Britain and authors earned more money from publishing their books than their British colleagues. Thus Höffner comes to the conclusion that 'the almost unanimously held opinion about the beneficial effect of copyright is empirically not tenable' (Höffner 2010: vol. 2, 387, my translation).

These findings are corroborated in Josh Lerner's historical comparative study in which he examined the effect of increasing patent protection on the rate of patenting. He found that in 177 of the most significant shifts in patent policy across 60 countries and 150 years, 'the impact of patent protection-enhancing shifts on applications by residents was actually negative' (Lerner 2002: 29) – stronger intellectual property rights did lead to fewer patent applications by domestic firms and individuals, but had a positive effect on patent applications by foreign applicants. In a similar vein Peter Drahos has argued that there is no linear relationship between social welfare and patent protection. Instead there is more likely an inverted U-shape relationship, where for each economy social welfare reaches a maximum at a certain level of IP protection after which the social costs of high IP standards exceed the benefits (Drahos 2005).

Critics of the trade and development narrative have argued that the negative effect of stronger intellectual property rights will be especially salient in developing countries. Since strong intellectual property rights favour IP owners over IP users, and since developing countries are net importers of knowledge goods, strong intellectual property rights will not have the beneficial effect its supporters predict, but lead to a transfer of wealth from developing to developed countries. The main beneficiaries of TRIPS will thus be the USA, Europe and Japan (Drahos 1995; Correa 2000; Dixon and Bauhardt 2002).

(2) The *myth of innovation* argument questions the second – often only implicit – assumption on which the utilitarian IP protection narrative rests: the independence of inventions. While the disclosure requirement is often cited as one major advantage of the patent system, because it would stimulate further technological innovation, the fact that inventive and creative activities build upon each other is usually not systematically taken into account. The argument that if one accounts for the cumulative nature of knowledge generation, the current IP system may actually have detrimental effects on innovation and creativity, has been put forward by several authors (Scotchmer 1991; David 1993; Benkler 2006; Lessig 2008). One line of argument is that the disclosure function of the patent system is generally overrated because on the one hand firms tend to circumvent the disclosure requirement by leaving out important information in the patent application. According to Peter Drahos and John Braithwaite patent lawyers have developed the art of drafting patent application 'in ways that satisfied the patent office, but were virtually useless to public readers of the documents' (Drahos and Braithwaite 2003: 47). On the other hand it has been argued, that the benefit of the disclosure requirement is limited because, since an invention only becomes valuable if it is used, in most fields of technology the product, once it is available, will reveal its functionality to any knowledgeable observer anyway (Machlup 1958: 24; Andersen 2004: 435). The myth of innovation argument is also at the core of Philippe

Aigrain's argumentation about the benefits and social values of sharing cultural goods (Aigrain 2012).

(3) A less fundamental critique of current intellectual property rights addresses problems of *partial failure of the IP system*. In its more moderate form this criticism has addressed the inconsistencies of the current legal and institutional setting. Adam Jaffe and Josh Lerner have argued that the patent system is not working properly because several groups of actors are using it to further their own private interests to the detriment of its overall welfare-enhancing function. Patent lawyers have a strong interest in high litigation costs and self-funded patent offices are structurally inclined to grant high numbers of patents because this automatically increases user fees (Jaffe and Lerner 2004). Sivaramjani Thambisetty has shown that national patent legislation follows dynamics of increasing returns and path dependency, making them resistant to external reform impulses (Thambisetty 2009).

Several authors, moreover, have argued that firms increasingly use patents as blocking devices by creating patent thickets that effectively keep newcomers from entering a market (Shapiro 2001; Drahos and Braithwaite 2003; May and Sell 2006; Boldrin and Levine 2008). Related to this is the increasing propagation of defensive patenting strategies in which firms build large patent portfolios that can be used as bargaining chips to protect against litigation. The rationale is that in the case of litigation the large enough patent portfolio will likely contain a patent that will allow the defendant to counter-sue the plaintiff, or that patent portfolios can be used in cross-licensing agreements to limit the chance of litigation between the contracting parties (Blind, Edler and Friedewald 2003).

A more fundamental structural deficiency of property rights systems in general and intellectual property rights systems in particular has been discussed by Michael Heller in his article on the tragedy of the anti-commons. Starting from Garrett Hardin's classical argument that unregulated common-pool resources will be subject to overuse, if too many owners have the privilege to use the resource, leading to the *tragedy of the commons* (Hardin 1968), Heller shows that under certain conditions private property rights can have the opposite effect and lead to underuse of the property. This happens when too many owners have overlapping entitlements to exclude others from using a resource, resulting in the *tragedy of the anti-commons* (Heller 1998). To illustrate his general claim, Heller uses the example of empty storefronts in Moscow in 1990 after the transition from socialism to capitalism. He shows that the privatization of former state-property resulted in a constellation in which multiple 'owners' held overlapping rights – one organization acquired the right to sell a property, another one the right to lease it and a third the right to occupy it – and each of these rights was, moreover, often held by multiple organizations. In this situation 'almost any use of the storefront requires the agreement of multiple parties' (Heller 1998: 639), and because it was often either impossible or too expensive to get the multiple parties to agree, potential users refrained from opening their businesses in the empty storefronts and, instead, opened kiosks for which a much more straightforward property regime existed. The resource remains underused because too many overlapping and competing property rights exist that make assembling a usable bundle of property rights too costly.

Several authors have argued that patents in the field of computer software, an area that is a prime example of a cumulative innovation process, are especially prone to lead to such an anti-commons problem, when further development is blocked by patents on existing software components (Hart, Holmes and Reid 2000: 36), and because the complexity of the software multiplies the possibilities for patent infringement beyond the grasp of the software developer (Bödeker, Moldenhauer and Rubbel 2005: 68). But unlike in Hardin's storefront example, the fact that it is often impossible to reliably judge which existing patents a specific piece of software would infringe, there is no reliable evidence that programmers would refrain from creating a program. Instead individual programmers often ignore the threat of possible infringement, and large software companies are building defensive patent portfolios, allowing them to threaten to counter-sue potential plaintiffs, or come to cross-licensing agreements with potential rights-holders.

Also under the rubric 'failure of the IP system' falls James Bessen and Michael Meurer's claim that, in the US patent system, patents are increasingly incapable of fulfilling their central property function: to provide non-owners with clear and unambiguous notice of the boundary of the property (Bessen and Meurer 2008). In their book *Patent Failure*, they make the rather bold claim that since the 1990s the US patent system has deteriorated in such a way that 'the average public firm outside the chemical and pharmaceutical industries would be better off if patents did not exist' (2008: 16). Instead of providing incentives for innovation and investment, the patent system is – except for pharmaceutical and chemical industries – providing disincentives to invest in R&D because the costs it creates by far outweigh its added value. The authors argue that the core task of a patent system must be to provide a boundary function that works as well as fences or titles in the world of tangible goods. But the current system provides only boundary information which is often fuzzy and unpredictable, not fixed in scope, and which may even change over time. This insecurity over the boundaries of intellectual property rights is rooted in the ambiguity of the patent claims. A land title uses geographical information to describe the limits of property it designates. This information is relatively unambiguous and does not change over time. A pharmaceutical patent usually contains a chemical formula or a detailed description of the chemical ingredients, a patent for a machine will often contain a blueprint that sketches the function of the patented machine. These types of information are also relatively unambiguous. But patent claims also use natural language to describe the claimed invention. And the more patent claims rely on this kind of information, the less precise the information becomes, and the more open it is to interpretation about what exactly may be included in the description. Taking into account that patentees will have a strong interest in formulating a patent claim as broadly as possible, to get as much protection as possible, the scope of the problem of fuzzy property boundaries becomes obvious.

(4) Finally a fourth line of criticism does not deny that current IP systems generate incentives for the private production of knowledge and innovation, but argues that the system provides incentives for the *wrong kind of innovation*, or – in a weaker version – has deficiencies in specific areas where inventions are socially desirable but not produced under a patent regime. Most authors agree that patents do not work effectively where research costs are high and potential revenues low. A standard example is often basic research where important groundwork for further innovation is laid but where only a very low probability exists that such research will lead to marketable results in the short run (Arrow 1962; Pugatch 2004). The consequence that is not only proposed in the literature but also realized in the political realm is state-financed basic research. Thus social resources that are necessary for carrying out basic research are usually provided through an alternative mechanism that does not rely on ex-post recuperation of research expenditures, but on ex-ante public financing of researchers and research institutions. Similar mechanisms exist as stipends for writers and artists or as subsidies for theatres, operas or more general cultural productions.

The opposite problem to the market under-provision of basic research is rent-seeking behaviour by rights-owners. The problem here is that strong monopoly rights tend to foster unproductive use of the property. Rights-owners will have a strong incentive to get as much as possible out of their privilege without caring about the social costs of such a behaviour. An example that is often used in the literature to illustrate this problem is the 1998 US Sonny Bono Copyright Term Extension Act where, as the result of intensive lobbying, the copyright term was extended another twenty years, preventing many well-known works, such as the Mickey Mouse character or George Gershwin's compositions, from falling into the public domain. Critics argued that the successful lobbying for the term extension was a prime example of rent-seeking behaviour because the additional income for the rights-owners did not incentivize the creation of new works but channelled money to rights-owners for works whose creators often were already dead (Drahos 2005: 146).

Another detrimental dynamic is what authors have called 'race to the patent' (e.g. David 1993: 55). Because innovation is usually a cumulative process where current research builds on existing knowledge in any given situation most likely multiple firms or researchers are independently but concurrently trying to find a solution to a known problem. A patent rewards only the one inventor who is able to add the (temporarily) finishing touch to this process. From an economic perspective this leads to inefficient resource allocation, because the patent will devalue the investments by those who were not the first to reach the patentable solution. Moreover, the exclusive patent right then creates an incentive to invent around an existing patent, instead of using the newly created knowledge for further innovation.

2.4.3.   Balancing monopoly rights

The shortcomings of patents and copyrights have not only been criticized in the academic literature, but are – at least to some degree – also addressed in several countervailing or balancing measures, realized in national IP laws and policies aimed to secure the provision of and access to knowledge.

For this purpose many countries provide in their intellectual property laws exemptions which allow for example copying of texts for purposes of research and education. In countries with a statutory law tradition this is usually realized in the form of specific limitations; in countries with a common law tradition this often takes the form of a more general 'fair use' provision (Samuelson 1994). Compulsory licences – that is state-enforced regulations that allow third parties to use a patented product or process without paying licensing fees or with only nominal compensation for the rights-holder – are common measures provided in many national patent laws to counter anti-competitive effects of the patent system or to prioritize other preferences (e.g. national security or health concerns) over IP remuneration. Anti-monopoly legislation is another way to limit the scope of monopoly powers a single company can exert. Historically, for example in the USA, periods of strong intellectual property rights have followed periods of strong anti-monopoly legislation and vice versa.

The fact that ex-post financing systems based upon patents or copyrights lead to under-provision of basic theoretical knowledge that cannot be immediately turned into profitable goods is one reason among others to maintain state-financed university systems and basic research facilities.

Moreover, alternative invention-reward models have been proposed by several authors with the aim to enhance access to the newly created knowledge. One such proposition is the allocation of prices that would honour the actual value of an invention – either after its creation (Polanvyi 1944) or by offering a fixed sum in anticipation of the social value of a desired invention, so-called ex-ante R&D grand prices (Davis 2004).

More recently the idea of prize funds has been taken up to address another inefficiency problem of the patent system: that patents only incentivize research for products for which a sufficiently big market with affluent buyers exists. This leads to the under-provision of medical research for illnesses that mainly affect people living in developing countries, who cannot afford to spend significant sums on drugs. Instead medical research focuses on drugs for the treatment of often less severe illnesses in the richer part of the world addressing the medical needs of more affluent customers. Proposals to spur the development of drugs for the so-called neglected diseases range from completely abolishing patent protection for medical innovation and replacing it with a system based on prize funds to maintaining the current system but enhancing competition by simplifying the granting of compulsory licences and offering prizes as additional incentives (Love and Hubbard 2009; Gombe and Love 2010).

All in all the legitimatory narratives of intellectual property rights today are dominated by the utilitarian discourse that without intellectual property rights innovation and thus economic competitiveness would come to a standstill. Even in the creative industries, arguments that focus on just compensation for intellectual labour or natural authors' rights are less important than the utilitarian narratives. The International Federation of the Phonographic Industry (IFPI), the international umbrella organization of the national recording industry associations, for example states on its website that intellectual property is needed to 'ensure there are proper incentives for companies to continue investing in the creation, production, promotion and marketing of sound recordings'[9] without mentioning the artists as possible beneficiaries.

---

[9] www.ifpi.org/content/section_views/why_is_piracy_illegal.html (accessed 15 May 2011).

More than 500 years after the Venice patent statute, knowledge about the social benefits of intellectual property rights is still ambiguous at best. It is obvious that certain industries – especially the US film and music industry and the European, US and Japanese pharmaceutical companies – profit immensely from strong intellectual property rights, and it is therefore no wonder that these industries are relentlessly pushing for ever-stronger intellectual property rights worldwide (Sell 2003, 2008). Whether their profits offset the social costs of strong intellectual property rights and whether intellectual property rights really fuel innovation is doubtful. A serious roadblock to answering the latter question is that scientists so far have not been able to directly measure innovation. The proxy that is usually used is patenting rates (Archibugi and Pianta 1996). This already assumes that innovation will be expressed in patents and such a measure is therefore a priori incapable of capturing those innovations that do not result in patent applications.

The growing scepticism about the universal benefits of strong intellectual property rights is reflected in the various developments that are pushing the course of IP politics at the international level in partially contradictory directions.

2.5.   Current developments and conflicts

At the international level three broad trends are visible that shape the development of current IP policies: (1) As attempts to further strengthen the international legal framework of intellectual property protection are increasingly met with resistance from developing countries, the USA and Europe are increasingly pushing their IP agenda in bi- and multilateral trade agreements. (2) This is accompanied by a growing focus on IP enforcement where emphasis is shifted from the creation of further legal frameworks to the implementation of existing rules in a maximally restrictive manner. (3) Against this, a third trend emerges that starts to establish alternative structures of regulation that emphasize access to and dissemination of knowledge over exclusion and appropriation.

The first trend, the *bi- and multilateralization of IP politics,* is a result of the stalemate between developing and developed countries at the level of international institutions after TRIPS. The attempts of especially the USA and to a lesser degree Europe to further harmonize and strengthen IP protection at the international level is met by increasingly vocal and increasingly well-organized resistance by developing countries led by Brazil, South Africa and India (Yu 2009b). As a consequence of this, the USA and Europe have increasingly focused their efforts on bi- and multilateral trade agreements in which they were able to include IP provisions that go far beyond what is required under TRIPS (Katz and Hinze 2009).

This strategy has been combined with the second trend, the *emphasis on enforcement*, in the process that led to the multilateral Anti-Counterfeiting Trade Agreement (ACTA). The ACTA process started in 2005 on the initiative of Japan and involved the USA, the European Union, Australia, Canada, Japan, the Republic of Korea, Mexico, Morocco, New Zealand, Singapore and Switzerland (Brenni 2010). In several secretive negotiation rounds between 2008 and November 2010 a text was agreed that presumably aims at fighting piracy and counterfeiting but de facto confers far-reaching rights on national customs administrations and establishes a priority of IP rights over other concerns. While after its rejection by the European Parliament ACTA has ultimately failed, the enforcement strategy stays alive in several bi- and multilateral trade negotiations, for example between the European Union and Canada (Geist 2012) or in the Trans-Pacific Partnership Agreement on Intellectual Property (Rossini and Opsahl 2012).

Against these trends of further maximalization of IP protection emerges a third trend that starts to establish alternative governance structures for knowledge, based on principles of *access and sharing*. The most visible part of this trend is the open source software movement that has created an alternative to the proprietary closed software paradigm and has created an operating system on which large parts of the internet infrastructure is built (Grassmuck 2002; Lutterbeck, Bärwolff and Gehring 2008). To secure universal access to the open source software the programmers developed a so-called 'copyleft' licence, the GNU General Public License (GPL). Inspired by the GPL's success in the field of software, in 2002 a group of US academics around Lawrence Lessig, Hal Abelson and Eric Eldred adopted the underlying idea of using the existing copyright system not to restrict but to guarantee unlimited access to literary and artistic productions in general by establishing the Creative Commons (CC) project (Boyle 2008: 8). Creative Commons offers a set of licences for digital creative goods which are more flexible than the GPL and offer authors more options to gradually place their work somewhere between the continuum of completely exclusive and completely open access. A more detailed discussion of the GPL and the mobilization around Creative Commons can be found in section 6.4.

In this context here, it is important to note that both projects have successfully established alternative rules that legally built upon the existing copyright regime, but that function in a way that effectively inverses the intention of the existing copyright system. They exploit a feature of the copyright system that automatically gives authors exclusive rights over their works as soon as the work is created, without the need to register these rights, or apply for these rights to be granted. Once in possession of the exclusive rights, individual creators are free to waive some or all of their rights, and to allow unrestricted use of their works. This option was not really envisioned in the perspective of the dominant legitimatory narratives, but the success of open source software and Creative Commons shows that, once such an option is offered in the form of an easy-to-use licence, a large number of individuals are willing to waive substantive parts of their exclusive rights in favour of public access to the knowledge goods they have created. Wikipedia is possibly the most prominent example of Creative Commons licensed content, and beyond this, millions of blog-posts, photos and increasingly also scientific articles have been made available under one of the Creative Commons licences.

Advocates of 'culture flat rates' (Grassmuck 2009) or 'creative contribution' (Aigrain 2012) follow a different path. They propose a general permission for non-commercial sharing of creative works that should go along with an alternative financing system for those works. This alternative system would not necessarily rest on existing copyrights, although it would go along with them.

In the scientific world the trend of access and sharing is strongly supported by university libraries and national science organizations. Starting with the Budapest Open Access Initiative, a growing number of institutional actors are pushing for the free availability of research results (Budapest Open Access Initiative 2002). The most prominent example here is the US National Institutes of Health's open access policy. Since 2006 it has requested and since 2008 it requires 'all investigators funded by the NIH [to] submit or have submitted for them to the National Library of Medicine's PubMed Central an electronic version of their final peer-reviewed manuscripts upon acceptance for publication, to be made publicly available no later than 12 months after the official date of publication' (National Institutes of Health 2008). Taking into account that the NIH is responsible for half of the US\$32 billion of federal research funding in 2010 in the USA (Britt 2010), the full scope of this step becomes visible: the largest government funding agency in the USA now requires scientists to make the results of their publicly funded research freely available. The Swiss National Science Foundation requires scientists in a similar way to publish the results of their research in institutional or disciplinary open access repositories (SNF 2008), and in a less stringent approach the German Research Foundation only suggests that scientists should publish their research in open access repositories and supports this option financially (Deutsche Forschungsgemeinschaft 2009).

Another part of this counter-trend against ever-stronger intellectual property rights is the establishment of the Medicines Patent Pool, a Geneva-based NGO financed by UNITAID with the purpose of 'negotiating with patent holders to share their intellectual property with the Pool, and then licensing it to other producers to facilitate the production of affordable generic medicines well-adapted for use in resource-poor settings'.[10] Similar to the GPL and Creative Commons, the Medicines Patent Pool was devised by a group of health activists around James Love to use aspects of the existing patent law to create knowledge with less restrictive exclusion rights. In all cases this is possible because rights-holders can always voluntarily renounce some or all of their rights. To the extent that this is done in a standardized process and with reliable results these initiatives thereby establish an alternative legal framework that piggybacks on the existing law and at the same time turns it on its head by accomplishing the opposite effect of the one for which the legal framework was originally devised. These grassroots attempts rely on voluntary adoption and can only thrive if enough actors contribute their works, or, in the case of the patent pool, contribute their patents.

Overall these contradictory developments are happening against the background of a fundamental politicization of intellectual property rights since the 1990s. Obviously decisions that shape the structure of intellectual property rights were always political decisions since they establish general rules and norms which have to be legitimized and which apply to all citizens within a given state. When I speak of politicization of intellectual property rights I refer to the fact that more recently conflicts about these rules and norms are emerging that involve a much wider constituency than hitherto known, and that the issue of intellectual property rights receives attention at the highest levels of political decision-making and in the general public sphere. The debates about the merits and problems of current IP regimes that I have discussed in this chapter are thus more than scholarly disputes. The arguments of the proponents of a strong intellectual property rights system and those of their critics built the foundation on which the claims about the future of the IP system are based. And often the academic authors are not just providing scholarly arguments, but are actively engaged in the struggles about the direction in which the current IP system shall evolve.

---

[10] www.medicinespatentpool.org/WHO-WE-ARE2/Mission (accessed 15 May 2011).

In the following chapter I will show that this politicization of IP should be interpreted within a wider framework of processes of social change associated with the transformation of modern societies to knowledge societies. I maintain that, to understand the current conflicts about intellectual property rights, it is not enough to look at the institutions that govern intellectual property rights, but it is necessary to look for the changing configuration of social conflicts, and to ask how these conflicts are related to large-scale processes of social change that are transforming our current societies.

3 Conflict and change in the knowledge society

The politicization of IP that I have described in the previous chapter is embedded in more fundamental processes of social change. It is no coincidence that in the late twentieth century contentious mobilizations emerged, addressing the rules and practices that govern the ways knowledge is produced, exploited and disseminated.

In this chapter I will locate the emerging conflicts about intellectual property rights in the broader processes of social change that are associated with the knowledge, information, post-industrial or network society. My analysis starts from the general assumption that large-scale social change alters the overall structures of social conflicts in a society. Changes in important parts of the social structure will lead to the emergence of new cleavages which may bring about new kinds of conflicts and may also bring about or facilitate the emergence of new collective actors. These new cleavages will not necessarily replace the old cleavages, but more likely add another dimension to the universe of social conflicts. Old cleavages will only gradually lose their centrality and will become less prominent vehicles for collective action. But the structure of social conflicts only partially reflects social structure. There is no mechanistic relation in which structural change automatically leads to corresponding conflicts. Social structures influence only conditions for the possibility of social conflicts, but these conditions are neither necessary nor sufficient. Conflicts can arise from many kinds of grievances which may or may not be related to structural inequalities in a society, and not all grievances will lead to conflicts that entail contentious collective mobilizations.

This chapter starts with a quick explanation of my terminology. To understand how the politicization of IP is related to processes of social change in our current societies I will then review the most influential theories of the post-industrial (Bell 1999 [1973]), network (Castells 2010b [1996]) and knowledge society (Stehr 1994b), focusing on the conflicts that these authors have analysed and/or envisioned in their theories. These considerations will be embedded in a more general discussion of the relationship between conflicts and social change, which is necessary because the three authors are surprisingly silent on the mechanisms of how the claimed large-scale social changes would be connected to changing social conflicts or political cleavages in current societies. Based on these discussions I will present some preliminary thoughts about a general model of the relationship between social conflicts and social change, and present a systematic assessment of the core new conflict lines that one might expect, based on the existing theories of the knowledge society.

3.1. Information, network or knowledge society?

Contemporary social theories are using numerous labels to characterize our current societies. Some of the more prominent are information society (Lyon 1988), network society (Castells 2010b [1996]), post-industrial society (Bell 1999 [1973]), knowledge society (Stehr 1994b), risk society (Beck 1986) or programmed society (Touraine 1972). Behind this abundance of concepts lies the notion that somehow the world today seems to differ significantly from the world about half a century ago, and that this change is somehow related to the enhanced role knowledge, information and computer technologies play in current societies.

The changes that many observers describe comprise the economy, the political institutions and the cultural realm. While nation-states still are the dominant form of social organization, their autonomy and power seem to be diminishing. Transnational corporations, international organizations and other non-governmental actors are competing with governments for overlapping 'spheres of authority', which only occasionally still coincide neatly with territorial borders (Rosenau 2002). The industrial sector with its production based on the transformation of raw materials into mass-produced consumer goods is losing its role as the prime source of wealth and productivity in the countries of the global North. Instead the service sector and the production of immaterial goods are becoming the main pillars of prosperity and economic growth (Bell 1999). Even the remotest regions of the world are subjugated under the command of the global economic order, although this integration is far from equal. Global cities are becoming the hubs of the global economy and are profiting immensely from this integration process, whereas other regions are marginalized and are practically decoupled from the global flows of goods and money (Sassen 2002). Global communication networks have expanded the possibilities of information-exchange, allowing the integration of financial markets in what Castells has called 'timeless time' (Castells 2010a: 7) and laying the ground for cultural globalization processes that detach communities from the constraints of physical proximity (Held and McGrew 2002: 3).

While the various theories disagree on many aspects there is widespread agreement that knowledge and information play a very important role in current societies and some even argue that they would be their decisive features. Even those who criticize the labels knowledge and information society, and who argue that these terms are neither distinctive nor precise enough to characterize current societies, concede that knowledge and information are without question enormously important in all realms of economy, politics and culture today. Krishan Kumar, for example, argues that the term *information society* is misleading because it suggests a radical change in core societal structures, but he nevertheless concedes that information technology has accelerated processes that have begun some time ago, and that have changed and are still changing the organization of the economy, the nature of work and patterns of culture and consumption (Kumar 2005: 174), or as Frank Webster writes in his insightful discussion of theories of the information society: 'The informational capitalism we have today is significantly different from the corporate capitalism that was established in the opening decades of the twentieth century' (Webster 2006: 267).

Knowledge capitalism might be a good term to describe the social constellations in which the production, appropriation and distribution of knowledge have become core defining features of economic and social relations. It highlights that the most important process driving the development and change of social and economic structures is not the multiplication of knowledge per se but the quest to maximize profits (Nuss 2006). These profits may today depend much more than in earlier periods on the systematic generation and application of theoretical knowledge, but it is the profit-maximizing logic and not an internal logic of knowledge that centrally fuels the expansion of knowledge.

But the term knowledge capitalism also overemphasizes the centrality of the economy. It is not only the quest for profit that drives the expansion of knowledge in unprecedented ways. Dynamics inherent to the scientific process are contributing to the accelerating growth of knowledge. Collaborative networks enable non-market processes of social knowledge and cultural production, involving large numbers of individuals, creating what Yochai Benkler has dubbed 'The Wealth of Networks' (Benkler 2006).

Throughout this book I will use the term 'knowledge societies' to describe those large-scale social structures in which core social dynamics depend on the production, appropriation, propertization and distribution of knowledge. Apparently this term does not describe a finite and unitary empirical object. Societies are analytical abstractions to describe complex social structures, and like most analytical concepts they have no direct equivalence in the empirical world. In this sense knowledge society is a metaphor that tries to capture one core aspect that drives current processes of social change. It is – like every metaphor – incomplete, because in any empirical social structure knowledge dynamics are never the only mechanisms that structure the relationships among actors, organizations and institutions.

Several renowned authors have pointed to the fallacies of the sociological use of the concept of society (e.g. Tilly 1984; Urry 2000). In his brilliant essay on the merits of a comparative historical approach, Charles Tilly has mounted a forceful critique on what he calls the nineteenth-century incubus of assumptions about large-scale social structures and processes. From the eight 'Pernicious Postulates' (Tilly 1984: 11) that he identifies, three are especially relevant for the notion of knowledge societies: the idea that 'society' is a thing apart, the assumption that social change is a general and unitary phenomenon, and the notion that societies evolve in a linear movement through a set of defined stages. Tilly claims that these assumptions (and the other five) are mistakes that obscure the possibility of an adequate understanding of social change and the processes that lie behind it.

He argues, that society is a highly problematic concept as long as the term is meant to describe a unitary object, because, upon closer inspection, every 'society' immediately disintegrates into many, often incongruent, pieces. The social relations that are said to define a society usually have different boundaries that only seldom coincide. Citizenship, economy, friendship and culture delimit different social structures that usually do not share the same geographical boundaries. The often implicit standard assumption in the social sciences is that societies coincide with nation-states. It is common to speak about German or American 'society' even though it is unclear which relation should define this social structure. Citizenship, residence or culture would each include different sets of people, organizations and institutions within the respective society. This problem multiplies if societies are defined through a core structuring principle. Where does the 'information society' start and where does it end? Is Germany an information society? Or Europe, the OECD countries, or the whole world? Do the limits of the information or knowledge society coincide with national borders? Or does it consist only of the highly connected hubs of financial and informational capitalism? The concept that was already problematic under the assumptions of a methodological nationalism becomes even more fuzzy if one tries to describe a globally interconnected structure of variable geography.

In a similar vein John Urry (2000) reminds us about the close association of society and nation-state in the history of sociology, an association that is clearly visible in Bell's post-industrial society that he develops based on data about the USA. Bell is aware of this limitation and argues that the USA is only the most advanced example of a trend other states will follow. Others have questioned the generalizability of Bell's observations and argued that for example the German and Japanese development paths differ significantly from the US one (Castells 2010a: 4), but the post-industrial society may not even be a reality in the USA as a whole. The trends Bell describes are most pronounced in the coastal agglomerations and selected mainland hubs. The contribution of the service sector to the average gross state product between 1992 and 1999 ranged between 49.5 per cent (Wyoming) and 76.0 per cent (New York) (Beemiller and Downey 2001). More fine-grained data would certainly show even greater differences between rural areas and mega-cities.

For Manuel Castells society is defined as the 'organizational arrangements of humans in relationships of production/consumption, experience, and power, as expressed in meaningful interaction framed by culture' (Castells 2000: 5). A network society would then be the social structure in which these organizational arrangements are governed by a networking logic. Here again it is highly improbable that any empirical social structure would exist in which all relations of production/ consumption, experience and power are governed by a networking logic and in which the limits described by all three relations coincide. Despite the impossibility of finding an empirical match for the post-industrial or network society, as abstractions and metaphors these terms help us to make sense of some large-scale processes of social change in current societies. While they may not offer a sufficient model they direct our attention to the pacemakers of social change. The knowledge society may still be a myth (Kübler 2005), but this does not belie the growing importance of knowledge and information that Drucker, Bell, Touraine, Stehr, Castells and others have diagnosed.

Bell was right in his claim that in many regions of the world manufacturing and classical industries are no longer the driving forces behind societal change, nor the most dynamic motor of economic development (Bell 1999). Even if manufacturing and agriculture are not going away and even if they still provide employment for large portions of the population, national economies may be called post-industrial insofar as the industries that dominated the period from the industrial revolution to the post-WWII reconstruction have lost their transformatory power. The existence of a developed industrial manufacturing sector also no longer distinguishes the rich and powerful countries of the global North from the developing countries of the global South. Many of the latter now have levels of industrialization comparable to the leading economies, although this has not diminished the gap between rich and poor countries which is growing even though some developing countries have ascended to the club of the wealthy (Castells 1998: 2; OECD 2008). But at the same time post-industrialism is too indeterminate (Stehr 1994a; Kübler 2005), overemphasizes the transition from manufacturing to services (Webster 2006; Castells 2010a) and underexposes the continuities of the capitalist economic base-structure (Kumar 2005; Webster 2006).

I concur with Castells' argument that today's information processing capabilities have allowed network forms of governance and decision-making to (partially) replace the established hierarchical organization of power (Castells 1998, 2000, 2004, 2010a). In his writings on the 'network society' Castells has developed an impressive and convincing theory that goes a long way towards explaining the direction of current processes of social change. But as Castells notes, his network society is also an information and knowledge society, because it is characterized by a new informational mode of development that differs from the industrial mode of development in that the main source of productivity no longer is the action of knowledge upon nature but now is the action of knowledge upon knowledge (Castells 2010a: 17).

Knowledge better captures the element of agency and abstraction while information is generally linked to the structured presentation and/or organization of data.[1] Stehr emphasizes the aspect of agency in his definition of knowledge as 'capacity for social action' (1994a: 95) – a somewhat unfortunate definition that suggests a necessary link between social action and knowledge. While it is certainly true that knowledge generates the possibility for social action, social action can also be based on power which has more sources than knowledge. Bell, on the other hand, largely omits the aspect of agency in his definition of knowledge as 'a set of organized statements of facts or ideas, presenting a reasoned judgment or an experimental result, which is transmitted to

---

[1] Porat, in his classical work, emphasizes the communicative aspect and defines information as 'data that have been organized and communicated' (Porat 1977: 2), the general definition of information used in computer science and philosophy provides the following formal definition 'σ is an instance of information, understood as semantic content, if and only if: σ consists of n data, for $n \geq 1$; the data are well formed; the well-formed data are meaningful' (Floridi 2010: 21).

others through some communication medium in some systematic form' (1999: 175). While this definition – as many others have commented before – is too narrow to capture the aspects of practical and tacit knowledge that escape the strict requirements of reason and explicitness, it defines the form of knowledge that is most important for the social changes associated with knowledge capitalism: theoretical knowledge.

Echoing Tilly's criticism one should therefore not confound the metaphor with empirical social structures of the real world. Germany is not a knowledge society, neither is the USA or any other nation-state, even if politicians and social scientists do not tire of claiming so. In any given concrete social structure, relations of production, consumption, experience and power follow multiple, often contradictory, and in any case historically specific logics. But the idea of a knowledge society emphasizes that in core economic sectors knowledge no longer mainly serves to develop new machines that further automate production processes in order to raise productivity, but that knowledge has become a surplus-generating production factor itself.

Knowledge society, thus, is not the next step in a historical sequence where a society based on property is replaced by one based on labour that now is being replaced by a knowledge society with an economy based on symbolic production, as Stehr (1994a, 2002) proposes. In the empirical world these stages are neither universal nor unidirectional (according to the World Bank's World Development Indicators, in China the service sector's share of GDP first decreased through the 1960s and only increased again in the mid 1980s at the expense of the agricultural, and not the manufacturing sector). Such a sequential notion also obscures the fact that, instead of a symbolic economy following a property and a labour-based economy, one crucial element of the knowledge society lies in the propertization of knowledge, keeping the core pillar of capitalist production alive: the private property of the means of production.

But despite these caveats it is obvious that the world we live in today differs significantly in many respects from the world in the heyday of industrial capitalism and also from the world thirty years ago, before computer technology started to permeate every aspect of society. The growing importance of theoretical knowledge, the increasing propertization of knowledge, the shifts in economic and occupational structures, the technological developments associated with the information revolution are processes that create new and shift old structural inequalities in societies. Throughout this book I argue that it is not just technology that has changed, but that processes of change at various levels of society have altered the cleavage structure of current societies and thus alter the conditions, limits and opportunities for social conflict. And with these changed cleavage structures the field of opportunities and constraints for existing collective actors has shifted. Moreover, if these changes are as epochal as many commentators think, they will most likely create the conditions for the formation of new collective actors in struggles that address the new conflicts of the knowledge society.

To get an idea about which conflicts might accompany the knowledge societies I will discuss three prominent conceptualizations that address the current processes of social change: Daniel Bell's analysis of the *post-industrial society* (Bell 1976, 1999), Manuel Castells' theory of the *network society* (Castells 2000, 2004, 2010a, 2010b) and Nico Stehr's theory of the *knowledge society* (Stehr 1994a, 2002*)*. My aim here is not to discuss those theories in full. Others have done this (Stehr 1994a; May 2002; Mattelart 2003; Kübler 2005; Kumar 2005; Webster 2006) and not much can be gained from another general discussion of the value of the concepts 'information society' or 'knowledge society'. Instead, since I am interested in the conflicts that have developed around the governance of knowledge and information, my discussion will be focused on the social changes that have been associated with the advent of the knowledge or information society, and the social conflicts that are expected to develop as a consequence of these changes.

3.2.   Theories of the knowledge society

All authors who have written about the knowledge or information society assume that the transition to the new form of society is marked by far-reaching and even fundamental changes in the social structure of current societies.

3.2.1.   Bell's post-industrial society

While the US sociologist Daniel Bell was not the first to use the term *knowledge society*, his venture in social forecasting *The Coming of Post-Industrial Society* (1999 [originally published 1973]) is certainly the most influential work that has been written about the knowledge or information society so far. Bell calls the society, which he claims is gradually replacing the industrial society in the second half of the twentieth century in the USA and to a lesser degree also in Europe and Japan, 'post-industrial society' to highlight its transitory and not yet fixed character. But this post-industrial society is above all a knowledge society because 'the major source of structural change … is the change in the character of knowledge' (Bell 1999: 44). Theoretical knowledge is for Bell the 'axial principle' of the post-industrial society, replacing machine technology as the axial principle of the industrial society. Innovation and policy formulation in the post-industrial society are guided by theoretical knowledge. Bell diagnoses and predicts an exponential growth of scientific knowledge, accelerated by the incessant branching of science. This scientific knowledge is used in a new 'intellectual technology' that substitutes algorithms for intuitive judgements and changes economic and political decision-making processes. It replaces judgements based on tradition, tacit knowledge or experience with judgements based on deductions from codified theoretical knowledge. Bell claims that 'after the Second World War, the scientific capacity of a country has become a determinant of its potential and power' (Bell 1999: 117).

The transition to the post-industrial society has far-reaching consequences for the social structure of current societies and Bell identifies three broad areas of social change: economy, occupational structure and power structure. At the level of the economy Bell predicts a shift from predominantly goods-producing industrial production to a service economy based on processing information and knowledge with the help of telecommunications and computer technologies. The tertiary (and quaternary and quinary) sector would take precedence over the industrial (secondary) sector as the major source of wealth and employment.

These changes in the economy in turn alter the occupational structures and with them the class structures of society. In the post-industrial society white-collar workers replace industrial (or blue-collar) workers as the core occupational category. Drawing upon US labour market statistics, Bell states that since the 1950s the fastest growing occupational groups are professional and technical workers, especially teachers and engineers. Their growth rate is topped only by the growth of scientific jobs, reflecting the changing economic relevance of scientists in the post-industrial society. The profile of this changing labour market requires tertiary education for a much larger segment of the working population than was necessary in the industrial society, and therefore results in a rapid expansion of the educational sector. University education, which was in the first half of the twentieth century a privilege of the few, has become the rule rather than the exception with one-third of the age group between 18 and 24 enrolled in higher education institutions in the USA by 1970 (Bell 1999: 221). In a new edition of his book that came out twenty-six years after the original publication Bell sees both developments confirmed. The trend from manufacturing to services and the extraordinary rise of professional and technical employment had continued with a further decline in manufacturing employment in the USA and nearly 60 per cent of the labour force in the professional, technical and managerial category.

For Bell the changing economic and occupational structure holds the promise of a more rational society, in which scientists and engineers will 'form the key group in the post-industrial society' (Bell 1999: 17) and will make decisions based on science and reason. Technical skill will become the base of power and education will be the key to acquiring it and gaining access to power (Bell 1999: 358). Whereas land was the source of power in the pre-industrial society, in the industrial society power is based on the ownership of machinery, and in the post-industrial society it is based on the control and ownership of knowledge. Bell does not claim that in the post-industrial society power based on land that is acquired or inherited, or power based on ownership of industrial production facilities ceases to play a role. But he insists that, just as in industrial societies the power of the gentry was gradually replaced by the power of capital, so will these power bases gradually give way to the new power of knowledge. This knowledge-based power will be able to control economic dynamics in an unprecedented way. His trust in the power of science and reason lets him assume a high level of steering capacity of the political domain leading to 'the subordination of the economic function to the political order' (Bell 1999: 373).

Bell's findings have been challenged by many authors who have criticized his use of the term service sector as being too unspecific as it essentially contains everything that is not agriculture and manufacturing – throwing cleaners and stockbrokers into the same category. Notably Castells, drawing on Singelmann (1978), argues that the main transformation between 1920 and 1970 was not from manufacturing to services but from agriculture to services. Only after 1970 did employment levels in manufacturing decline in most western societies – although with different speeds and starting from different levels. Moreover, the sharp decline in manufacturing with the concurrent rise of the service sector really only happened in the USA and Canada, whereas Germany and Japan – the two most competitive economies in the 1980s – retained high levels of manufacturing employment (Castells 2010a: 4). I will come back to these criticisms and to Castells' alternative interpretation of the social changes in the economy and occupational structure of western societies in the next section.

Bell's theory of social change   Bell nowhere develops explicitly a general theory of social change. But his underlying model is one of incremental and evolutionary change, a model in which societies over time become more developed and also more rational. The driving force behind social change, for him, is technology and rationalization. His model stands in a long tradition of social theories that regard social change generally as a continuous and cumulative process in which human societies have progressed from primitive to modern.

This perspective is present in the classical sociological theories of evolutionary change (Comte 1875; Spencer 1893; Tönnies 1926; Durkheim 1933) which see social change in general as a continuous process in which human society as a whole evolves along a singular trajectory from primitive to complex from simple to differentiated. The evolution may be ruptured and accompanied by phases of disorder, and the development may proceed in waves, but in the long run social change is seen as a linear process along an identifiable trajectory. In general this process of change is equated with progress, increasing rationality and the development of a more profound base of social cohesion. Only Tönnies has a more sceptical view and sees the transition from community (Gemeinschaft) to society (Gesellschaft) as a deterioration of the human condition (for a more detailed discussion see Sztompka 1993). Conflicts have no systematic place in these theories or can only result from disorder. In Durkheim's theory the growing division of labour leads to a dissolution of the traditional 'mechanic solidarity' based on kinship bonds. While new forms of 'organic solidarity' based on shared consciousness emerge only slowly, anomie spreads and upsets the foundations of social order (Durkheim 1933). Conflicts in Durkheim's perspective have their place as expressions of this anomie, of the 'gap between the degree of differentiation and the extent of regulation of social relations' (Tilly 1978: 17), which is for him a transitory phase on the way to a new social order based on shared beliefs.

Parsons departs from the earlier evolutionary theories and allows for greater variation, claiming that socio-cultural evolution 'has not proceeded in a single neatly definable line, but at every level has included a rather wide variety of different forms and types' (Parsons 1966: 2). But his structural-functional theory is nevertheless based on the premise that behind this variation four evolutionary mechanisms (differentiation, adaptive upgrading, inclusion and value generalization) propel society from the primitive to the advanced primitive, to the intermediate and finally the modern stage (Sztompka 1993: 121). Social conflict has no systematic place in this theory where social development is driven by a functional logic.

Later incorporations of this evolutionary model are, for example, modernization theories (Rostow 1959; Huntington 1968) which assume that the western path of industrialization will eventually be followed by all countries. In these theories, which gained some currency in international relations in the mid twentieth century and guided US and some European countries' trade policies in the 1970s and 1980s, conflicts are present – but not as social conflicts but rather as conflicts between societies or civilizations.

Bell's assumptions about social change are clearly influenced by the ideas of functional differentiation and contain also elements of the naïve hopes of modernization theorists that technology will lead to increasing welfare. Marx's famous claim that 'the history of all hitherto existing society is the history of class struggles' (Marx and Engels 1888) is not shared by Bell. Instead he argues that the ideologies of the nineteenth century are exhausted and that future societies will be pluralist and not structured by class conflicts but by diverse competing interests (Bell 1960).

Conflicts in the knowledge society according to Bell   While Bell diagnoses and predicts far-reaching changes in the social structure of current societies that will have repercussions in the political and cultural sphere, he remains surprisingly silent when it comes to potential conflicts that might accompany or even result from these changes. According to Bell, the fundamental conflict between labour and capital, which shaped the cleavages of the industrial societies in the nineteenth and early twentieth centuries, has lost its centrality as the working class is fragmenting and as power no longer primarily resides in the ownership of the means of production. But this old conflict line is not replaced by a new conflict line of the post-industrial society. Bell envisions the post-industrial society as a complex society in which a large number of interest groups will formulate their often competing claims, but he does not identify the economic or occupational structure as a specific source of social conflict (Bell 1999: 154 ff.).

But even if the notion of conflict is curiously missing in Bell's otherwise impressive work, his argumentation offers at least two links where one would have to look for possible conflict lines in the post-industrial society. Both are related to the supposed changes in the society's power structure:

(1) Bell argues that the succession of pre-industrial, industrial and post-industrial societies coincides with a shift in the societies' core power structure. In pre-industrial societies power was based on the ownership of land, and consequently the control of land was a constant source of often violent conflicts. In industrial societies the control of the means of production – or, as Bell calls it, the control

of machinery – is a constant source of social conflict that brought about the workers' movement and dominated world politics for half a century in the juxtaposition of socialist and capitalist regimes. If it is true that in the post-industrial society power will be based on theoretical knowledge, conflicts should develop over the control of scientific and technical knowledge.

Bell recognizes this conflict, but only in a limited way. He describes state control of science in socialist states and the problem of bureaucratization of science in the USA. He notes the importance of the military in the development of today's large-scale scientific institutions and highlights the key role of scientific knowledge for economic success. But he locates the core area of scientific production in the universities and is confident that at least in democratic societies the inherent logic of scientific knowledge to branch and develop in unexpected ways would prevent centralized control of science. He sees the incentives of powerful actors to control the production of scientific knowledge, but in the end remains ambivalent about the extent to which this might endanger the scientific ethos of striving for knowledge and truth (Bell 1999: 408).

(2) The second conflict line that one can glean from Bell's description of the post-industrial society is closely related to the first and concerns the possibility of access to knowledge – or more concretely – access to education. In Bell's model the post-industrial society is characterized by a rapid expansion of the tertiary education system. The tiered structure of the US higher education system with community colleges and public universities providing education for the masses and private universities catering for the elite does not escape Bell, but his enthusiasm for the extraordinary expansion of the higher education system that has thoroughly democratized access to universities in many developed countries impairs his perception of possible consequences that lead to growing inequalities despite more equal access to education.

Current studies consistently show that in those countries that Bell sees as being at the forefront of the development to post-industrial societies, income inequality has significantly increased over time. In the USA, Germany and Japan the gap between rich and poor steadily increased between the mid 1980s and mid 2000s (OECD 2008). In the USA the Gini coefficient, which measures the inequality of income distribution, with a value of 0 expressing total equality and a value of 1 maximum inequality, increased from 0.32 in the mid 1970s to 0.38 in the mid 2000s. This seemingly small increase translates to a 12 per cent transfer from the lower half of the income distribution to the upper half (Blackburn 1989). Taking into account that in the USA the top half earns on average three times as much as the bottom half (OECD 2008: 28), the increase in the Gini coefficient from 0.32 to 0.38 translates to an effective transfer of 24 per cent of income from the average person in the bottom half to the top half. Because the transfer was spread over thirty years this represents a relatively small annual income redistribution but one that nevertheless has significantly increased inequality in the long run.

So if we follow Bell that in a post-industrial society theoretical knowledge is the base of power and education the key to gain access to power, then we can expect conflicts to develop about access to education and knowledge. While knowledge as such is in principle a public good that is non-rivalrous and non-exhaustible, its provision in institutions of higher education comes with significant costs. This creates a possible area of conflict about the commodification of knowledge and restriction of access.

3.2.2. Castells' network society

In Manuel Castells' *network society* conflicts play a very prominent role. The entire second volume of his trilogy on the economy, society and culture of the information age is devoted to the possible sites and forms of social conflict in a network society, and it ends on an almost dystopian note that '[a]t the dawn of the information age, a crisis of legitimacy is voiding of meaning and function the institutions of the industrial era' (Castells 2004: 419). In his description of the changing economic and occupational structure, Castells also highlights the conflictual and uneven nature of the current transformations (Castells 2000, 2010a).

Like Bell, who argues that the post-industrial society is essentially a knowledge society, Castells states that the network society is characterized by a new mode of development that he calls 'informationalism' or 'informational mode of development' (Castells 2010a: 14, 17), in which knowledge generation, information processing and symbol communication are the sources of productivity. The transition from the industrial to the informational mode of development is driven by a technological revolution centred around micro-electronic information and communication technologies, and genetic engineering (Castells 2000: 9). Castells sees this information technology revolution as being on a par with the industrial revolution in its power to restructure social relations in current societies. The availability of new, flexible information technologies coincides with several other developments: the deregulation and liberalization of the economy in general and of trade in particular, the failed restructuring of the socialist state economies (or, as Castells calls it, of 'statism'), a libertarian ideology arising from the social movements of the 1960s and 1970s and the development of a new electronic media system. Together, these developments are responsible for the emergence of the network society.

In the network society relationships of production are reconfigured in an economy that is informational, global and networked. It is informational because productivity and competitiveness are a result of the ability to generate knowledge and process information. It is global because its core activities have the capability to work on a global scale, and it is networked because the firm is no longer the relevant unit but the business project that is realized in networked enterprises of varying shape. Castells argues that these changes in the economy have profound consequences for the occupational structure, leading to a flexibilization of work and an individualization of the relationship between capital and labour, and thereby 'reversing the process of socialization of production characteristic of the industrial era' (Castells 2000: 12).

The networked economy introduces a new cleavage between what Castells calls 'networked' and 'switched-off' labour. The first is integrated into the circuits of the network, the second limited to non-interactive, specific and local tasks. Within the first group a second cleavage develops between 'self-programmable' and 'generic' labour (Castells 2000: 18). The latter is constantly threatened with being replaced by automation, whereas the former could be interpreted as the core knowledge-based work.

The individualization of labour is mirrored by an individualization of consumption that goes along with growing inequalities where the goods of the global economy become available almost everywhere on the planet, but where the ability to purchase them becomes even more unequally distributed than in the industrial era.

The network society reconfigures established power relationships. Castells' phrase that 'the power of flows takes precedence over the flows of power' (Castells 2000: 20) expresses that in a networked economy hierarchical and place-bound power structures are replaced by decentralized power structures based in information networks. He claims that the institutions (bureaucracies, military, churches, etc.) in which power was concentrated are being sidelined by information networks of capital, production, trade, science and crime; and have to adapt so that they become networked institutions themselves. The state becomes a network state, that is, a node in a power-sharing network, and even the mighty US military is no longer able to fight and win wars on its own.

These changes in power relations, and the economic and occupational structure coincide with transformations of relationships of experience and culture. Castells maintains that the latter are not simply consequences of the economic and political changes, but are – at least to some extent – independent processes of social change. The co-evolution of women's struggles, the feminist movement, the network economy, and reproduction technology, together lead to what Castells calls 'the end of patriachalism' (Castells 2004: 4), which, in turn, has strong repercussions for the structures of power and occupation in current societies. At the cultural level Castells sees the advent of a 'culture of real virtuality' in which symbols become dissociated from place and experience. Compared to economy, occupation, power and experience, where Castells presents abundant data to support his claims about fundamental social change, his discussion of cultural change is based solely on his perception of the internet (or digital multimedia communication systems) as universal carrier of delocalized and disembodied cultural expression and experience.

While Castells emphasizes the conflictual nature of the transformations in the wake of the network society, he is ambiguous about whether or to what extent they can become crystallization points for conflictual collective action. The reason for this is that the rise of the network society changes the base for the construction of collective identities which are the prerequisite for the establishment of collective actors.

Castells claims that the systematic disjunction between the local and the global in the network society destroys the foundations of civil societies where conflicts about hegemony were fought in the industrial age. Drawing on Gramsci (1992), Castells defines civil society as 'a set of organizations and institutions, as well as a series of structured and organized social actors, which reproduce, albeit sometimes in a conflictive manner, the identity that rationalizes the sources of structural domination' (Castells 2004: 8). The civil society is thus structured by the dominant institutions or 'apparatuses' of the society. In the civil society power relations and dominance are actualized and reproduced through active consent, backed up by the shadow of coercion, guaranteeing the relative stability of the dominant order. But precisely because civil society is not separated as a super-structure from the base-structure of material power relations, power can be challenged and is constantly challenged in the civil society in struggles for hegemony.

In the network society, according to Castells, civil society is no longer the base for collective identities, which, instead have to be built on defensive communal identities of those devalued and/or stigmatized by the logic of domination. These 'resistance identities' form outside civil society in cultural communes, and do not necessarily develop a political project beyond the celebration of the community's norms and values. They may still seek the transformation of core social structures, and if they do so, they become, according to Castells, 'project identities' with the potential to politicize structures of domination and exclusion of the network society. But the necessary link between collective action struggles for hegemony in the civil society no longer exists (Castells 2004: 1).

Castells develops, with a broad brush, a general model that offers an explanation for why we seem to be witnessing a growing number of communal or identitarian movements at the end of the twentieth century and the beginning of the twenty-first. The problem is that this model builds on two general assumptions that are only weakly substantiated in Castells' otherwise impressive analysis of the network society.

The first assumption is that within civil society collective identities are formed around the core identities of modern societies. Unfortunately Castells remains rather vague about what these are. He mentions citizenship, democracy, politicization of social change and confinement of power of the state (Castells 2004: 9), but not the labour–capital cleavage as sources for collective identities. Even more problematic is that he does not explain why counter-hegemonic struggles should necessarily be based on collective identities already present in the institutions of civil society. I doubt that, besides the workers' movement, the two most important social movements of the late nineteenth and early twentieth centuries that have fundamentally transformed social relationships, the anti-slavery movement and the women's movement, were built on legitimizing collective identities of the civil society. While it is certainly true that citizenship was a core element in both of them, their appeal went far beyond the state and its institutions. So while arguably in the industrial age civil society was the *site* of struggles for hegemony, social movements were not just built on identities of the civil society but created subjects that were previously not part of the hegemonic order.

The second assumption is that the network society creates an inescapable logic of inclusion/exclusion that makes the development of project identities (according to Castells the only form of collective identity with the potential to transform the power structures in society) within the network society's civil society impossible. Resistance to the network, in Castells' model, is only possible by either denying the logic of the network and retreating into cultural communes or by building alternative networks outside the existing network. This model has surprising similarities with Luhmann's theory of autopoietic systems that are constituted by differentiating themselves from the environment and where each subsystem functions by its specific binary code – power/no power in the political system, legal/illegal in the legal system, money/no money in the economic system, true/false in the scientific system (Luhmann 1987). As in Castells' network metaphor the most significant difference is between inside and outside. Everything inside the system/network functions according to the system's code or the network's logic and everything outside is alien to the system/network. In Luhmann's theory the binary code follows from the functional differentiation of the subsystems. An element can only be processed in the economic system as long as it can be commodified. If it cannot be exchanged for money, it cannot be processed in the economic system.

In Castells' theory the binary logic of the networks is based on the network's ability to replace every node as soon as it becomes dysfunctional for the network. Castells writes: 'If a node in the network ceases to perform a useful function it is phased out from the network, and the network rearranges itself – as cells do in biological processes' (Castells 2000: 15). He combines here two metaphors: the network and the biological system. The network stands for flexibility and redundancy whereas the (biological) system guarantees that every activity which is alien to the system's logic is eliminated, if it cannot be incorporated. The problem with this dual metaphor is that real-world social systems and networks may function differently. The 'logic' of the internet is commodification, control, creativity and freedom (of information) at the same time. There is very little indication that networks in general have to follow only one single logic. They may more aptly be described as multiplex networks in which nodes can be connected by different relations. This does not deny the at the same time inclusive and exclusionary power of economic and other networks. But it questions the notion that alternative networks have to be built necessarily outside the existing networks.

Moreover, the claim that in a network every node can be replaced is highly questionable. The current financial crisis clearly demonstrated that in the banking network, through which the flows of international financial transactions are channelled, some banks are 'too big to fail'. These hubs in the financial network could not be replaced without compromising the functioning of the network. The concept of 'scale-free networks' captures this feature that is characteristic for many real-world networks: they exhibit a high degree of error tolerance, and thus are able to survive failure or removal of a large number of random nodes, but they are very vulnerable to attacks on a small number of highly connected nodes (Albert, Jeong and Barabási 2000).

In his theory of the network society Castells offers an impressive framework to interpret the fundamental social changes of the last decades. The fact that networks may be more complex and less unitary than Castells claims does not invalidate his theory. It merely suggests that conflicts in the network society may develop in more diverse forms than Castells expects.

Castells' theory of social change   Castells' and Bell's underlying models of social change are similar in that they both assume a stage model of society and see technology as the main driving mechanism of social change. Castells' 'axial principle' is the binary logic of the network that characterizes the network society and differentiates it clearly from preceding social formations. But Castells' model is much closer to the Marxist theory of society than to modernization theory or functionalism.

From a Marxist perspective conflict is the essence of historical change. In the dialectical model societies progress through the stages of their development in a series of conflicts in which the immanent contradictions of the society's class structure are actualized. An actor's class position is determined by the relationship to the means of production, and history is a history of a growing polarization of class relations. In this model macro changes are brought about by human action, but they follow a clear historical trajectory from primitive community through slavery, feudalism and capitalism, finally to communism. Each socio-economic formation contains its own specific and inherent contradictions that determine the core areas of social conflict in a society (Marx and Engels 1888).

The important idea is that history is not seen as a disembodied history of ideas nor as driven by 'great men' – historical leaders following their own personal agenda. History in the Marxian perspective is collectively produced within the structural constraints of the socio-economic system that define the contradictions and antagonisms along which, in a succession of social conflicts, social change proceeds.

Piotr Sztompka has argued that Marx's theory is a complex multidimensional theory of history-making that combines theories of social action and history at three levels: world-historical, socio-structural and action-individual. These three levels are connected neither through a simple top-down nor through a straight bottom-up process. The world-historical level does not (completely) determine individual actions and socio-structural change nor do individuals have complete autonomy to determine their fate. Sztompka argues that Marx assumes strong determinism at the world-historical level, where history ultimately follows its prescribed path; much weaker determinism at the socio-structural level, where class action may escape its historical determination; and strong elements of voluntarism at the individual level, where choice is possible (Sztompka 1993: 11). But conversely this also means that the contingency on the lower levels is limited by the structural constraints of the world-historical level, in that in the end collective action must address the fundamental historical antagonisms to advance history.

Thus the Marxist fallacy is twofold. First, the exclusive focus on the binary opposition between ownership and lack of ownership of the means of production does not capture the complexity of social conflicts in societies. Instead of the expected growing simplification of social conflicts, the twentieth century clearly brought a multiplication of the sites and fault-lines of contention. Second, the model is at its core still very much a stage model of evolutionary progress. While it allows for some contingency at the level of collective action, the contradictions, which in the end have to be solved in the historical progression of societies through the stages of development, are more than structural limits for action. They contain their own directional developmental logic. In the Marxist theoretical framework social struggles can succeed or fail, but progress is a priori defined and thus the success of social struggles is in the end not an empirical question, but depends on the fulfilment of the theoretical expectations.

Contemporary Marxist thinkers have tried to broaden the perspective of the theoretical framework in order to incorporate a greater variety of social struggles. Gramsci's theory of hegemony expanded the focus from a narrow economistic perspective to an incorporation of struggles for cultural hegemony. But as Ernesto Laclau and Chantal Mouffe have argued, the Gramscian notion of hegemony still depends on a single unifying principle that hold every hegemonic formation together, 'and this can only be a fundamental class' (Laclau and Mouffe 1985: 69). Thus the class division in bourgeois society between capital and labour remains the final defining element.

Castells' theory of society is closer to these neo- and post-Marxist theories that dismiss the deterministic and teleologic assumptions, allow for more than one conflict line and no longer reduce the cultural realm to an appendix of the economy. Speaking of modes of production and modes of development, Castells borrows not only some of his terminology from regulation theory (Hirsch and Roth 1986; Aglietta 2001; Jessop 2001) but also their assumptions about capitalism's inherent flexibility to restructure its mode of regulation and about the co-dependence of the economic and cultural sphere. But the strongest influence on Castells' theory of society comes from the French sociologist Alain Touraine.

In his search for the new historical actor that would replace the proletariat of the industrial age in a post-industrial society that is no longer marked by the antagonism between capital and labour but between technocratic domination and alienation, Touraine modifies the classical Marxist agenda (Touraine 1968, 1981, 1988). His social theory is based on the assumption that every historical social formation is characterized by a central conflict and that historical progress is advanced through the conflictual interaction of the antagonists. In industrial capitalism this was the working class and the bourgeoisie, in the post-industrial (or elsewhere: programmed or technocratic) society they are replaced by new actors who are not yet defined. Touraine expected to find this potential, to take on the role of the historical social movement, first in the French student movement (Touraine 1968) and later in the anti-nuclear movement, which, he believed, would be better suited than the students' or women's movements to inherit the central role that was taken in the industrial society by the labour movement.

Touraine departs from Marx in that he sees social actors no longer as passive bearers but as active producers and reproducers of social relations (Scott 1996: 80) but his binary framework remains locked in the nineteenth-century logic of a unified society characterized by a single core principle and obscures rather than enlightens an understanding of the movements which Touraine was investigating. It nevertheless inspired a number of authors to reflect more thoroughly on the possible relationship between structural social change and social movements. Touraine's contribution lies in his insistence that social movements are not just articulations of interests whose success depends on the availability of elite allies, favourable institutional settings and movement entrepreneurs, but develop in specific historical circumstances along changing societal fault-lines. Apart from their concrete policy goals, social movements sometimes express more fundamental cleavages that become political issues only though their conflictual interventions.

The idea of social movements as historically situated actors is present in Claus Offe's writings as well (Offe 1985). For him structural change is the reason for the emergence of new social movements which no longer focus on class-based redistributive politics but address a wider set of planetary (peace, environment), rights (human rights, feminism, racism) and life-world issues. Offe claims that the new movements displace the boundary between the private and the political and thereby politicize the institutions of the civil society, which in the old paradigm was founded on the neat separation of the political sphere of the state and the non-political spheres of the economy and the private. The characteristic of the 'new' movements is that they no longer are socio-economic groups acting as groups in distributive conflicts but socio-economic groups acting on behalf of ascriptive collectivities. This means the new social movements still have a distinct class-base (the new and old middle class and 'peripheral groups' – students, housewives, unemployed) but they do not act on behalf of this socio-economic base (Offe 1985: 852). Instead the new movements are based on ascriptive identities based on race, gender, age, locality and other aspects.

Castells' theory of social change combines structure and agency. For him, societies are always the product of 'conflictive interaction between humans organized in and around a given social structure' (Castells 2000: 7). But it is not always clear to what extent social structures can develop their own logic and effectively limit the possibilities for action. On the one hand Castells rejects the idea of an inherent or historical logic of differentiation or capital accumulation that drives the development of societies behind the back of the actors. This is why he focuses so much on social movements: they bear the potential for future social change. But on the other hand, especially when it comes to the emergence of the network society, Castells is less explicit about the agents of social change. Here the networking logic and the information and communication technology paradigm seem to develop their own dynamics and influence the direction of social development.

The important insight that Castells takes from social movement theory is that collective actors of the network society (and not only there) are not natural, or given categories. Collective actors have to establish themselves as collective actors by building collective identities. This process is a source for many conflicts, but how these conflicts are related to the structural changes in the knowledge society is not answered by Castells.

Conflicts in the knowledge society according to Castells   Nevertheless, Castells' analysis of current changes offers several cues where conflicts about the production, control and distribution of knowledge and information might be expected along the displaced or exacerbated old and new cleavages of the information age. Starting from his observation of the integration and exclusionary power of networks, one likely area of conflict will be located at the (always changing) line that separates those actors and regions that are integrated in the networks from those that are excluded or switched off. This conflict line, which Pippa Norris has called the 'digital divide' (Norris 2001), can be located within national societies and between regions of the world. In general, conflicts between the global North and the global South, between centre and periphery, between networked and generic labour are located at this cleavage.

Another of Castells' central claims is that the network society under-mines the state monopoly of power. The establishment of a new net-work-based power structure out of the reach of governmental actors will certainly generate conflicts. Access to the network and control over the content of the knowledge, information, money and power that flows though the network may be focal points of these conflicts. On the other side of the coin are conflicts that are related to the resurgence of communities eagerly protecting their communal (resistance) iden-tities. Here the conflicts are about limiting the reach of the network, about gaining and/or retaining autonomy, creating and/or maintaining exclusive control over values and knowledge. Religious-political fun-damentalism with its communitarian ideology and its quest to uphold distinctive knowledge that is often opposed to the dominant ideas of science and society is one expression of this conflict line.

3.2.3. Stehr's knowledge society

Stehr's description of knowledge societies (Stehr 1994a, 1994b, 2002, 2004) resembles in many aspects Bell's post-industrial and Castells' net-work society. Like them he diagnoses a profound process of change that affects core areas in modern, industrial societies, and in particular iden-tifies changes in the economic and occupational structure. He claims that 'the age of labor and property is at an end' (Stehr 1994a: viii), and that in current societies knowledge is the constitutive mechanism that defines their identity. He sees the knowledge society as the latest stage in the development of the bourgeois society that has changed from a society of owners to a labouring society (Arbeitsgesellschaft) and now to a knowledge society. In a corresponding development the economic base of the society changed from material to monetary to symbolic. He argues that in current societies knowledge has superseded labour and property/capital as the defining characteristics, and that today know-ledge is the motor of growth in the production process (1994a: 10). Stehr concedes that knowledge has not just recently become an import-ant factor in societies, but he argues that what distinguishes current societies from earlier modern and pre-modern societies is that today knowledge and science are penetrating *all* spheres of life.

Despite the many similarities Stehr positions his theory of know-ledge societies explicitly in opposition to Bell and Castells, although the grounds for his rejection of the terms post-industrial or network society are not always clear. He argues for example against the post-industrial society because industry and manufacturing would not vanish (1994a: 12), but at the same time is aware that Bell only claims a *relative* decline of the manufacturing vis-à-vis the service sector (1994a: 47). He rejects Castells' notion of the network society on the grounds of his alleged technological determinism and his 'conflation of knowledge and information' (2002: 70) without recognizing Castells' insistence on the historicity of several parallel technological, economic and social processes that are co-determinant for the rise of the network society (Castells 2000).

While Stehr rejects simplistic, deterministic models of social change driven by technological or scientific developments, the explanatory power of his own theory remains limited as he is not able to identify a mechanism (or a set of mechanisms) that would be responsible for the growing centrality of knowledge. In this sense Stehr's account remains descriptive. He discusses at length where and when knowledge increasingly permeates all social, political and economic spheres, and argues that the origin and development of knowledge societies 'is linked first and foremost to a radical transformation in the structure of the economy' (Stehr 1994a: 122), but is not able to explain why the economy is undergoing such a radical transformation apart from the somewhat circular argument that increasingly economic growth is depending on symbolic and knowledge-based inputs.

The strength of Stehr's work thus lies less in providing a theory of social change but more in clarifying the contradictory role of knowledge. Whereas Bell and Castells treat knowledge largely as a relatively unproblematic concept that organizes objectifiable facts, Stehr discusses the contradictory character of knowledge in current societies. He emphasizes the link between agency and knowledge and defines knowledge as 'a capacity for social action' (1994a: 95). This unusual definition is highly problematic. Stehr attempts to mirror in his definition Ludwig von Mises' sociological definition of property as 'the power to use economic goods' (Mises 1951: 37).[2] But unlike von Mises' definition Stehr's is not an equation: not all capacity for social action is knowledge, nor has it necessarily to be based on knowledge. It can also rest on power based on force, property or other means. But Stehr's association of knowledge and (the capacity for) social action nevertheless highlights an important aspect that is often ignored in definitions of knowledge, that knowledge is not only about something (or some things) but a social process that enables possibilities for action. It is social because it is meaningless beyond human interaction, and it is action oriented because it creates new possibilities for action. And,

---

[2] The German original reads 'das Vermögen, die Verwendung wirtschaftlicher Güter zu bestimmen', which is closer to Stehr's 'capacity'.

Stehr argues, it is above all scientific and technical knowledge that 'constitutes more than any other form of modern knowledge an incremental capacity for social action' (1994a: 97). In this capacity knowledge does not necessarily simplify decision-making and planing. In knowledge societies developments are increasingly 'made' whereas earlier they just 'happened'. He argues that increasing knowledge can create insecurities and risks as well as a liberating potential for action (Stehr 2001: 13). Knowledge is the base for authority but can also undermine it and therefore the social consequences of the growing importance of knowledge are far from clear.

These considerations lead Stehr to the assumption that in current societies access to knowledge becomes an issue of political and social struggles. He claims that knowledge will replace property and labour as the constitutive mechanisms of social inequality, reversing the relation between material and cognitive factors (Stehr 1999). One can therefore expect increasing legislative activity to regulate the production and distribution of knowledge. Stehr's argumentation here shows a close affinity to the theory of the post-industrial society advanced by Touraine, who had long before Stehr argued that in the post-industrial or programmed society economic growth and power increasingly depend directly on knowledge, and that therefore knowledge would replace property as the defining characteristic of the ruling class (Touraine 1972: 57).

Stehr's theory of social change   Despite Stehr's claim of developing a theory of knowledge societies it is almost impossible to identify a theory of social change that would underpin his writings. Like Bell his focus is on the economic sphere. For him 'the origin, social structure and development of knowledge societies is linked first and foremost to a radical transformation in the *structure of the economy*' (Stehr 1994a: 122). His model of social change is a stage model that puts ownership relations at its centre. Stehr argues against technological determinism or an overarching historical logic, but collective actors that might, in the absence of structural dynamics, drive historical development are also largely missing in Stehr's account. Where he claims that knowledge societies are characterized by their self-transforming capacity his description bears aspects of a system theory of society, but it remains again unclear which functional dynamic would drive this action of the system by itself.

Conflicts in the knowledge society according to Stehr   In his writings Stehr develops his claims mainly in critical discussion with existing theories and frameworks that have been proposed by other authors and offers only weak empirical support for his assumptions about the

growing conflictuality of the governance of knowledge. But nevertheless, his considerations point to several areas of (possible) conflict that
the other theories have neglected or only glossed over.

(1) If power is based on knowledge, then knowledge has to be fenced
in, hidden or protected from general access. Because power is a
relational concept, knowledge can only so long serve as its base as a
differential distribution is maintained. This collides with the inherent public-good characteristic of knowledge and therefore requires
serious efforts to establish excludability. Because knowledge can be
freely transferred and replicated, exclusivity for the general stock of
knowledge can never be reached. But Stehr argues that a decisive
feature of science is that it creates incremental knowledge (Stehr
2002: 29 ff.). And because advantages in productivity will depend
mainly on this newly added knowledge, it may therefore suffice to
secure (temporal) exclusivity for the latest increase in knowledge
in order to maintain the difference on which power can be based.
Intellectual property regimes provide exactly this functionality by
restricting access to the latest advances in knowledge and releas-
ing them to the public domain as soon as they have lost their differentiating potential. Building on Stehr's argumentation one may
therefore expect to see increasing conflicts about the rules that
propertize knowledge and thereby create intellectual property.

(2) A second point that Stehr mentions briefly and that Bell and Castells
also touch upon concerns the content of knowledge. It may be generally true that knowledge creates capacity for action, but not all
knowledge creates this capacity for all actors to the same extent. It
is therefore very likely that the content of knowledge will be an area
of struggle as well. That the content of knowledge is an embattled
terrain is nothing new. Systems of power were always constructed
to control what kind of knowledge is generated, by controlling education and research, establishing curricula and prosecuting those
who deviated from the prevailing opinion. On a much more general
level Foucault has argued that the order of discourse is embedded
in and reproduced by a complex set of (historically changing) institutions and practices, defining the areas of possible knowledge, the
rules of generating knowledge, and the limits and conditions for
cognition (Foucault 1981, 1991).

In a society in which economic development and political power depend
mainly on (new) knowledge, controlling the content of this knowledge
becomes at the same time more important and much more difficult.
The growing importance is evident, but the difficulty is related to the

social change → *conflict* → *social change '* → *conflict '* → *social change ' '* → ...

Figure 3.1 Linear model for conflict and social change.

necessary contingency of the scientific process. Because the outcome of research cannot be one hundred per cent foreseen we see on the one hand enormous efforts by authoritarian regimes to contain the uncontrolled sprawl of knowledge and on the other hand elaborated mechanisms to hedge the economic risks of research investments with unknown results.

3.3.   Going beyond the stage model

Despite the strong differences in terms of theoretical reference points and substantial claims, Bell, Castells and Stehr share one element that is common to their underlying theories of social change. Human history, for them, follows a clearly identifiable path. They may not all subscribe to the notion that the development of human societies is a continuous and directed evolution along a single master trajectory, and social conflict only a reflection of the structural changes with no life of its own. But the stage model of history in which one form of society is replaced by another, each structured by a single dominant logic, or axial principle, is essentially a cumulative model – although at least in Castells' and Stehr's accounts this historical progress is not necessarily associated with beneficial outcomes.

At their core many classical theories of social change argue that there is a direct connection between large-scale social change and conflict and assume a very simple causal chain as symbolized in Figure 3.1.

Social change leads to conflict, which leads to new social change, leading to new conflicts, and so on. While this is obviously a stark simplification and most models realize that conflicts have many more causes than social change, and that social change has more sources than social conflict, the assumption in many social theories is nevertheless that there is a simple relation between core processes of social change and core conflicts.

The three theorists of the knowledge society would most likely not subscribe to such a simple model of social change. Instead of one conflict associated with one process of social change they see multiple conflicts that develop in parallel. This leads to a somewhat more complex model that allows for multiple, independent conflicts (Figure 3.2).

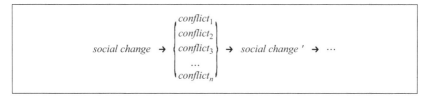

Figure 3.2 Model of multiple conflicts and social change.

But this model of multiple, parallel conflicts still remains a stage model of social history. This cumulative model and the corresponding idea of society and history in the singular has been attacked during the second half of the twentieth century by authors like Karl Popper, Robert Nisbet, Charles Tilly and Immanuel Wallerstein (for a more detailed discussion of their perspectives, see Sztompka 1993: 12). Their epistemological foundations vary, but their critical perspectives are united by the claim that history is neither a linear nor a unitary process, but rather develops in highly contingent and contradictory ways and is made through the concrete interaction of collective actors.

Popper rejects in his critique of historicism the idea of a universal history of humankind and insists that history is a highly contingent and fragmented process. He argues that history is essentially an open process, whose path cannot be predicted particularly because human action will always lead to unexpected results (Popper 1957). Another critic of a unidirectional notion of history is Robert Nisbet, who argued against the misleading metaphor of growth, insisting that in human history stagnation and discontinuity are as prevalent as growth (Nisbet 1970).

In a similar vein Charles Tilly argues against the idea of a single master process of social change. Instead, he claims, social development is characterized by numerous fragmentary processes, running parallel and sometimes in opposite directions. This perspective abandons the idea of a historical teleology. For Tilly social change is a complex process with contingent outcomes, propelled by conscious interventions of collective actors (Tilly 1984).

And finally Immanuel Wallerstein argues that the question whether the world system as a whole moves in a direction that could be regarded as progress should be an analytical question and not taken as a given. Within the current world system the 'progress' of single states depends usually on unequal relations of power and trade, so that the gains of some come with the losses of the others (Wallerstein 1991).

In all these theories conflicts play a prominent role. The rejection of the idea of history as a unified process with a clearly definable direction has shifted the perspective from a simple cause and effect model, in which conflict is seen as a direct result of social change, to more complex models in which social change alters the conditions and possibilities for conflictual interaction of various groups in society. This shift is particularly apparent in Tilly's works, which often take a broad historical perspective. Conflict appears here neither as the consequences of the breakdown of social order in historical processes of differentiation nor as the result of inherent social contradictions. For Tilly conflicts are rooted in concrete inequalities and power differences. Structural social changes affect the conditions for collective action, and his research tries to explain how the creation of nation-states, industrialization and democratization enhance or restrict possibilities for collective action, and influence the forms of action and the contents of public mobilizations (Tilly 1978, 1994, 2004).

Tilly and other critical historians have shifted the perspective on social change and conflicts in their research. They no longer primarily ask 'How does society work/function?' but, instead, are more interested in the question 'How do people make history?' The totalizing perspective of the classical theories of society is replaced by a detailed historical or sociological perspective that still is interested in patterns and mechanisms, but always in the plural.

But in this detailed historical picture no theory emerges that would link large-scale social change to specific social conflicts. In the classical social theories the relation between social change and conflict is under-complex as either conflict in general follows from processes of social change (Durkheim) or social change creates one specific core conflict (Marx). In Tilly's perspective social change alters the conditions for all kinds of social conflicts, and people develop tools and forms of collective action adapted to these changing circumstances, and with which they change the conditions for further collective action. But in this complex model social change, again, becomes unspecific with regard to social conflicts. Democratization may create favourable conditions for social movements, but this it does regardless of the issues specific movements address. So, the question, how social change and conflicts are related is still not answered.

Obviously one field of research that has addressed the relation of conflict and social change is the research on social movements. Large areas of current social movement research have abandoned the premise that social movements would be inherently linked to large-scale social change. Instead they are seen as an integral part of current societies in which a large variety of collective actors use protest to further their interests. Nevertheless, the idea that social movements would somehow be connected to more general processes of social change is still present in two rather different approaches: the political process and the new social movements approach.

The political process approach generally assumes that the ability for social movements to act, that is to mobilize adherents and to influence policies, depends strongly on the institutional environment and on the configuration of actors with whom the movements interact (Tilly 1978; McAdam 1982; Kriesi et al. 1992; Tarrow 1994; Kriesi 1995). While most studies from this perspective focus on the effects of political opportunity structures in terms of elite conflicts, institutional support, openness of the political system and political stability (McAdam 1996), the principal model of the policy process acknowledges that 'broad socio-economic processes' influence political opportunities and organizational capabilities. The latter create conditions for cognitive liberation and the emergence of social movements (McAdam 1982: 51). And in McAdam, Tarrow and Tilly's widely acclaimed model of the dynamics of contention, broad processes of change are at the origin of the proposed identifiable patterns of mechanisms of contentious interaction (McAdam et al. 2001: 45).

But while the reference to broad processes of change is still there, they remain somehow the dark matter of the political process model: they lurk in the background, but their function and the mechanisms of interaction remain obscure. Occasionally addressed is the opposite relation: social change as a result of collective action. While the models still contain the link from social change to conflict, analysis usually starts only with the activities of collective actors or addresses structural constraints at the level of the political (and sometimes cultural) system.

Researchers who have explicitly addressed the interrelation of social change and collective action are more likely associated with the 'new social movements' approach (Melucci 1980, 1989; Touraine 1981, 1988; Offe 1985; Roth 1994), a label that subsumes the de facto rather divergent perspectives from mostly European authors under a common name (Buechler 1995). Their attempts to understand how social change and social movements are structurally related grew out of the desire to make sense of the protests of the 1960s and 1970s. Confronted with protests that differed significantly in their demands, forms and participants from the protests of the nineteenth and the first half of the twentieth century, a number of authors developed frameworks that should better accommodate the role of these so-called 'new social movements' in processes of social change. I have presented some core elements of Touraine's and Offe's writings already above in the discussion of Castells' model of social change. Their shared starting point was the realization that the Marxist model of social change was no longer able to explain the dynamics of current protests. The new social movement theories differ significantly in their core assumptions and claims, but their common starting point is the notion that the Marxist model of class conflict was no longer sufficient to explain the emergence of current social movements and the cleavages these movements address.

The theoretical perspectives are united in the attempt to seek an explanation for current social movements in the contradictions of the social structure. Social movements – for them – were not just organized attempts of groups to further their interests, but products of the contradictions that are the necessary consequence of the structures of power and inequality in modern societies.

Alberto Melucci departs most clearly from the Marxist model of binary opposition and single historical movements and rather sees social movements as indicators of structural problems of current societies (Melucci 1980, 1985, 1989, 1996). He argues that to understand why social movements develop at a certain historical point in their specific forms, a theory of collective action and social change is needed. In his writings he develops elements for such a theory that goes beyond the Marxist determinism and the utilitarian indeterminacy.

His framework starts from the observation that in order to be able to analyse change the system in which change takes place has to be defined (Melucci 1996: 50). Change can only be observed in relation to a system in which change takes place, and the definition of the system's boundaries is ultimately an analytic decision since complex social systems do not have natural borders. Change is therefore an analytical category and depends on the reference points of the observer. This does not make change a subjective category, but is a reminder that theoretical and analytical decisions about the limits of the system influence the range of processes that can be interpreted as social change. If society is defined through the relations of production, social change will only be seen if those relations are altered. If society is defined through the structure and institutions of interpersonal relations, other processes of change that alter kinship relations or cultural meanings will possibly be interpreted as structural social change.

Melucci differentiates between adaptive and structural change and between endogenous and exogenous factors leading to change. Adaptive change is a reaction to change in some elements of the system that does not question the overall function of the system and thus can be integrated. Structural change involves a major reconfiguration of the system. Melucci maintains that even structural change usually does not involve all elements of a system, thus change will always be partial and multiple processes of change will likely happen at the same time, sometimes independent from each other, sometimes amplifying, and sometimes contradicting each other. Processes of change in different subsystems can, moreover, lead to incompatibilities among the elements or parts of a system if one subsystem is no longer able to maintain its function as a result of changes in another subsystem (Melucci 1996: 52).

This leads him to define social movements as those collective actors that at the same time set processes of social change in motion and are results of the ruptures that result from processes of change. They 'tie contradiction and conflict together; for they are situated at the intersection of structure and change' (1996: 53).

3.4.   Theories of social change and conflicts revisited

To get a clearer picture of how social change and conflict are related in existing theories of society it is helpful to compare the various perspectives along four axes:

(1) What are the *forces of change* that propel societies through history? Who are the (collective) subjects that drive processes of social change? Or which processes and functional mechanisms are responsible for the evolution of societies?

(2) The second dimension addresses the *processes* that structure social change. Which underlying logics of social change do the various theories assume? Which mechanisms are identified that structure social change?

(3) The third level addresses the role the theories assign to *conflicts*. Are conflicts a systematic part of social transformations? Are they seen as temporary disturbances in an essentially stable and well-ordered system, or are they seen as productive forces of social development?

(4) And finally, the fourth level addresses the anticipated *results*. What follows from conflicts and social change? Does social change serve a purpose, are conflicts to be overcome, or are they an indispensable part of the social?

Table 3.1 summarizes the core assumptions of the four main theoretical perspectives that I have discussed in this chapter so far. Individual authors often fit only partially into this scheme. As I have

Table 3.1 *Social change and conflict*

	Forces of change	Processes	Conflicts	Results
Classical theories of society	Functional or ideational logic	Development/ evolution along a series of stages with increasing differentiation	Results of changes	Progress
Marxism	Historical actors	Dialectical development driven by class antagonisms	Expression of contradictions	Classless society
'Critical perspectives'	Multiple actors	Contradictory processes driven by collective actors' interests	Integral part of society	More conflicts
New social movement theories	Social movements	Undirected process driven by the interplay between system and antagonist movements	Signs of contradictions	More conflicts

argued above, all three theorists of the knowledge society built on a stage model of social development but they do not necessarily adopt the perspective that social change is driven by a functional or ideational logic.

This schematic overview highlights several aspects:

- While the classical theories of society assumed that history would follow a (teleological) meta logic, driven by ideas or an inherent logic of functional differentiation, current theories of societies have largely abandoned this idea. In theories of the information and knowledge society such an evolutionary logic sometimes reappears in the form of technological determinism.
- The lasting contribution of Marx and Engels consists in the idea that history is made by collective actors in social conflicts. This notion is today shared by a variety of approaches from the post-Marxist new social movements and regulation theories to theories of rational political action.
- Although the authors that I summarized under the label 'critical perspectives' (Tilly, Nisbet, Popper, Wallerstein) and the new social movement theories (Melucci, Offe, Touraine) have much in common,

only the latter maintain a direct link between conflicts and processes of change.

In the absence of a consistent theory of conflict and social change, several aspects that are contained in the various theories of society, social change and collective action merit attention:

(1) Every analysis that sees social relations as more than an aggregation of arbitrarily moving monads has to address the structural conditions on which power is based in societies. The most important contribution of historical materialism is the insight that societies generate fundamental contradictions not because they lack the capacity to produce order but because power relies on the differential access to resources. Social cleavages that run along power and resource differentials are thus an integral part of modern societies. These cleavages change over time with the result that structural change alters the structure of conflict.

(2) The important contribution from the critical historical perspective is, first, that the organic metaphor is fundamentally flawed and, second, that social research should abandon the teleological models. The idea that the various elements of society work together like organs in a body or like parts in a machine can accommodate conflict only as a (temporary) disruption of the meta-social order that assigns every unit a function in a unified system. But societies are neither on a local nor at the global level integrated systems that follow a single logic. They are contradictory and are not held together by a unifying principle and they do not follow any simple developmental logic.

(3) A recurring theme among actor-oriented approaches is the conviction that conflicts are fundamentally social, that is, they are created through contentious interactions of collective actors, who do not enact their prescribed role on the stage of history but who produce history through their actions.

(4) In a weak version these three aspects are compatible with the pluralist idea of a society composed of competing interests. It acknowledges the multiplicity of sites of conflicts and the notion that conflicts do not share a common theme, but address various issues with competing and sometimes contradictory goals. The political process model subscribes to this perspective. Constraints in this model are localized mainly on the institutional level where (political) opportunity structures influence the emergence and the trajectory of conflicts.

(5) A strong version maintains that the pattern of conflicts in a given society is neither arbitrary – dependent only on the ability of

movement entrepreneurs to mobilize adherents – nor only structured through institutional opportunities and constraints. Instead
authors like Melucci, Touraine and Offe but also Giddens, Beck
and others argue that conflict patterns reflect core social cleavages,
ruptures that are associated with far-reaching changes in the social
fabric.

The problem is that as soon as these authors start to identify core social
cleavages the shadow of the unifying master narrative returns. Instead
of developing a complex model that would be able to accommodate
competing or even contradictory cleavages, they fall back on models
centred around one single core process or cleavage. Differentiation is
replaced by reflexivity, the labour–capital antagonism is replaced by the
struggle for control over knowledge and/or the process of the coloniza-
tion of the life-world.

But a model that would be able to account for the interrelation of
various processes of social change and social conflicts that have their
source in multiple cleavages and also influence in non-linear ways more
than one element of the social structure has yet to be developed. It
would have to account for the interaction between different processes of
social change, the interaction between social change and conflicts and
between conflicts. Such a model would possibly resemble the network
sketched in Figure 3.3.

Such a model would acknowledge that one process of social change
can lead to multiple conflicts, that several processes of change happen concurrently, that conflicts may not be related to social change,
that conflicts interact and that processes of social change interact.
Obviously such a model would not claim that every conflict will lead to
social change. And it may be possible that some social changes will not
lead to conflicts. Although it can safely be assumed that at least those
processes of social change that involve a society's power structures will
only in rare cases take place without the old power-holders trying to
hang on to their power.

The model depicted in Figure 3.3 is only a first sketch. Structural
constraints and other factors that influence the development of social
conflicts and the trajectories of social change are missing. Also the fact
that some conflicts persist over long periods while others dissolve more
quickly is not reflected in this simple graph. But the core idea this model
expresses is that even a model that allows for multiple parallel and/or
contradictory conflicts does not have to abandon the idea of causal relationships between conflict and change – the relation becomes 'only'
more complex.

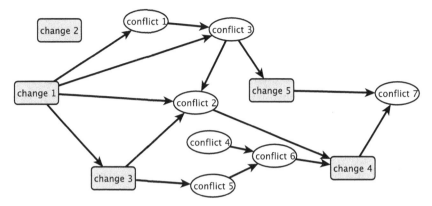

Figure 3.3 A network model of conflicts and social change.

As long as a more developed model that would integrate all these factors is still missing, every conceptualization of the relationship of conflict and large-scale or structural social change should at least be sensitive to the following points:

- Society is not a unitary object and does not develop along a linear trajectory.
- Social change is a fragmented process that has multiple and often contradictory outcomes.
- Structural change is a relative, not an absolute term – it depends on the analytical definition of a system's boundaries.
- Social change can occur in several areas. In the literature it is often qualified as structural or large-scale social change if it affects:
  - the economic and political base of power,
  - cultural values,
  - social practices,
  - the occupational structure,
  - and structures of participation.
- Within each area multiple, and sometimes contradictory, processes of change can take place concurrently.
- Processes of change in one area can have effects in other areas.
- Conflicts will often have more than one cause and sometimes produce effects in multiple areas.

Because of the complexity of the interactions any empirical study of conflicts and social change will have to limit its scope to a selection of relationships. But it will have to bear in mind that the conflicts under study are not autonomous entities that exist in isolation and independent from other social processes. In every society conflicts will always develop for specific reasons and under idiosyncratic conditions. Their trajectories will follow recurring patterns that are created by mechanisms of contention that structure collective action. And they will always be related to and dependent upon other past and concurrent conflicts.

3.5.   Change and conflict in the knowledge society

None of the theories of the knowledge society presents a consistent model of conflicts and social change, but the three authors each identify several processes of change and also some areas of conflict. In line with the idea of the network model of social change sketched in Figure 3.3, it is thus possible to at least identify some nodes in the network that characterize the processes of conflict and social change in the knowledge society. Missing a fully specified theoretical model, the relations between the nodes may best be identified in the empirical conflicts that we currently see unfolding around issues of intellectual property rights, privacy and access to knowledge.

The different authors emphasize different processes of change. Table 3.2 summarizes the main processes that Bell, Castells and Stehr identify. In this overview they are each – for the sake of simplicity – associated with one author only. In reality some of them appear in several of the theories, but here, the reference is only given to the author in whose work the respective process plays the most important role.

Overall, the authors assume that *power structures* change within nation-states and at the international level. Within societies power increasingly depends on the command over theoretical knowledge. Education, and especially tertiary education that imparts theoretical knowledge, therefore gains importance as a base for power in society. Until the mid twentieth century a clear distinction existed between money-based and education-based elites where the former held more powerful positions in industrialized countries (Ringer 1980). In contrast to this today's political and economic elites almost always have completed tertiary education, and often come from prestigious universities. In France a large part of the country's elite has attended the École Nationale d'Administration (ENA) and all US Senators have studied at tertiary education institutions.

Castells identifies another tectonic change in current societies' power structures. He argues that power is no longer based on the top-down control of hierarchical power structures, but on the control of much

Table 3.2 *Processes of change in the knowledge society*

Area	Process of change
Power structure	• Skill and education are the new base of power (Bell) • Knowledge replaces property as the source of power (Stehr) • The power of flows takes precedence over the flows of power. Power is based on networks outside the nation-state (Castells) • Power depends on the ability to program the network (Castells)
Economy	• The service sector replaces manufacturing (Bell) • Network enterprises replace the large hierarchical firms (Castells)
Occupational structure	• White-collar jobs become the dominant form of employment (Bell) • Access to tertiary education becomes a mass phenomenon and determines the position in the labour market (Bell) • A new cleavage develops between networked and switched-off labour (Castells) • Women are increasingly included into the formal labour market (Castells)
Culture	• The growing importance of experts and expertise • The end of patriachalism fundamentally alters social relations on all levels (Castells) • Knowledge about what is not known creates new fundamental uncertainties (Stehr) • A culture of real virtuality disconnects cultural practices from their local base (Castells)

more fluent and less hierarchical network structures. Power here depends on the ability to define a network's logic. These networks increasingly develop independently from nation-states and thus change the distribution of power in the international system.

At the level of the *economy* all authors agree that at the heart of knowledge societies lies a transition from industrial manufacturing to knowledge-based production. They disagree about the globality of this change and about the appropriateness of the term service economy, but they all are convinced that in the most competitive economies manufacturing is on the wane and that services, symbolic production and the virtual economy of financial markets become the defining elements of national economies and of the global economic order.

This has important repercussions in the *occupational structure*. The predominance of white-collar jobs goes hand in hand with a differentiation and individualization of the workforce. The dynamics of the network economy reverse the process of socialization of working conditions in the industrial age. The growing 'middle class' is a very inhomogeneous category with a huge income spread and strongly differing living and working conditions. The flexibilization imperative individualizes the social condition and thus undermines the foundation of industrial-age collective action. The growing inclusion of women into the formal labour market is, according to Castells, a parallel process that is connected but also partly independent from the dynamics of the transition to a knowledge society. It contributes to the fundamental change in the occupational structure of current societies, alters conflict structures and has far-reaching consequences in the cultural realm.

All authors argue that the emergence of knowledge societies is accompanied by changes at the level of *culture*, but the contours of these expected changes remain relatively vague. Castells' claim that we are witnessing the unfolding of the end of patriachalism is the most concrete process, but he argues that its source is not primarily the advent of the network society but the mobilization of the women's movement and the technological developments that enable women for the first time in human history to control the process of reproduction (Castells 2004: 4).

The changing role of experts and expertise is often mentioned in the literature about knowledge societies. But the tangible contours of this change are often not clear. Especially because the accelerating production of knowledge also produces new uncertainties that may even multiply at a higher rate than the knowledge (Stehr 2002: 9).

A third process of change is related to virtualization that not only affects the flows of money and power but also disembeds cultural practices from their local roots. Cultural practices that were always place-bound are becoming part of a globalized culture transmitted via global media and the internet.

Several conflict lines are either explicitly mentioned in the theories or can be deduced from the writings. Table 3.3 summarizes them in a similar fashion to the processes of change in Table 3.2. The conflicts are related to the changes discussed above, but most of them can neither be neatly allocated to only one of the realms of power, economy, occupational structure and culture, nor are they always the result of one specific process of change. Instead, and in line with the network model of conflict and social change, they are often related to more than

Table 3.3 *Conflicts in the knowledge society*

Level	Conflicts
Societal principles	• Control over the networking logic (Castells)
	• Autonomy (Castells)
	• Inclusion/Exclusion (Castells)
	• Redistribution of wealth (Stehr/Castells)
Generation and production of knowledge	• Content of scientific and technical knowledge (Bell)
	• Modes of innovation (Castells)
	• Propertization of knowledge (Stehr)
Access to and distribution of knowledge	• Access to education (Bell)
	• Digital divide (Castells)

one process of change and often span multiple spheres. To systematize them I have sorted them roughly according to the level on which they may be located – starting which conflicts that address basic societal principles, going then to conflicts that are located at the level of knowledge production, and going then to conflicts that address access, use and distribution of knowledge. Again, this categorization is a stark simplification and does not do justice to the fact that some (if not all) of the conflicts may have repercussions on multiple levels.

At the most fundamental level are the conflicts that address the general conditions for the generation of knowledge. These are conflicts about the programming and control of the networks and about the criteria and mechanisms that determine inclusion in or exclusion from the networks of power, production and financial flows. Conflicts about autonomy are for example those that Castells predicts between self-programmable and generic labour (Castells 2000: 12). An assumption that is prominent in Stehr's and Castells' writings is that at the socio-economic level knowledge replaces labour as the main source of inequality. It is thus reasonable to expect new conflicts about the (re-) distribution of wealth, involving other actors than those of the industrial age.

One level above are conflicts that address the modes of generation and production of knowledge. Conflicts at this level are about the content and the limits of accepted knowledge. Bell mentions here for example government attempts to control research and curricula. It is apparent from the writings of all three authors that the transition from the industrial and manufacturing mode of innovation will not happen without conflicts. And Stehr points to the conflictual nature of struggles about the possibilities of and limits to propertizing and thus privatizing knowledge that is generated in societies.

Finally another group of conflicts revolve around the rules that govern access to and the distribution of knowledge. Here we see conflicts about access to education, access to information, about limits for the access to private, privatized and public information, about the creation and maintenance of (digital) commons, and about the inequalities of access rooted in social and/or geographic conditions.

The two lists of processes of change and conflict lines roughly mark the field of conflicts and social change in the knowledge society that is present in the most prominent theories of the knowledge society. These lists give a first set of nodes that define processes of change and conflicts that may or may not be connected in a causal relation.

This is still far away from a theory of conflict and social change, and based on the sometimes speculative, sometimes contradictory literature on the processes of social change that accompany the transition to the knowledge society, no general theory of conflicts in the knowledge society can be developed – although some general structures can be recognized.

Taken together the processes of change and the areas of conflict that are associated with the knowledge society revolve around two meta issues: inclusion/exclusion and the mode of production. The conflicts and processes of change are on the most abstract level about the rules, conditions and processes of inclusion into the knowledge society. Changes in the economy, culture and occupational structure and conflicts related to these changes alter the conditions that define the position of collectivities in society. They shift the power structure among collective actors and the ability of collective actors to control the direction of their action. They are also about the opening-up and closing of possibilities for the establishment of collective actors. In these conflicts and processes of change the (relevant) actors in the knowledge society are defined.

The conflicts and processes of change that revolve around the second meta issue address the conditions for the production of knowledge. This second area is dominated by one core mechanism around which conflicts and change gravitate: the propertization of knowledge. I maintain that the transformation from a material to a symbolic economy does not – as Stehr has argued – lead to knowledge replacing property as the core source of power and inequality. On the contrary: the transformation upgrades the economic relations of the industrial age, but the economy remains capitalist, i.e. driven by the need to maximize profits and to commodify every relation within its reach. If immaterial goods become the base of the economy they have to be transformed into private property – otherwise they cannot be processed in a capitalist economy. The mechanism that provides the tools for this transformation is intellectual property. It is thus no surprise that many conflicts of the knowledge society revolve around the rules that govern the creation of intellectual property rights.

How – beyond this meta-level – processes of change and conflicts in the knowledge society are connected is now foremost an empirical question. Only an analysis of the concrete conflicts that have developed around core elements of the knowledge society will be able to uncover whether and how these conflicts are related to more fundamental processes of social change. Based on this analysis it will be possible to refine the – for now – rather crude model of conflict and change, and to specify with more accuracy how conflicts and social change are related in the knowledge society.

In the next chapters I will thus analyse the four most visible conflicts that have addressed the modes of production, valorization, use and dissemination of knowledge. All these conflicts question elements of the current worldwide system of intellectual property rights.

4   Software patents in Europe

The conflict about software patents in Europe turned out to be one of the most contentious issues that the European Parliament has seen so far (Interview 9). From its beginning in 1997 to its end in 2005 more and more actors became involved in a conflictual mobilization that brought the previously specialist issue into the TV evening news. The conflict started in June 1997 when the European Commission published a Green Paper on the Community patent and the patent system in Europe (COM 1997). It ended eight years later on 6 June 2005 when the European Parliament rejected the directive with a majority of 648 to 14 votes. Between these dates lies a contentious mobilization in which new collective actors emerged and entered the area of IP politics in Europe, and which has lastingly altered the power relations in this field.

The European conflict about software patents involved more actors than any other conflict in this policy field. The only other conflict that has developed a comparably strong mobilization is the conflict about access to medicines that will be analysed in the following chapter (Chapter 5). In order to analyse the social and institutional context of the conflict, the constellation of actors and the lines of conflict, this chapter proceeds as follows: I will start with a brief overview of the legal and institutional context in which the conflict was embedded (4.1). Then a thick description of the chronological development of the conflict follows, in which the main actor coalitions and their positions are highlighted (4.2). Building on this contextual information, and based on data about their cooperative relationships, the concrete interaction networks among the various actors (4.3) and their framing strategies (4.4) will be analysed. After summing up the findings of the analysis so far (4.5), I will finally discuss what the software patents conflict tells us about conflicts in the knowledge society on a more general level (4.6). The argumentation in this chapter builds on a discourse and network analysis of 170 newspaper articles published in Germany, the UK, France and Poland, several hundred primary documents published online by actors involved in the conflict, interviews with twenty-five key actors (Interviews 1–22), and evaluation of a questionnaire sent to the actors involved in the conflict (see section 4.3 for more details).

4.1.　The institutional context of the software patents conflict

In the European Union the publication of a Green Paper is usually the first step in a legislative process initiated by the Commission. In a Green Paper the Commission outlines its perspective on policy problems in a specific area, suggests possible points of intervention and tentative solutions, and asks stakeholders for input on the questions raised in the paper. In the run-up to a Green Paper selected stakeholders and experts are often already consulted and a more general and open consultation usually follows its publication. This was no different in the case of the Green Paper that addressed several perceived shortcomings of the European patent system.

The Commission bureaucrats had followed the debates in the legal community, had consulted selected stakeholders via a questionnaire on industrial property rights and had identified several areas of concern. Its title 'Promoting innovation through patents' reflected the mainstream position in the legal community that stronger intellectual property rights would promote innovation and, as a consequence, economic growth. The main focus of the paper was on the precarious relation between the European patent and the still not existing Community patent.

In Europe there is still no unitary patent system. Innovators can apply at the European Patent Office (EPO) for a European patent that, once granted, is essentially a group of independent nationally-enforceable patents which are valid in the member states of the European Patent Convention (EPC) – an international treaty, whose members only partially overlap with the European Union.[1] Numerous attempts to install a more encompassing Community patent within the European Union have failed. The Convention for the European Patent for the common market that was signed in 1975 in Luxembourg has never been ratified by enough member states and none of the attempts since then to revive the Community patent has been successful (Guellec and van Pottelsberghe de la Potterie 2007). At the time the Green Paper was published in 1997, the stalled Community patent was generally regarded as a major political nuisance. In the Green Paper the Commission lamented that

---

[1] Since January 2008 the member states of the European Economic Area and the EU are automatically EPC members. But the EPC also includes non-EU or EEA members, notably Switzerland, Turkey and a number of Eastern European states.

'almost forty years after the Treaty of Rome was signed, companies doing business within the Community still do not have access to a single system of patent protection' (COM 1997: 1).

The result of this situation is that a patent granted by the EPO may nevertheless not be enforceable in some European countries because of diverging national IP legislation. This is especially true for a specific group of patents that cover innovations in the area of computer software – and this was a second major point addressed in the Green Paper.

The European Patent Convention excludes in Article 52(2) discoveries, scientific theories, mathematical methods, aesthetic creations, schemes, rules and methods for performing mental acts, playing games or doing business, programs for computers and presentations of information from patentability. But Article 52(3) qualifies this exclusion by stating that the subject matter referred to in paragraph 2 should only be excluded from patentability to the extent that the patent application relates to them 'as such'. What this qualification actually means is still contentious, has changed over the years in the EPO patent grant practice and differs between national legislations in Europe.

The EPO has gradually broadened the scope of patentable subject matter under Article 52 to the extent that now a computer program can be patented if the claim refers to any hardware (Laub 2006; Ballardini 2008). A computer program on its own is still not patentable in Europe, but software running on a computer can be patented as long as the computer is mentioned in the patent application. Or as Simon Davies puts it, 'all inventions that might reasonably be considered as within the realm of computer science, for example procedures at the operating system level to improve machine operation, or generic algorithms, techniques and functionality at the application level, would normally be regarded as outside the exclusion of Article 52(2) EPC' (Davies 2003). This practice has led to 20,000–30,000 software patents being granted by the EPO up to 2004 (FFII 2004; Diver 2008).

But patents only have an economic and practical value if they are enforceable. And since patent enforcement rests in Europe with the national courts, many EPO-granted patents have de facto only dubious value in Europe. The legal practice in Germany, for example, largely resembles the EPO practice. Software patents are possible here and have mostly been granted in the field of engineering. In the past decade the Bundesgerichtshof (Federal Court of Justice, BGH) in several decisions[2] has further broadened the scope of patentable subject matter

---

[2] The landmark decisions highlighted in the literature are 'Logikverfahren' (BGH, *GRUR* 2000, p. 498), 'Sprachanalyseeinrichtungen' (BGH, *GRUR* 2000, p. 1007)

(Blind et al. 2001; Ensthaler 2010). In the UK, on the other hand, the UK Patent and Trademark Office (UK-PTO) usually rejects computer program claims and has refused to grant patents in many cases where the EPO had granted them, on the grounds that the claimed invention was a computer program as such (Ballardini 2008).

Solutions for this situation were sought on two parallel tracks: via a reform of the EPC and via legislation within the EU. On the first track, in preparation for an intergovernmental conference to revise the EPC, the EPO Administrative Council had prepared a proposal to remove computer programs from the list of exclusions in Article 52(2) of the EPC. But the national delegations were reluctant to follow the EPO proposal. Following the intervention of the French, Danish and German delegations, Article 52(2) was left untouched. They argued that the publication of the Commission Green Paper had started a deliberation process about the merits and possible limits of software patents within the European Union which they would not want to pre-empt. The French delegation went even further, arguing that they wanted to make sure that the 'risk of uncontrolled drift towards patents for business methods in particular must be avoided' (French Delegation 2000: 3). Ralf Nack and Bruno Phélip, in their report written for the International Association for the Protection of Intellectual Property (AIPPI), attributed this to 'the massive protests against software patents by a number of software developers' (Nack and Phélip 2000: 4). Whether or not this was true – leaving Article 52(2) EPC untouched left only the second track, the EU legislation.

In the 1997 Green Paper the Commission, aware of the diverging positions, conceded that the input it had received from stakeholders varied widely. But the differences that the Commission was concerned about were only between those who wanted the status quo without the legal uncertainties of the diverging national case law, and those who wanted to get rid of the limitations of Article 52(2) of the European Patent Convention completely (COM 1997: 17). So the only relevant difference the Commission was aware of was a difference between stakeholders who were satisfied with the EPO practice of granting software patents and stakeholders who wanted an even more liberal US or Japan-style practice. Under these conditions, finding a solution that would suit most stakeholders seemed to be largely a technical problem.

In accordance with this perception, the Commission published in the following years two separate proposals: in August 2000 a proposal for a

and more recently 'Steuerungseinrichtung für Untersuchungsmodalitäten' (BGH, *GRUR* 2009, p. 479).

Community patent (COM 2000a) and in February 2002 a *Proposal for a Directive of the European Parliament and of the Council on the Patentability of Computer-Implemented Inventions* (COM 2002). The first never made it through the Council. The member states were not able to come to an agreement and the proposal was finally abolished in 2004. A recent Council statement that proposes the creation of a unified patent litigation system in the form of a European and EU Patents Court (EEUPC) and that calls for an EU patent as a unitary legal instrument for granting patents valid in the EU as a whole (COUNCIL 2009) has also been met with scepticism by commentators who have followed the debate (Horns 2010).

The second, the so-called software patents directive, generated – to the surprise of almost all observers – one of the most contentious controversies in the recent history of the European Union. It finally failed in the European Parliament's second reading in July 2005, which is itself a remarkable fact. Among the 521 directives that have been decided in the codecision II procedure[3] in Europe between 1997 and 2008 only 19 failed, and among these 19 only one, the software patents directive, was rejected in the Parliament's second reading without an option of further conciliation (Biesenbender and Holzinger 2009).

But the software patents directive is exceptional for other reasons as well. In its course intellectual property rights have become politicized in Europe in an unprecedented way. The issue that until then had been seen as arcane and accessible only to a specialized tiny minority within the patent community became a major rallying point in a political conflict that involved EU policy-makers, experts, lobbyists and normal citizens with forms of political action ranging from behind-closed-doors lobbying to demonstrations in Brussels and Strasbourg. Before the software patents conflict patent policies were largely handled within the patent community, a term that comprises the 'patent attorneys and lawyers, patent administrators, and other specialists who play a part in the exploitation, administration and enforcement of the patent system. They form a community by virtue of their technical expertise and general pro-patent values' (Drahos 1999: 441). After a massive mobilization, in 2004 the issue reached the science and technology, the feuilleton and finally also the politics sections of large, national

---

[3] In the codecision procedure that was introduced in 1993 under the Maastricht Treaty (codecision I) and revised in 1997 under the Amsterdam Treaty (codecision II), the European Parliament effectively gains equal footing with the Council in the legislative process. Both institutions now have unconditional veto power, and legislation that falls under the codecision procedure can only be adopted if both institutions approve the proposal (Greenwood 2003; Burns 2004).

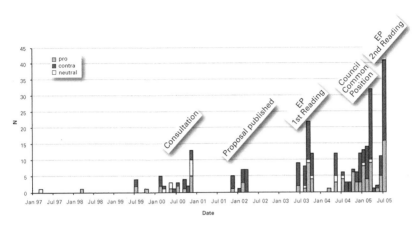

Figure 4.1 Timeline of the claims-making in the software patents conflict 1997–2005. Claims per month based on an analysis of newspaper articles in four countries (Germany, France, Great Britain, Poland); see section 4.4 for a description of the data on which this graph is based.

newspapers and even the TV news. It had turned from a specialist to a general political issue.

4.2.   The development of the conflict

In the following sections I will describe in more detail how the conflict evolved and analyse how it became such a political issue. The mobilization took place in five discernible waves that follow closely the formal decision-making process in the European institutions. Figure 4.1, showing the number of claims per month that were reported in the newspapers, illustrates this dynamic. In section 4.4 I will elaborate on the data on which this figure is based. Here it is only important to note that the conflict evolved in five waves. The first wave of contention developed around the consultation of the Commission Green Paper, the second started with the publication of the proposal for the directive, the third wave developed around the European Parliament's first reading of the directive, the fourth and fifth waves comprise the deliberation in the Council, and the second reading in the Parliament.

Overall the intensity of the conflict increased over time. The following discussion of the evolution of the conflict follows these waves. Julian Eckl (2005), Thomas Eimer (2011) and Eric Albers (2009) have created excellent analyses of specific aspects of the institutional decision-making process around the software patents directive. My focus here is the main actors, their interests and the forms of action.

4.2.1.   From the Green Paper to the proposal

The EPO's patent grant practice and the Commission's eagerness to facilitate software patenting in Europe has to be seen against the backdrop of the US – and to a lesser degree the Japanese – patent practice, where software patents and even patents on business methods are possible and where such patents are granted. In the USA, where software patents have been possible since the Supreme Court decision in *Diamond* v. *Diehr* (1981), this development has been regarded with great suspicion by software programmers and some civil society organizations (Laub 2006; Tysver 2008). In 1989 two computer programmers, John Gilmore and Richard Stallman, founded the League for Programming Freedom whose aim was to fight against interface copyrights and software patents. While they attracted some attention from the science and technology community and managed to place some articles in general interest magazines in this area (Garfinkel, Stallman and Kapor 1991; Garfinkel 1994), their impact remained limited and they were not able to generate any political momentum. The critical debate remained largely confined to some legal and economic scholars and a handful of activists in the free and open source community. But their argumentation about the negative effects of software patents laid out many of the issues that were raised ten years later in the European conflict.

In Europe, the formation of the Federation for a Free Information Infrastructure (FFII) and of the EuroLinux alliance was a response to the parallel efforts of the EPO and the Commission to liberalize the patenting practice with regard to software patents, either via the removal of the limiting clause in the EPC or via a 'harmonization' of the national legislations that would bring all member states in line with the EPO practice. The Commission, in its 1999 follow-up communication to the 1997 Green Paper, clearly stated this two-pronged strategy: 'On the one hand ... the Commission will present, as soon as possible, a draft Directive based on Article 100A of the EC Treaty aimed at harmonising Member States' legislation on the patentability of computer programs. In parallel with this legal action, the contracting states to the Munich Convention will need to take steps to modify Article 52(2)(c) of the European Patent Convention, in particular to abolish computer programs from the list of non-patentable inventions' (COM 1999: 14).

Five days after the publication of this paper in February 1999, FFII was officially founded in Munich as a registered association under German law. In June 1999 the EuroLinux alliance was founded by FFII and the francophone Linux user group AFUL (Association Francophone des Utilisateurs de Linux et des Logiciels Libres). Hartmut Pilch, a simultaneous interpreter for Chinese, Japanese, English and German and software programmer who has worked for the EPO in Munich, was the driving force behind the founding of FFII. Jean-Paul Smets, a software programmer, French Linux activist and author of an early book on the new free/open source business model (Smets-Solanes and Faucon 1999), was pivotal in the creation of the EuroLinux alliance. Coming from a free and open source software (F/OSS) background, both Pilch and Smets had picked up the debates that had existed within the Linux community since the early 1990s.

The Commission was supported in its efforts by several industry associations, notably the Union of Industrial and Employers' Confederations of Europe (UNICE, now BUSINESSEUROPE) and the European Information and Communications Technology Industry Association (EICTA). But the activities of FFII and EuroLinux were soon noticed as well. In October 1999 DG Internal Market organized a meeting with EuroLinux and other representatives of the F/OSS community, where they were able to voice their concerns (EuroLinux Alliance 1999; COM 2000b). But while their concerns were heard, they had no immediate policy impact. In a report on the implementation and effects of the directive governing the copyright protection of computer programs (Directive 91/250/EEC) the Commission reiterated its position without any change (COM 2000c).

In the F/OSS community meanwhile a remarkable virtual and real mobilization started. On 14 June the EuroLinux alliance published an online petition on its website, directed at the European Parliament, in which virtual signatories were able to voice their concern about the software patent plans of the Commission and 'urge decisionmakers at all levels in Europe to enforce the law, which clearly prohibits patenting pure computer programs, instead of changing it' (EuroLinux Alliance 2000). This petition quickly gathered support. After less than two months more than 30,000 people had signed it (Schulzki-Haddouti 2000), and another two months later the number of supporters surpassed 60,000. But the protests did not remain confined to the virtual realm. On 29 August 2000, at the official opening of amazon.fr, about twenty-five activists distributed 'unpatented cookies' and leaflets denouncing Amazon's '1-Click' patent[4] that served in the mobilization as an especially hideous example of a broad software/business methods patent.

---

[4] http://en.wikipedia.org/wiki/1-Click.

Probably owing to these mobilizations some of the software patent critics' concerns were mentioned in the Commission's consultation paper published in October 2000, which, instead of eulogizing the advanced US and Japanese patent system, concedes that the impact of patents for 'computer-implemented inventions' on the economy is ambiguous, and that there is no consensus on whether introducing software patents would strengthen or weaken the competitiveness of the European economy (COM 2000b: 12). In the two months in which the consultation was open, the Commission received 1,447 responses, 91 per cent of them rejecting the proposed patentability of software, and many of them motivated by the EuroLinux petition. Almost 1,200 of the responses were forwarded to the Commission by EuroLinux, who had offered this form of collective submission on their website. The consultation, which overlapped with the intergovernmental conference to revise the EPC, also received a surprising amount of attention in the general media.

This high number of opposing statements was not what the Commission had expected and wanted, and in a report done by PbT Consultants for the Commission the overwhelming rejection of software patents is euphemized by arguing that while there may have been a numerical majority against software patents 'there is an "economic" majority in favour of patents on computer-implemented inventions' (PbT Consultants 2001: 4).[5] Responses to the consultation came from all EU and EEA member states apart from Liechtenstein, some CEEC countries, the USA, Australia and South Africa. On a substantive level the report sorts the responses into two camps, opponents of software patents and supporters of software-related patents, merging the three options suggested in the consultation paper (more restrictive, status quo, and more liberal) into two categories that more aptly reflect the fact that the EPO status quo was already a strong pro-software-patents position.

After the consultation the first mobilization wave abated. In 2001 the conflict largely retreated from the public stage. Figure 4.1 shows that after a first wave of public attention that peaked in December 2000 no articles were published in the mainstream press until the end of 2001 (for a detailed discussion see Haunss and Kohlmorgen 2009). After

---

[5] At first sight the pie-charts showing the organization types in the two camps seem to confirm this reasoning, indicating that only 8 per cent of the opponents compared to 30 per cent of the supporters were large firms. Since absolute numbers of the two camps are not given anywhere, one has to recalculate them from the overall number of responses and the proportion of the two camps to see that actually 105 large firms opposed software patents whereas only 39 supported them.

the consultation the actors tried – with varying success – to lobby the Commission and national governments. Commission officials met with various interest groups, among them UNICE, EICTA, the Business Software Association (BSA), the Computing Technology Industry Association (CompTIA), several representatives from large firms, and also, a second time with FFII (Interview 1). The Commission also actively sought expertise and cooperated closely with the European Patent Office. Eric Noteboom, the head of the industrial property unit in the DG Internal Market, and Bernhard Müller, the administrator responsible for drafting the directive, travelled to Munich to discuss the details of the directive with patent examiners, judges and high ranking officials (Interviews 1, 21).

Within the Commission the directive was far from consensual. DG Competition suggested internally that the directive should be renounced completely (Eimer 2011). Criticism came also from DG Information Society, which was more open to the arguments of the F/OSS community. In a contribution to a conference on software and business method patents at the University of Maryland, Philippe Aigrain, at that time head of the sector 'Software Technologies' in the unit 'Technologies and Engineering for Software, Systems and Services' of the DG Information Society, cautiously voiced strong concerns about the negative consequences of software patents (Aigrain 2001). Later, in 2003 Aigrain left the Commission and became actively involved in the mobilization against the directive.

Despite the clearly visible conflict DG Internal Market adhered to its course and published on 20 February 2002 a 'proposal for a Directive of the European Parliament and of the Council on the patentability of computer-implemented inventions' in which it follows its maximalist position to 'harmonize' the EPO practice of granting patents for anything that runs on a computer.

The proposal states in its core Article 3 that 'Member States shall ensure that a computer-implemented invention is considered to belong to a field of technology', after defining computer-implemented invention in Article 2 as 'any invention the performance of which involves the use of a computer, computer network or other programmable apparatus' (COM 2002: 20). In other words anything that runs on a computer or similar device is 'computer-implemented', and anything that is 'computer-implemented' is technical. And if it is technical, it can be patented, provided that it is new and involves an inventive step. The only limit this directive sets is that a computer has to be involved somehow. In this version the directive may have excluded pure business method patents – those are possible in the USA but no group involved in the conflict had claimed that they should be introduced in Europe – but it would have secured the patentability of software as long as the patent claim mentioned the computer on which the software would run. With this proposal the Commission obviously neglected all the concerns that had been voiced from the F/OSS community and many academics, and followed completely the patent community and the large business associations, whose position on this issue was again strongly influenced by the patent departments of the large member companies.

The unwillingness of the Commission to seriously consider concerns of software patent critics is especially visible in the explanatory part of the proposal where the Commission assesses the impact of the patentability of software-related inventions on innovation, competition and businesses. Citing a study that was conducted by the Intellectual Property Institute, London – a think-tank of the patent movement – on behalf of the Commission, they argue that 'the patentability of computer program related inventions has helped the growth of computer program related industries in the States, in particular the growth of SMEs and independent software developers into sizeable indeed major companies' (COM 2002: 5). While this is indeed stated in the executive summary of the study, the chapter, written by Peter Holmes, containing the economic analysis does not substantiate this statement. On the contrary, the author repeatedly refers to the danger of 'blocking-patents' and the possible negative effects of software patents, and that 'any move to strengthen IP protection in the software industry cannot claim to rest on solid economic evidence' (Hart, Holmes and Reid 2000: 32).

The configuration at this point of the conflict can be summarized as follows: at the international level the issue of software patents in Europe was embedded in a constellation where the two other most important economic powers, the USA and Japan, had introduced software patents in their legislations, whereas in Europe software was formally excluded from patentability although EPO practice had gradually allowed software patents to be granted – with limited enforceability in the member states. This situation was seen as an economic disadvantage by the large industry associations, especially those representing technology and software companies. The patent community had a strong interest in getting rid of the software exemption clause in the EPC or at least in harmonizing the legislation in the member states to follow the EPO practice. Both interest groups were well connected to the responsible ministries in the European member states and to the European Commission. Business associations and the patent community not only shared the same beliefs but overlapped also on the level of personnel, since IP policies of large companies are usually shaped by their patent department. Oppositional voices were not represented by established formal organizations and were not included in the relevant policy networks shaping IP policies.

Against this background it was not very surprising that the conflict that began in 1999 continued and even intensified. What *was* surprising was the trajectory and the outcome of the conflict in which in the end the resource-poor and inexperienced F/OSS activists prevailed against the resource-rich and well-established business associations.

4.2.2. The strength of the European Parliament

With the publication of the proposed directive the ball was in the European Parliament's court. Since the legal basis for the proposed directive was Article 95 of the EC Treaty it had to be decided in the codecision procedure. This means the proposal is passed to the Parliament, which can accept or amend it. Formally the EP cannot reject the directive at first reading, but in practice it can either amend it in a way that contradicts the directive's meaning or reject the amendments of the responsible committee to stop a directive at this stage. Amendments can be made with simple majority at first reading. The directive is then passed back to the Commission, which can pass the (amended) directive directly to the Council or rewrite the directive in a way that incorporates those amendments the Commission deems acceptable and then pass it to the Council. The Council can now accept the results of the EP's first reading with qualified majority if they have been incorporated into the amended proposal by the Commission. If not all the EP's amendments have been incorporated in the text, or if the Council wants to change the Commission's text, it has to adopt a common position about which the Parliament then decides in a second reading. At this stage it can accept, amend or reject it, whereupon amendments can only be made with absolute majority, that means every absent or abstaining MEP counts de facto against an amendment. If the Parliament amends the directive, it is then again sent to the Council for a second reading, and if the Council does not agree with the amendments a conciliation procedure follows in which a committee consisting of MEPs, Council representatives and the Commissioner responsible try to find a compromise (for a detailed discussion of the decision-making process see Council General Secretariat 2010).

The software patents directive only made it to the Parliament's second reading in which it was rejected with a huge majority of 648 to 14 votes.

But before it got there a fierce conflict developed that had repercussions for the politics of intellectual property in Europe and beyond.

After the proposal was published the bureau of the European Parliament decided that the leading committee responsible for the proposed directive would be the committee on Legal Affairs and Internal Market (JURI), and that additional opinions should be given by the committees for Industry, External Trade, Research and Energy (ITRE) and for Culture, Youth, Education, Media and Sport (CULT). The British Labour MEP Arlene McCarthy became rapporteur for JURI, the Dutch liberal Elly Plooij-van Gorsel rapporteur for ITRE, and, after the conservatives abstained from naming a representative in the culture committee, Michel Rocard, former French prime minister and like McCarthy a member of the social democratic group in the EP (PSE), became rapporteur for CULT.

For most of 2002 the issue of software patents remained largely below the general public radar. Specialized public groups were addressed through several conferences organized by interest groups and academics. Only in France did the issue gain some prominence in the presidential election in which all candidates publicly took a position against software patents (Latrive and Mauriac 2002).

In the European Parliament the issue was discussed for the first time in the JURI committee four months after publication of the proposal. In Arlene McCarthy's first working document, she briefly mentions but largely discounts the objections of the F/OSS community (McCarthy 2002). She also mentions, but without giving any details, a study on the desirability of EU level legislation in the area of software patents that had been commissioned by the European Parliament (Bakels and Hugenholtz 2002). In this study, which was commissioned before the proposal for the directive was published, the authors summarized the findings of the relevant scientific literature and drew several conclusions. Among them are the very cautionary notes that so far, '[i]t has not been demonstrated that software patents contribute to innovation. The opposite may be true as well' (Bakels and Hugenholtz 2002: 22), that the proposed directive would not prohibit business methods patents, and – most importantly – that it would not solve the problem of trivial patents and poor patent quality.

While McCarthy tried in JURI to gloss over the opponents' concerns, in general the European Parliament was very open-minded towards their arguments and listened to all sides involved in the issue. In two Parliamentary hearings in May and November 2002 representatives from FFII and other critics of software patents as well as representatives from the Commission, the EPO, patent attorneys and from industry associations had been invited to present their position to the MEPs (EP 2002).

How much the debate had already changed since the 1997 Green Paper became visible in September 2002 in the first official position paper by an EU institution on the directive – the opinion of the Economic and Social Council (ESC). In stark contrast to its earlier opinion on the Green Paper (ESC 1998) which showed support for the EPO practice of granting software patents, the – non-binding and only consultative – position of the ESC on the proposed directive was highly critical, questioning its 'de facto acceptance and justification of the a posteriori drift of EPO jurisprudence' (ESC 2003: 157), and recommending a serious revision of the proposed directive that would limit instead of broadening the scope of software patents. On the other hand, the Permanent Representatives Committee of the Council (COREPER) – the national civil servants preparing the work for the Council meetings in Brussels – supported the Commission's position and even suggested extending the scope of patentability beyond the proposed directive (Albers 2009).

These developments show that the political opportunity structure for the opponents of software patents offered at least some avenues for access to the European institutions. Also the clear-cut division between opponents and proponents of software patents that was already visible in the consultation phase persisted. The Commission and the Council were clearly positioned in the proponents' camp, and their willingness to consider the opponents' position was minimal or even non-existent.

The first deliberations in the European Parliament revealed divisions between and within the political groups and strong incertitudes towards the issue. The culture and industry committees took a critical position, suggesting that the directive should be amended in a way that would effectively prohibit software patents (CULT) or would strictly limit the scope of software patents, secure interoperability and exclude generic software running on a computer from patentability (ITRE) (Plooij-van Gorsel 2003; Rocard 2003). In both committees these opinions were contested. A strong minority of MEPs supported the Commission's proposal or even suggested amendments that would have further liberalized software patenting in Europe. In JURI the members were also divided, but here a majority supported the position put forward by Arlene McCarthy. From the other committees' amendments only those that were meant to secure interoperability were integrated in JURI's recommendations; all those that would effectively prohibit software patents or significantly impede broad and general software patents were rejected (McCarthy 2003).

In the average decision-making process the European Parliament would have followed in its first reading the recommendations of the responsible committee, especially on matters that are regarded as being narrow and technical. But this time the Parliament did not follow JURI, and the reason for this lies in the political mobilization of the opponents of software patents in the months before the Parliament's first reading on 24 September 2003.

While the attempts to influence the decision-making process so far had relied largely on the classical lobbying repertoire, the mobilization dynamics changed significantly in spring and summer 2003. On 4 April Alexandre Dulaunoy from the Belgian Association Electronique Libre (AEL) and Hartmut Pilch from FFII submitted the EuroLinux petition with 140,000 signatures to the European Parliament. The number of signatures already showed that the mobilization had reached far beyond the F/OSS community. Among the other actors that were getting involved independently were the German section of Attac, who wrote an open letter to the MEPs (Attac Deutschland 2003), and a group of scientists working in the field of intellectual property, who wrote to the MEPs urging them 'to reject the proposed Directive in its present form' (researchineurope.com 2003). The forms of action also changed. The lobbying repertoire of contacting decision-makers via letters, email or direct visits, organizing conferences and formal and informal meetings, writing open letters and petitions, and the like, were complemented by more conflictual forms of action usually associated with social movements.

On 27 August 2003, 500 people demonstrated in Brussels against software patents, staging a street performance and a manifestation. The real demonstration at the Place de Luxembourg in front of the Parliament was accompanied by a virtual demonstration on the internet in which between 1,500 and 3,000 participants symbolically closed their websites, replacing their entry page with a black page sporting the slogan 'closed due to software patents'. This virtual demonstration in particular received widespread attention in the general media. Many of the activists who came to Brussels in the last weeks before the EP's first reading of the directive had no prior experience of lobbying or political protest. 'For many this was the first political action in their lives', wrote Markus Beckedahl in his report on how he, together with twenty-five other activists from the F/OSS community, came to Brussels in the last week of August 2003 (Beckedahl 2003: 43). The activists discussed their strategies on public mailing lists and relied on volunteers for most activities. In Brussels they received some support from the European Greens, who provided passes for the Parliament and co-organized a

conference and press conferences with them. Of the four largest political groups in the European Parliament the Greens were the only one
with a widely supported anti-software-patent position. The majority
of the liberals (ALDE) were also for stricter limits on software patentability, whereas the two largest groups, the social democrats (PSE) and
the conservatives (EPP-ED), were split. Within the social democrats'
faction Michel Rocard led the opposition against Arlene McCarthy
and, after several internal votes, was able to establish his position as
the social democrats' majority position. In the EPP-ED the Finnish
MEP Piia-Noora Kauppi was the crystallization point for the directive's opponents.

The exceptional conflictual dynamic was highlighted in the plenary debate on 23 September 2003 in which several MEPs mentioned
the unusual attention the directive had gathered and in which Arlene
McCarthy complained that in her ten years as MEP she had 'never
encountered such a personal, aggressive and abusive campaign' (EP
2003a). Others, like the Spanish social democrat Luis Berenguer
Fuster, were more positive about the attempts by lobbyists, activists
and many individuals involved in the mobilization to contact and lobby
the MEPs. Remarkable on a different level were Commissioner Frits
Bolkestein's opening words in the parliamentary debate on this day:
a thinly veiled threat to the Parliament that, if it would not follow the
Commission's proposal, 'we may well be confronted with a renegotiation of the European Patent Convention' (EP 2003a) in which the
EP would have no say. In the vote on the following day the Parliament
had to vote on 129 amendments to the proposed directive, 28 tabled
by JURI, the others proposed by the political groups and individual
MEPs. To provide some orientation among all these amendments the
Greens/EFA, GUE/NGL and ALDE had prepared voting lists for
their groups, EPP-ED and PSE – divided on the issue – each produced
two voting lists, prepared by Arlene McCarthy (PSE) and Joachim
Würmeling (EPP-ED) in support of the Commission's proposal and by
Michel Rocard (PSE) and Piia-Noora Kauppi (EPP-ED) in opposition.
In addition FFII had also prepared a voting list which it had sent to all
MEPs. After consolidating the partially overlapping amendments the
EP adopted 64 of them in the vote on the following day, turning the directive effectively on its head. Instead of codifying the recent practice of
the EPO, the directive in its form after the EP's first reading would have
strictly limited the possibility of software patents, especially through
the introduction of a sentence in Article 2(b) by which the processing,
handling and presentation of information was excluded from patentability, even where technical devices are employed for such purposes,

by excluding computer programs that implement business, mathematical or other methods from patentability if they produce no other technical effect than running on a computer or network (Article 4a), and by requiring industrial application of the patentable invention (EP 2003b). With the EP's decision to adopt a substantially changed directive with a large majority of 361 to 157 votes (with 28 abstentions) that largely reversed the Commission's intentions, the next round in the conflict about software patents in Europe began.

4.2.3.   Trouble in the Council

The Parliament's decision was welcomed by FFII and others involved in the mobilization against software patents but set off alarm bells at other industry lobbyists and in the patent community. The industry associations and the Commission had seriously underestimated the determination of the European Parliament, and the successful intervention of FFII and others had taken them by surprise (Gehlen 2006; Interview 1).

The Council's General Secretariat quickly evaluated the Parliament's decision and on 28 October concluded that nineteen of the amendments could be accepted unconditionally, and another three with reformulation. Thirteen amendments might be susceptible to compromise, but the largest part (twenty-seven) would be unacceptable, the last being all the amendments that would restrict the scope of patentability (Council General Secretariat 2003). The Irish Council presidency that took office in January 2004 had intellectual property rights in general and software patents in particular prominently on its agenda (Irish Presidency 2004: 6). It quickly proposed a 'compromise' that, on closer examination, really was no compromise at all. Apart from some cosmetic changes the proposal ignored all changes made by the EP and essentially rolled back the text to its status before the Parliament's first reading (Albers 2009). But in contrast to the Irish presidency other member states were rather reluctant to push the issue. The European conflict had made politicians at the national level aware of the scope of the issue and Sweden and France announced that they would first hold national consultations before acting in the Council. It thus soon became clear that the majority of the member states were not willing to rush through legislation before the European election in spring 2004 (Krempl 2003).

Despite its efforts the Irish presidency therefore failed to get the issue through the Council before the fifth EU enlargement came into effect on 1 May 2004, which brought ten new member states – most of them from Eastern Europe – into the Union and changed the distribution of votes in the Council. On 18 May the directive was set on the agenda of the Competitiveness Council where it was not formally adopted, but – officially due to missing translations – only a 'political agreement' was reached with the Austrian, Italian and Belgian delegations abstaining and Spain voting against the proposal. Under usual circumstances a political agreement would mean that the decision would have to be formally confirmed at a later date. But this time it took another ten months before the Council finally agreed on a common position.

One reason for this delay was the odd circumstances under which the agreement was reached. In the Council meeting a first deliberation did not secure the needed qualified majority of 88 out of 124 votes since Belgium and Spain indicated that they would vote against the proposed text and Poland, Denmark, Austria, Germany, Latvia, Italy, Luxembourg, and Hungary that they would abstain. After an intervention by Commissioner Bolkestein a minimal change was introduced in the text that partially satisfied Germany's reservations. The Council president and Irish Minister for Enterprise Trade and Employment, Mary Harney, now asked which countries would not be able to support the modified text. She then asked some but not all of the countries who originally had abstained or opposed the proposal about their vote, urging Denmark especially to support the text (Müller 2006: 42). Abstentions were not separately polled, and all countries that had not signalled that they would not support the proposal were counted as supporters – a procedure that obviously surprised some of the delegations of the new member states. Jarosław Pietras, the Polish delegate, claimed on the following day that the Polish delegation did not change from abstention to yes (Pietras 2004). But as long as no other delegation claimed to be misinterpreted this did not change the qualified majority that now consisted, even without Poland's support, of exactly the required 88 votes.[6]

The actual instability of the political agreement resulted in multiple failed attempts to set the issue as an A item on the Council's agenda.[7] The Dutch presidency that took over in July 2004 announced several times that the directive would be on the Council's agenda, only to

---

[6] A video of the Council session is available on the FFII website at http://media.ffii.org/ Council18may/council18may04.avi. An edited version is available at http://video.google.com/videoplay?docid=-4116399771660063665.

[7] In the Council A items are those issues on which a consensus has already been reached in the COREPER or which only have to be formally adopted. A items are voted on without discussion and usually en bloc. Only B items are discussed in the Council meetings.

remove it again at the last minute. At the 2,633th Council (Agriculture and Fisheries) it was finally on the agenda, but after the Polish delegate Vladimir Marciński, Secretary of State at the Ministry of Science and Information Technology, insisted on removing the item from the agenda the decision was once again postponed (Eckl 2005) – an unprecedented act, since despite the formal possibility of withdrawing an A item from the agenda, until then no government had ever actually used this option in the Council (Gehlen 2006: 12). The entry into force of the new voting weights in November 2004 complicated the situation even more. Under the changed rules the Spanish 'no' and the Austrian, Italian, Belgian and Polish abstentions would have led to a result that would have fallen short of the necessary limit of a qualified majority of now 232 votes by 16 votes.

The situation became even more intricate after the European Parliament decided to intervene in an unforeseen way in the decision-making process. In reference to Article 55(4) of its rules of procedure, a group of nine MEPs launched in December 2004 an initiative to restart the directive (Buzek et al. 2004). Under the relevant article the president of the Parliament can request that a proposal shall be referred again to Parliament if the Commission substantially amends its initial proposal, if the problem substantially changes, or if new elections to Parliament have taken place since it adopted its position (EP 2004). JURI supported this initiative and on 17 February 2005 the Parliament's presidency officially asked the Commission to refer the directive back to the EP (Marson 2005), a request that was quickly declined by Commission President José Manuel Barroso (Barroso 2005).

After the issue was left undecided for such a long time it was for most observers no small surprise when the Council on 7 March 2004 in its 2,645th meeting (Competitiveness Council) decided to accept the political agreement without changes as an A item despite Denmark's and Portugal's wish to discuss it as a B item (Eckl 2005: fn. 46). As in the first decision, Austria, Italy and Belgium abstained and Spain voted against the proposal. Denmark, Cyprus, Latvia, Hungary, the Netherlands and Poland entered declarations into the minutes in which they expressed discomfort especially with the unclear definition of the scope of patentability and the lack of an interoperability requirement. While the delegations did not want to further block the directive in the Council, these declarations can be read as signals that respective member states would possibly like to see changes in line with the changes introduced in the EP's first reading. Nevertheless, the overall message of the Council decision was blatant disrespect for the Parliament since all substantial changes that would have limited the patentability of software had been removed and a newly introduced Article 5(2) even allowed patent claims to a computer program, either on its own or on a carrier (Council General Secretariat 2004). This put the Council's common position in an even more software patent friendly position than the original Commission proposal (Albers 2009: 65).

The dynamics of the conflict in the one and a half years in which the directive lingered in the Council can only be understood by taking into account the interventions of the various stakeholders outside the European institutions. If the result of the Parliament's first reading reflected the successful mobilization of the F/OSS community, the conflict in this phase of the dispute was heavily influenced by even more intense interventions by industry and civil society groups.

After the European Parliament's first reading, business associations and large firms in favour of software patents quickly realized that they would have to become more active if they wanted to archive a result in line with their preferences. EICTA acted quickly and initiated in November 2003 a letter from the CEOs of Alcatel, Ericsson, Nokia, Philips and Siemens to the, at that time, Italian Council presidency and the European Commission, urging them to send 'a strong counter signal' against the EP's decision that would remove effective patent protection for their R&D investment (Nokia et al. 2003). The German high-tech business association BITKOM seconded them with a press release on the same day claiming that the EP's directive would contradict not just established patent rights but the foundations of a property-based economy (BITKOM 2003). To counter the F/OSS community's mobilization EICTA also decided to establish a Computer-Implemented Inventions (CII) taskforce, headed by EICTA's public affairs director Leo Baumann, with a special budget of €400,000 to which Nokia, Ericsson, Intel, SAP, Microsoft, IBM, Siemens and Philips each contributed €50,000 (Gehlen 2006: 10). In the final phase of the conflict in spring 2005 this campaign war chest was once more significantly updated: Alcatel, Nokia, Philips, Ericsson, Siemens, SAP, Microsoft and Intel contributed another €250,000 each, providing EICTA with a special lobbying budget of about the size of its usual overall annual budget (Gehlen 2006: 15). The Business Software Alliance (BSA), the other big, more US-centric, IT business association in Brussels, had a similar amount at its disposal. Seven out of eight large IT member firms contributed €250,000 each (Interview 17), so that the two business associations alone disposed of about four million euros for lobbying on the software patents directive. FFII, in comparison, had to manage with an annual budget between €70,000 (2003) and €180,000 (2005).[8]

The business associations urged their members to intensify their lobbying efforts at the national level. They also created two campaign websites: Patents4innovation (patents4innovation.org), a site set up by EICTA featuring 'inventor stories' by Philips, Nokia, Siemens and Alcatel employees, and Campaign for Creativity (campaignforcreativity.org), an astroturf website managed by Simon Gentry and financed at least partly by Microsoft, SAP and CompTIA (LobbyControl 2006).[9] The latter website claimed to be a genuine effort by individuals and SMEs from the creative/innovative industries and linked to an online campaign site which provided an option to send emails in support of software patents to MEPs.[10] In retrospect the value of these efforts in reaching out to the internet public remains dubious. The Campaign for Creativity in particular was later seen more as a hindrance than as advancing the interests of its creators.

At the national level the opponents of software patents scored a number of spectacular but ultimately inconsequential points. Several national parliaments passed motions and decisions against software patents and in support of the European Parliament's position. The Dutch House of Representatives (Tweede Kamer) passed a resolution requesting the government to abstain in the Council in future votes on the directive, and requested the government again in February 2005 not to agree to the common position. The German Parliament (Bundestag) adopted a cross-party resolution against a broader scope of software patents criticizing the political agreement in the Council. The Spanish Senate and the Hungarian and Latvian parliaments also adopted resolutions against the directive (Eckl 2005; Gehlen 2006). And in Denmark the EU committee of the Danish Parliament gave the Minister of Economy the binding instruction to demand renegotiation in the Council. Against this backdrop the decision in the Council in which, of those countries, only Spain voted against the directive, was an instructive example of the limited power of national parliaments in intergovernmental negotiations.

The most visible activities of the opponents of software patents were several demonstrations. On 12 May 2004, FFII organized demonstrations in several European cities. On 24 June 2004, about 1,000 people

[8] http://old.ffii.org/geld/log/index.de.html (accessed 13 May 2010).
[9] Astroturfing refers to a form of political campaigning in which usually an industry actor presents itself falsely as an unbiased or grassroots initiative.
[10] In December 2005 the Campaign for Creativity won the first 'Worst EU Lobbying Award' for its misleading campaign.

attended a demonstration against software patents in Brussels organized by FFII and the Free Software Foundation Europe (FSFE) and supported by a big coalition of organizations, companies and NGOs. On 6 and 7 July, smaller demonstrations took place in Munich and Bordeaux, and on 17 February 2005 there was a demonstration with 300 participants in Brussels. These real demonstrations were accompanied by several virtual demonstrations and banner campaigns and usually were covered in the mainstream press and sometimes even made the TV news.

In the summer of 2004 FFII launched a postcard campaign in which participants were asked to send holiday postcards with texts about software patents to their MEPs. Also in summer, a delegation headed by the prominent free software developer and founder of the GNU project, Richard Stallman, travelled through Eastern Europe to try to influence the new eastern member states, which were seen as potential allies due to the lack of a developed IT industry sector with big firms like Siemens, Alcatel or Nokia, but often with a relatively active F/OSS community.

Additional support for FFII and the F/OSS activists came in October 2004 when Florian Müller launched the NoSoftwarePatents.com website. So far FFII had used the internet extensively, but its website was mainly a wiki, a site that contained large amounts of more or less ordered information, contributed by activists. It served mainly as a knowledge base for those active in the campaign, but it did not present information in an easy-to-understand way to interested internet users. With NoSoftwarePatents.com Florian Müller, a software programmer working for MySQL AB,[11] who had been involved in the campaign since April 2004, set up a multilingual dedicated campaign website geared to the general public, similar to EICTA's Patents4innovation.org website. For his campaign he received initial support from the database software company MySQL AB, from the biggest European internet provider 1&1, and from the biggest Linux distributor Red Hat.

In sum, the one and a half years between the Parliament's initial decision and the Council's common position had introduced an additional intra-institutional conflict line to the issue. The complete disrespect for the Parliament's position by the Commission and by the member states' governments structured the relatively short last phase of the conflict. Moreover, the rejection of the Parliament's restart request

---

[11] MySQL AB is a Swedish software company (bought in 2008 by Sun Microsystems) that produces the most popular open source database application with a market share of 25 per cent.

further deepened the rift between Commission and Parliament. So far the conflict had gained visibility in each phase. In the first and second phases the F/OSS community became for the first time visible as a relevant actor, in the third phase in the European Parliament the issue became a political issue of general interest, and in the fourth phase the political conflict became manifest, broader and also more entrenched. The fifth phase turned out to be the shortest phase at only a little over four months, but also the most intense.

4.2.4. *The Parliament's rejection*

In the Parliament's first reading a large majority had adopted the amendments that would have limited software patents. But the changes after the election in 2004 (which brought EPP-ED fifty-four additional seats and shifted the Parliament more to the right) and the requirements of an absolute majority in the second reading made the outcome in this fifth phase of the conflict very unpredictable. Moreover, the pro-patent lobbyists now focused significant energy on the Parliament, which they had largely neglected in the second and third phase. EICTA, BSA, other industry associations and several large firms were now sending legions of lobbyists to the Parliament to get MEPs to support the Council's common position (Müller 2006).

But the changes in the Parliament had not all been in favour of the pro-software-patent camp. Michel Rocard had replaced Arlene McCarthy as rapporteur in JURI and Piia-Noora Kauppi had replaced Joachim Würmeling as the EPP-ED's shadow rapporteur – two outspoken critics of software patents replacing two strong supporters.

The various interest groups all intensified their lobbying efforts, and interestingly the action forms of the conflicting parties in this fifth and last phase became more similar. Apart from demonstrations, which were used only by the F/OSS community, both sides employed the same lobbying methods – they directly contacted MEPs, initiated email and postal mailing campaigns, set up websites and organized conferences and hearings. In some weeks several conferences/information events at which experts and activists presented their positions took place concurrently or one immediately after the other. The political groups in the Parliament and the responsible committees also organized several hearings to which experts and activists from both sides were invited. The anti-software-patent camp received support from the Green/EFA group, especially from Laurence Vandewalle, an assistant to the group and adviser on industrial politics. The other side was supported by the British MEP Malcolm Harbour's office whose assistant sent an email from the Campaign for Creativity to all MEPs on 1 June 2005, inviting them to free ice cream in support of software patents.[12]

Other lobbying efforts were exhibits of high-technology products by Siemens and the truck manufacturer Scania to demonstrate that the patenting of computer-implemented inventions would be necessary to protect these products. EICTA and some of its member firms also placed a number of large advertisements in several Brussels newspapers. One of them, a full-page advertisement from SAP, proved to be rather counter-productive, since SAP strongly urged MEPs to leave the Council's common position unamended as it would provide the patents needed by SAP. The only problem was that the proponents otherwise always argued that they would not want pure software patents, but only patents for 'computer-implemented inventions' – even though SAP is a pure software company, producing nothing but software.

How closely big industry associations monitored FFII's tactics became visible in April 2005 when EICTA mimicked the opponents' SME mobilization and initiated an 'SME Manifesto on Patents for Computer-Implemented Inventions' (EICTA et al. 2005), a text written by EICTA and signed by fifty-four SMEs calling for the adoption of the Council version of the directive. FFII, on the other hand, tried with its much more limited funds to expand its presence in Brussels and in the final phase rented an apartment in the city where lobbyists and activists could stay to avoid the high costs of hotel accommodation.

In the Parliament the situation became increasingly unstable. While the replacement of McCarthy and Würmeling by Rocard and Kauppi in the legal affairs committee was interpreted as a victory of the anti-software-patent camp, their influence in the committee remained limited. Rocard initially tabled amendments that would have by and large reinstated the EP's restrictive position from its first reading (Rocard 2005a). But in the decisive vote on 20 June 2005 in the committee a majority of MEPs led by Klaus-Heiner Lehne, the legal affairs coordinator of the EPP-ED, rejected many of Rocard's amendments and instead approved several of the 256 proposed amendments that had been tabled by pro-software-patent MEPs (JURI 2005). Rocard's last-minute attempt to table a list of seventeen compromise amendments (Rocard 2005b) was also rejected. The overall outcome of the vote in JURI was received with reservations from both sides. FFII strongly

---

[12] The email sent from Malcolm Harbour's assistant's account read: 'Dear Members and Assistants, Yes its true! If you go down to Place du Luxembourg from now until 3pm, you can collect your free icecream and support the Computer Implemented Inventions Common Position! Hope to see you soon.' It generated some commotion about the misuse of EP infrastructure for lobbying purposes.

criticized the result, claiming that the result would leave the Council position largely unchanged (FFII 2005), but BSA also complained 'that some of the amendments proposed by the Socialist rapporteur, Michel Rocard, could drag Europe's patent regime back to the 19th century' (BSA 2005).

The showdown finally came on 6 July 2005. Outside the Parliament in Strasbourg FFII and others had organized another demonstration against software patents. But for once the other side also used demonstrative forms. The Campaign for Creativity had chartered a motor boat and moored it at a bridge connecting the two buildings of the European Parliament. It carried a banner with the slogan 'Patents = European innovation'. The anti-software-patent activists, wearing yellow t-shirts with the slogan 'Power to the Parliament', soon reacted by renting small canoes, symbolically attacking the motorboat, and unfurling banners saying 'Software patents kill innovation' (Banks 2005; Müller 2006).

Meanwhile in the Parliament an unexpected solution was receiving growing support: rejection of the directive. With no camp happy about the proposed amendments from JURI, political groups and groups of individual MEPs had again submitted additional amendments for the Parliament's final vote on 6 July 2006, leading to a list of 178 amendments. But no side was sure whether it would have the necessary absolute majority for its preferred amendments. Instead the chances were high that some amendments of the pro- and some of the anti-software-patent camp would be accepted, leading to an inconsistent or even contradictory directive. Therefore both sides finally chose the safe strategy of rejecting the directive altogether.

The inter-institutional conflict dimension once more surfaced in the parliamentary debates on 5 and 6 July. On Tuesday, 5 July, Joaquín Almunia, Commissioner for Economic and Financial Affairs, again warned the Parliament that the Commission would not accept any substantial changes to the directive that would restrict the EPO patent practice (EP 2005a). On Wednesday Michel Rocard responded by saying that one reason for the rejection was 'a collective and unanimous anger on the part of the entire Parliament at the unacceptable way it has been treated by the Commission and the Council' (EP 2005b). In the ensuing vote the directive was rejected with a majority of 648 to 14 votes (with 18 abstentions).

Already on this descriptive level several aspects of the contentious dimensions of the European software patents conflict are visible:

• The conflict is essentially a conflict about the locus and the mode of innovation. Both sides claimed to represent the innovative core of

European industries. The large firms and their industry associations advocated a model of *centralized, capital-intensive innovation* that needs monopoly rights to secure incentives for the necessary R&D investments. The opponents proposed a model of *decentralized and mainly cumulative innovation* that relies on unhindered access to the existing stock of knowledge.

- The conflict is also a conflict about democratic and administrative control over innovation processes. The controversy between Parliament and Commission escalated because both sides disagreed on the legitimacy criteria of the decision-making process. The Commission acted as if the decision about the proposed directive could only be based on the expertise of the established stakeholders, i.e. patent lawyers and industry associations. For them the decision was in essence an administrative decision. A significant number of MEPs did not agree with this interpretation. For them the decision was a political decision, structured by general normative concerns and in need of democratic legitimation.
- During the conflict the context and the political opportunity structure changed significantly. At the beginning the opponents of software patents were confronted with a closed institutional structure in the Commission that did not take their objection seriously and relied on its established relations with industry associations and the patent community. Through their intervention the opponents were able to exploit differences within the Parliament and increasingly also between the European institutions and between member states, creating avenues of intervention that previously did not exist.

But maybe the most important aspect that makes the European software patents conflict relevant beyond the concrete policy conflict is that within the conflict we witness the emergence of a collective actor that previously did not exist, intervening in the politics of intellectual property. In the next section I will thus take a closer look at the actors involved in the conflict, at the relationships between the actors, and at the collective action networks that formed during the conflict.

4.3. The network of actors

The number of actors involved in the software patents controversy was remarkable. The EuroLinux petition alone was signed by more than 300,000 individuals and firms. Several large membership organizations and a number of national parliaments were involved in the conflict, and all 732 MEPs were contacted by lobbyists. But even the core collective action networks of persons and organizations actively involved in the conflict comprised about 800 actors.

To systematically analyse this huge mass of actors I rely in this chapter on some of the tools provided by social network analysis (Carrington, Scott and Wasserman 2005; de Nooy, Mrvar and Batagelj 2005; Knoke and Yang 2008). Graph theoretical methods are used mainly to identify core actors and cohesive subgroups. The dataset on which this analysis is based combines information about cooperation relationships among actors involved in this conflict from various sources.

- Newspaper articles in major national newspapers are the first source. Using the political claims analysis framework developed by Koopmans and Statham (1999b), my collaborators and I have conducted a content analysis of all newspaper articles published in selected quality newspapers[13] of four countries that mentioned the conflict. A total of 170 articles (Germany 56, UK 37, France 45, Poland 32) were coded in this step. This data is also the source for the frame analysis presented in the next section (4.4). From the newspaper data a list of actors that have been mentioned in the press was generated.
- A second source are semi-structured interviews with twenty-five key actors (Interviews 1–22) about their perception of the conflict, their role in it, and their cooperation networks. These interviews were transcribed and statements about the actors' cooperation relationships were extracted.
- A third source is a qualitative content analysis of documents published by actors involved in the conflict on the web. These were press releases, conference announcements, strategy papers, memos, blog posts and other documents in which the actors identified who they cooperated with in the conflict.
- A fourth data source is the evaluation of a questionnaire that was sent to all actors identified in the previous three data sources. In these questionnaires actors were asked to provide information about their cooperation relationships with other actors involved in the conflict.

Information from these four sources was combined into one dataset, containing information about the cooperation relationships between actors, about their organizational affiliations, and their position in the conflict (if available). To mitigate possible errors and overstatement

---

[13] *Süddeutsche Zeitung, die tageszeitung, Frankfurter Rundschau, Die Welt, Stuttgarter Zeitung* for Germany; *Daily Mail, The Times, The Guardian, Financial Times, Western Mail, Morning Star, Daily Telegraph, The Business, The Independent, The Observer* for the UK; *Le Figaro, Liberation, Les Echos, Le Monde* for France; *Gazeta Wyborcza, Polityka, Rzeczpospolita, Wprost* for Poland.

of self-reported cooperation, ties reported in written documents were weighted by a factor of two while ties from interviews and question-naires were weighted by a factor of one. This data describes the collect-ive action networks of the conflict. I define *collective action networks* as those networks that include all interacting actors involved in a conflict, ranging from civil society organizations and firms to public institutions (such as parliaments and the European Commission), and including individuals. In the network graphs, nodes represent actors and edges represent cooperative relationships as indicated by any kind of joint activity, such as membership in a formal coalition, organizing a hearing together or signing a petition or letter together. Because one can assume that cooperation is reciprocal, edges in the graphs are undirected.

The full network (Figure 4.2) consists of six large membership and support networks. On the side of the proponents these are the formal membership network of the European Information and Communications Technology Industry Association (EICTA), which includes thirty-seven different national associations and fifty individual corporations, and the Business Software Alliance (BSA), which presents itself on its website as 'the voice of the world's commercial software industry and its hard-ware partners'. Even though a number of relevant companies (e.g. SAP, Intel, Adobe Systems, Apple and Symantec) belong to both EICTA and BSA, the network data shows only limited cooperation between the two associations. This may be due to the latent rivalry between the two associations about leadership in representing the major high-tech industries in Europe.

On the opponents' side, there is FFII's formal membership network and three large informal support networks, the EuroLinux Alliance, Economic-Majority.com and patentfrei.de. The two European SME associations, Confédération Européenne des Associations de Petites et Moyennes Entreprises (CEA-PME) and Union Européenne de l'Artisanat et des Petites et Moyennes Entreprises (UEAPME), were also involved but played only a minor role. In addition at least two established social movement organizations (SMOs), Attac Germany and Campact, were actively mobilizing against software patents. Other important actors in the collective action network are the three European institutions: the European Commission, the Council of the European Union, and the European Parliament with its political par-ties and administration. The EPO also played an important role at least in the first phase of the conflict. Actors in this network are in general organizations, associations, political parties and firms – that is collective or institutional actors. Only two individuals are shown in the network graphs: Hartmut Pilch and Florian Müller. Florian Müller

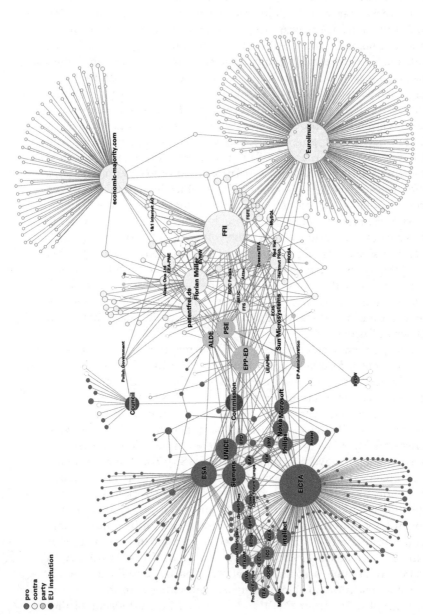

Figure 4.2 Cooperation network of actors involved in the conflict over the software patents directive.

Note: Edges represent cooperation, vertex size represents betweenness centrality, different shades indicate political position in the conflict.

was an important individual actor without institutional affiliation, and Hartmut Pilch, the founder of FFII, also had many individual cooperation relationships beyond his role in FFII.

The following analysis will take a closer look at various core networks of this complete collective action network. Network cores can be obtained by reducing the original network to a sub-network that consists only of those nodes that have more than a certain number of ties with other nodes (their degree is above a certain threshold), or by reducing it to a sub-network that consists only of those nodes that are connected by ties with a weight above a certain minimum level (i.e. the cooperation relationship has been confirmed by multiple sources). Both criteria can be combined in so-called (k,m)-cores: if a k-core is a maximal sub-network in which each node has at least degree k within the sub-network and if an m-slice is a maximal sub-network containing the lines with a value of at least m and the nodes incident with these lines (de Nooy, Mrvar and Batagelj 2005: 70, 109), a (k,m)-core is a maximal sub-network in which each node has at least degree k and which contains the lines with a value of m and higher.

A closer look at the (2,2)-core (Figure 4.3) of the software patents directive network illustrates the uneven access the two camps had to the European institutions. Only those in the proponents' camp were able to establish stable cooperative relationships with the European Commission. This fact supports the contention in the EU interest groups' literature that European associations and single large firms would have the best access to the Commission (Bouwen 2002, 2004). Neither camp was able to establish direct cooperative links with the Council. This, too, is in line with the research on interest representation in the EU, which sees the Council as the institution most open to the lobbying efforts of national interest groups via the national lobbying route. This strategy is visible in the network where FFII activists established links to members of the Polish government who acted against the directive in the Council.

A closer look at the direct links between MEPs, the Commission and interest groups (Figure 4.4) shows that both sides established close cooperation relationships with the two biggest political groups (conservatives and social democrats). The liberals were a bit more closely linked to the software patent advocates while the Greens were firmly rooted in the oppositional camp. Overall the opponents had more and stronger links to the political parties in the European Parliament. Moreover, although it is not visible in the graphs, which present only a static illustration of the conflict, the opponents established their links with the MEPs earlier in the conflict. This is because, unlike the other

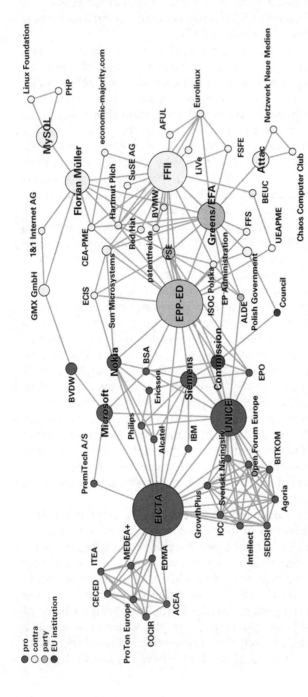

Figure 4.3 Close cooperation in the (2,2)-core of the collective actor network.

Note: Edges represent cooperation, node size represents betweenness centrality, different shades indicate political positions; (2,2)-core (degree ≥2, line value ≥2), 63 vertices.

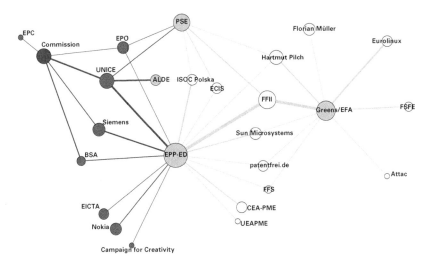

Figure 4.4 Direct neighbours of European parties and Commission.

Note: Maximal sub-network consisting of all nodes with direct connections to the political parties in the European Parliament, (1,2)-core, node sizes indicate degree, different shades indicate political positions.

side, they immediately understood the importance of the Parliament in the codecision procedure, whereas the business associations relied for a long time on their established connections to the Commission.

To better understand the internal structure of the two collective action networks which mobilized for and against the directive I will now compare the networks of those actors who were unambiguously positioned in one of the two camps. In order to limit this comparison to those actors most actively involved in the conflict, I will compare the two sub-networks at the level of their respective 3-cores, i.e. the two sub-networks in which each node is connected to at least three other nodes in the respective coalition (Figure 4.5). Both sub-networks contain thirty-four actors, and are similar in several aspects. They are both relatively dense (pro 0.27, contra 0.20) and show a moderately high degree of centralization (pro 0.68, contra 0.66), indicating a clear centre–periphery structure. Judging from the network analysis, the central organization in the proponents' network was the high-tech industry association EICTA, and the central player in the oppositional network was FFII.

The two networks differ significantly in their betweenness centralization (pro 0.51, contra 0.36), which is a measure of the hierarchical structure of the network. This affirms what is clearly visible in the

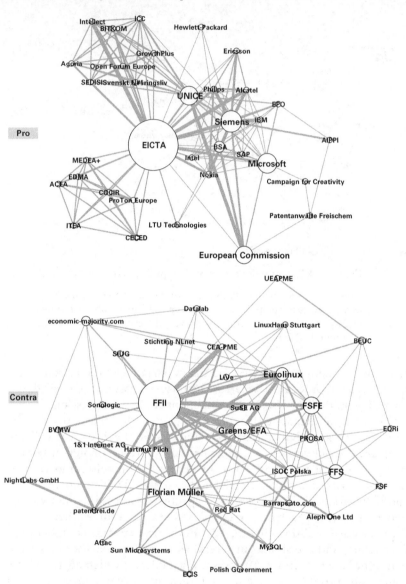

Figure 4.5 3-cores of lobbying networks in the software patents conflict.

Note: 3-core, pro-network (34 nodes; top) and contra-network (34 nodes; bottom), node sizes indicate betweenness centrality.

graphical representation, that the core of the pro-network is more hierarchical than the core of the oppositional network. EICTA connects two networks of associations to the network who are otherwise not or only weakly connected to other actors in favour of software patents. Apart from EICTA, BSA and UNICE, the densely connected core of the proponents' network consists of a handful of large IT firms who actively lobbied in favour of the directive. The oppositional network is clearly centred around FFII, but unlike the pro-network even without its three most central actors it would still remain strongly connected. With this, the oppositional network exhibits the main features of the decentralized, polycentric collective action networks that have been identified as typical for civil society networks by Baldassarri and Diani (2007).

Conclusions from the network analysis The network analysis shows that the opponents managed to build a broad and diversified, yet flexible network. The proponents' network was much more institutionalized and had only a few important nodes. For example, only a few lobbyists contacted the MEPs, whereas many actors from the opponents' network contacted them. These manifold avenues of influence certainly contributed to the success of the 'No Software Patents' campaign.

The successful mobilization against the software patents directive had many characteristics of a grassroots mobilization. The relatively low betweenness-centralization of the oppositional network can be interpreted as a sign that the mobilization was not driven solely by a central actor but through the initiative of many independently operating activists who each established their own cooperation relationships. Many committed actors who would have been directly affected by the directive's passage actively took part in the campaign by writing papers, uploading websites, organizing demonstrations, lobbying MEPs and connecting to other activists. The network was very open so that all interested actors were able to participate. This kind of grassroots mobilization also had an effect at the discursive level. The directive's opponents had a high level of credibility among many MEPs because they were seen as committed individuals and not as lobbyists sent by an organization.

The decentralized structure of the oppositional network, moreover, was broadly transnational, with bases in almost all EU member countries. The opponents utilized the multi-level structure of the EU. They were active at the European level and at the national level where they lobbied national governments, parliamentarians and parties. Thus, the diversified, transnational character of the network gave the campaign momentum and was clearly enhanced by the opponents' ability to influence the decision-making process.

The oppositional network shows many signs of a social movement in the making (Diani 1992; della Porta and Diani 2006: 20). It is a cohesive collective action network centred around FFII, an NGO that was founded to fight this political conflict, and that since the failure of the software patent directive, continues to mobilize around the issue of IP. Within the diversity of the network as a whole, the FFII was not only a critically important node in terms of connecting different actors and providing an infrastructure for the campaign. As will be shown in the next section (4.4), it also provided the opponents' network with expertise and played a central role in their collective action framing, especially with regard to interpretation and argumentation.

On the other side, the proponents' network was characterized by a small number of central actors who invested significant funds in professional lobbying, while the majority of network members showed a relatively low level of commitment. The proponents did not manage to build a mobilization of the type that creates and in turn is fuelled by a strong collective identity. However, once they realized what they were up against, they tried to mimic the methods and grassroots style of mobilization used by their opponents. EICTA gathered several SMEs to sign a petition arguing in favour of patents, and the Campaign for Creativity tried to stage an 'astroturf campaign' – they tried to set up campaigns that pretended to be driven by concerned individuals but were really top-down designed by marketing firms. In the end, EICTA and BSA were not able to overcome their rivalry and put little effort into building a strong common network.

The network analysis of the cooperation relationships between the actors involved in the software patents conflict strongly supports the notion that this conflict was not just a lobbying conflict between competing interest groups. Instead the oppositional mobilization shows clear signs of a social movement dynamic. Mario Diani defines social movements as those social processes in which actors engaged in collective action are involved in conflictual relations with clearly identified opponents, are linked by dense informal networks, and share a distinct collective identity (Diani 2003: 301; della Porta and Diani 2006: 20). The first two conditions were certainly fulfilled for the network of actors engaged in the struggle against software patents in Europe.

The conflict was characterized by dense, informal cooperation networks and a strong polarization between proponents and opponents of software patents. In the wider context of conflicts in the knowledge society it should be noted that this polarization does not run along existing cleavages of the industrial age. It was not possible to locate the two camps along a left–right axis, nor was it a capital–labor conflict, or a conflict between industry interest and other (e.g. civil society) groups. All political parties in the European Parliament – except the Greens – were split on the issue of software patents, and while civil society organizations sided with the opponents, the majority of the oppositional actors were corporate actors themselves.

Moreover, the oppositional network was not just a coalition of previously existing organizations. Within the conflict a new collective actor was created. The network analysis of the cooperation relationships is not able to tell us to what degree this new collective actor has started to develop a collective identity. An answer to this question will have to wait until in the next section the actors' framing processes are analysed.

4.4. Frames

The network analysis of cooperation relations in the software patents conflict reveals a cohesive collective action network among the opponents of software patents. But how was this network held together? The literature on collective action has long realized that collective action can only under very restrictive circumstances be explained as the aggregated action of self-interested individuals (Ostrom 1990). In the absence of formal organizations, one important mechanism that holds collective action networks together is a shared set of ideas, interpretations and aims. The thriving literature on framing provides many insights into how successful collective action frames are constructed (Snow 2004). An informal collective action network will likely be built around a shared set of convictions, a shared interpretation of the problem, and a shared perspective of how to act – or to use Benford and Snow's (2000) terminology: diagnostic, prognostic and motivational framing. In addition, the importance of consistent narratives or story lines has been highlighted by Hajer in his work on discourse coalitions (Hajer 1993) or Polletta in her work on narratives in social movements (Polletta 1998).

In this section I will analyse the frames and the framing strategies that have been used in the software patents conflict. The analysis is based on the content coding of 124 newspaper articles published in quality newspapers in Germany, Great Britain, France and Poland between 1997 and 2005.[14] In a first step all articles that addressed the software patents

---

[14] The newspapers from which the articles were taken are, in Germany, *Süddeutsche Zeitung, die tageszeitung, Frankfurter Rundschau, Die Welt, Stuttgarter Zeitung*; in the UK, *Daily Mail, The Times, The Guardian, Financial Times, Western Mail, Morning Star, Daily Telegraph, The Business, The Independent, The Observer*; in France, *Le Figaro, Liberation, Les Echos, Le Monde, La Tribune*; and in Poland, *Gazeta Wyborcza, Polityka, Rzeczpospolita, Wprost*.

conflict in Europe or the issue of software patents in general were selected. In these articles every instance of claims-making was coded according to a coding scheme (Haunss and Kohlmorgen 2008) on the basis of Koopmans' political claims analysis codebook (Koopmans 2002). A *claim* in this context is *any demand, proposal, criticism, decision, etc. made by actors active in the respective field of conflict in the form of statements or collective mobilizations*. This can be a parliamentary motion, a formal vote, a petition, a demonstration or any other act of public political intervention. For each claim the content of the claim, the date, name and organizational affiliation of the claimant, addressees (if explicitly mentioned) and the argumentative frame was recorded. Frames in this context are the reasons that are given for a specific instance of claims-making. They are the – sometimes explicit, often implicit – arguments or concepts used by the actors. To give an example: an article reports that an actor has published a press release in which he demands that the European Parliament should reject the directive, because it would disadvantage small IT companies and small software companies. This article contains a claim – the press release – and a frame – 'Software patents are bad *because they negatively affect the competitiveness of small and medium sized enterprises*'. In the database this is then coded as actor X making a claim (publishing a press release), using the frame 'competitiveness of SMEs'. It is furthermore recorded that the frame 'competitiveness of SMEs' is here used to argue against software patents in Europe.

For the frame analysis only those claims were considered where an interpretation of the claim was reported in the article. A report that simply states that on a certain date a demonstration against software patents with so and so many participants took place, contains a claim but no frame as it does not say anything about the motives of the demonstrators apart from their aim. The 124 articles contained 355 substantiated claims, that is claims which were accompanied by a corresponding frame. Among those 17 were neutral or ambiguous in relation to the introduction of software patents in Europe. But because it was often not clear whether the ambiguity stemmed from the actors or from the journalist's interpretation, only the 338 claims for which a clear actor position in the conflict was given are analysed in this section.

Coding only claims that are reported in newspapers limits the analysis to a subset of the total claims made in the conflict since not all claims-making activities are reported, and there is a selection bias towards certain actors and action forms in the newspapers. But it can reasonably be assumed that in a public political conflict claims that go unreported will be less important than reported claims, since they remain invisible for most of the decision-makers as well (for a more detailed discussion see Earl et al. 2004).

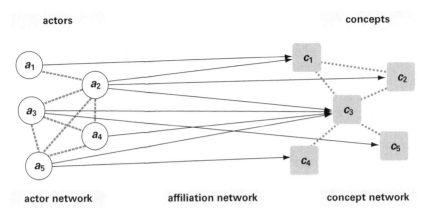

Figure 4.6 Illustration of the basic discourse network model.

The large number of claims makes it necessary to go beyond a qualitative text-analysis in order to grasp the underlying structures of the
discursive interaction. To analyse the actors' framing strategies I thus
use the methodological tools of discourse network analysis (Leifeld
2009; Leifeld and Haunss 2012). Discourse network analysis provides
a model to analyse discursive interaction over time. Every time an actor
uses a frame, a connection is created between this actor and the frame.
Figure 4.6 illustrates this model.

The affiliation network G_{aff} connects actors a_1, a_2, ... a_m with frames
or concepts c_1, c_2, ... c_n. In Figure 4.6 this is expressed by the solid lines
connecting actors and concepts. It is a 2-mode network because direct
connections exist only between nodes from the two different categories.
The lines are directed (arcs) because actors choose concepts. Moreover,
since a frame is used by an actor at a specific time t, for each point in
time a specific affiliation network G^t_{aff} exists. Finally actors can use a
frame affirmatively or negatively. Actor a_1 may, for example, argue for
software patents because she thinks that they would positively affect
innovation within the IT industry, while actor a_2 argues against software patents because he thinks that they would inhibit innovation. In
the network model this would be expressed by a positive or negative
sign of the value of the arc connecting actor and concept. The discourse network in this model is thus a directed temporal signed 2-mode
network.[15]

---

[15] In principle the model can also accommodate neutral or ambivalent statements by
assigning them the arc value 0. But in practice these cases occur very seldom (less
than 5 per cent of the claims in the software patents conflict).

From this original network two derivative 1-mode networks can be generated by connecting on the one side actors who share a concept and on the other side concepts that are used by the same actor. These two co-occurrence networks are undirected; they are visualized by the dotted lines in Figure 4.6. By accounting for negative or positive arc values, six more specific actor and concept networks can be generated: a positive and a negative congruence network connecting actors that use the same concepts in the same way, and a conflict network in which edges are formed if two actors disagree on a concept, and in the same manner two congruence networks of frames connected through like-minded actors and a conflict network of frames connected through disagreeing actors. Again, these derivative networks can be generated for each point in time t, making an analysis of the network evolution possible.

As I have shown earlier in this chapter (4.2), claims-making in the software patents conflict occurred in five waves that followed largely the institutional decision-making process described at the beginning of this chapter (see Figure 4.1). The first wave accompanied the consultation process with the Commission's launch of an internet consultation and the foundation of FFII and the EuroLinux Alliance. A short second wave followed the publication of the proposal for the directive in February 2002. The third wave culminated around the Parliament's first reading; the fourth wave comprised the deliberations in the Council, and the fifth wave the Parliament's second reading and the rejection of the directive. A simple frequency count shows a growing intensity of the conflict from low to moderate levels of claims-making in the early phases of the conflict to a high volume of claims-making and a high visibility of the conflict in the press in the last two phases. Overall 56 per cent of the reported claims were against software patents, 39 per cent supported the directive and 5 per cent were neutral or ambivalent. Forty-eight different frames were used to argue for or against software patents. The thirty-three most often used frames are depicted in Figure 4.7. Of these, twelve core frames were used in more than 80 per cent of the claims.

The discourse network analysis clearly identifies the frame 'competitiveness of SMEs' as the most central frame, used in 16.3 per cent of cases, followed by 'innovation and transfer of knowledge' (13.5 per cent). The discourse network graph in Figure 4.7 also shows that both frames were heavily contested. Both sides were using these frames to argue for or against the directive. Proponents argued that software patents would strengthen the competitiveness of SMEs because a patent portfolio would attract venture capital. Opponents argued that SMEs would not have the manpower and specialized knowledge necessary to check whether the software they produce or use would infringe existing

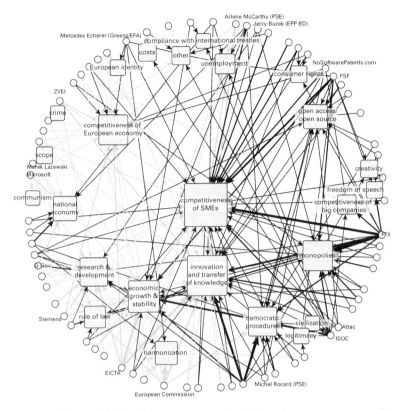

Figure 4.7 The discourse network of the software patents conflict.
Note: (2,2)-core (actors with outdegree ≥2 and concepts with
indegree ≥2) of the discourse network between 1999 and 2005.
Concepts are depicted as squares, actors as circles, node size
represents indegree. Black arcs (directed links) represent use of the
frame in a claim against software patents, grey arcs represent use
of the frame in favour of the directive. Layout: centrality layout
(Brandes et al. 1999).

patents, and that software patents would therefore negatively affect the
competitiveness of SMEs.

From the twelve core frames all except one were disputed. Only the
'open access/open source' frame was exclusively used by opponents of
software patents. Five of the core frames were dominated by the no software patents camp ('monopolies', 'democratic procedures', 'innovation
and transfer of knowledge', 'competitiveness of SMEs' and 'competitiveness of big companies'), three frames were dominated by the supporters

of the directive ('harmonization', 'competitiveness of the European economy' and 'research & development'). Frames in the network periphery were generally less contested. Consumer rights, legitimacy of the European institutions, promotion of creativity were issues raised only by the opponents, while supporters argued that globalization and a worldwide system of liberalized free trade would necessitate software patents in Europe as well, or that software patents would deter product piracy. But these undisputed frames were not at the centre of public attention.

The most often used and at the same time most contested frames refer to the economic sphere. The conflict was thus at its core a conflict about the expected economic consequences of software patents. It is remarkable that the F/OSS activists succeeded in dominating the discourse in the area where the specific strengths of their opponent lie. Traditional wisdom and the literature on EU interest representation assumes that economic matters would be the genuine field of expertise of industry associations and large transnational firms. But in the software patents conflict FFII and the other opponents of the directive succeeded in positioning the question of the economic welfare of SMEs at the centre of debate, sidelining the question of European competitiveness in global trade relations.

Moving from the 2-mode discourse network to the 1-mode congruence networks of frames connected through agreeing actors, the network analysis reveals distinct framing patterns for each side of the conflict. Figure 4.8 illustrates that the directive's supporters strongly connected innovation with competitiveness of the European economy, research and development, and harmonization. The opponents developed a frame bundle containing innovation, competitiveness of SMEs, economic growth, research and development, democracy, monopolies and open access/open source. In other words, they took up the original framing of the European Commission, that software patents would be an issue of strengthening innovation in the European economy, and made it an issue of SME competitiveness, democracy and open source.

The illustration reveals that the opponents had developed a coherent set of frames that were shared by a large number of activists. This frame bundle, this collection of strongly connected frames, outlines the argumentative consensus among the various actors that mobilized against software patents in Europe. It captures core elements of the opponents' collective identity. At its centre stand innovation, the competitiveness of SMEs, democracy, monopolies and growth. These core frames were embedded in a number of broader frames that address questions of

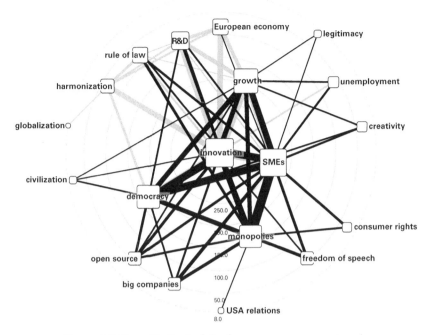

Figure 4.8 Core (5-slice) of the frame congruence network (1999–2005).

Note: Edges represent concepts shared by at least five like-minded actors (edge-value ≥5). Node size and position reflects degree of centrality, edge width expresses the number of actors that agree on the two adjacent frames. Grey lines reflect frame used in claims for the directive, black lines frame used against software patents.

creativity, freedom of speech, consumer rights and open access to knowledge and information. The discourse network analysis clearly shows that the conflict was framed by the actors as a conflict about the future mode of innovation, and thus addressed a core element of the knowledge society.

This frame bundle was cohesive enough to hold together a transnational mobilization of actors with very different political, institutional and personal backgrounds. It could accommodate Attac, Sun Microsystems, the F/OSS activists from the Free Software Foundation or the French AFUL, and liberals (in the economic sense) from the SME associations.

Based on the strong cohesion of the oppositional frame bundle it is appropriate to assume that the actors developed in the conflict a shared interpretation, based on which they were able to define the 'orientations of their action and the field of opportunities and constraints' (Melucci 1996: 70) – in other words they developed a collective identity.

4.5.   Bringing the threads together

The software patents conflict in Europe was remarkable for its outcome. Almost nobody would have expected that a bunch of open source activists would stand any chance against the united powers of the European Commission, the biggest firms in the IT sector and the patent community, who wanted to broaden the possibilities to gain software patents in Europe. But it is remarkable for other reasons as well. The conflict about software patents created one of the biggest controversies of the last decade in Europe. It involved many thousands of participants who signed petitions, lobbied their MEPs, organized conferences and demonstrated in Brussels and Strasbourg. Software patents are still a hot potato in Brussels and so far the Commission has only attempted to address this issue again through the back door, by advancing plans for a unified European patent and a central patent litigation court; and these attempts have been met with resistance from several member states.

But the software patents conflict is relevant beyond its concrete policy outcome. It has lastingly changed the conditions for politics of intellectual property in general within the European Union, and possibly even beyond. In the remaining pages of this chapter I will highlight these more general aspects by first summarizing the findings about the conflict's structural location and opportunity structures, the relevant actors and the interpretations and frames. I will then discuss which more abstract cleavages of the knowledge society surface in the software patents conflict.

4.5.1.   *Political opportunity structures*

The main arenas of the software patents conflict were the European institutions of transnational legislation. In the beginning this institutional setting was very unfavourable for the opponents of software patents. The EU institutions, and especially the Commission, provide privileged access to the established industry representatives. They are routinely consulted and are included in relevant discussions while a legal text is drafted. Some authors argue that the Commission also

provides access to civil society groups as a means to enhance its legitimacy (Greenwood 2003: 6; Saurugger 2008: 1,281). This may be true for
environmental policies and other areas (Biliouri 1999; Hallstrom 2004),
but it was certainly not true for intellectual property issues. Expertise
in this area was sought by the Commission initially only from the
European Patent Office and the large industry associations, whose IP
policies are determined by their large members' patent departments.

The Council was difficult to access for the opponents as well.
National policy preferences shape the decisions in the Council, and
the national administrations in the relevant ministries of justice and
economy have been tightly interwoven with the patent community. In
Germany, for example, Arno Körber, at the time of the conflict head of
Siemens patent department, was also head of the German trade association of the electronic industry (ZVEI) IP commission, deputy head
of the German industry association (BDI) IP commission, member of
the board of managing directors of the German Association for the
Protection of Intellectual Property (GRUR) and member of the expert
commission on IP at the German Ministry of Justice (Interview 20).

The ability of FFII and other opponents of software patents to gain
access to national administrations was inversely related to the existence of large IT firms with interests in software patents in that country.
In Poland, a country with an SME dominated IT sector and no large
patenting IT firms, the national patent office was sceptical about software patents and the administration open to the demands and criticisms of the F/OSS activists. In Ireland, a country in which several
large computer and software companies like Microsoft, IBM, Apple,
Dell or Cisco have their European headquarters or large subsidiaries,
the F/OSS activists were not able to gain access to the administration.

In contrast to the Commission and the Council, the European
Parliament was open to all sides from the beginning. Knowledge about
IP issues was limited among the MEPs and the need for expertise therefore strong. And since the Parliament did not have long-established
cooperation relationships with the patent community or industry associations on these issues, all political groups and parliamentary com-
missions sought expertise from a variety of sources, including critical
academics and F/OSS representatives. The Green/EFA group especially was very open to FFII and other activists, as they saw in the
open source approach an option to develop a distinct green industry
and research policy profile beyond environmentalism (Interview 7).

During the conflict, the stubborn ignorance of the Parliament's position shown by the Commission and the Council certainly played out

in favour of the software patent opponents. The inter-institutional rift gave the conflict an additional drive and strengthened the Parliament's resolve.

Another advantage for FFII was that it filled a niche in the Brussels interest groups landscape. IP issues were until then firmly in the hands of the patent community. The IP commission of the large trade associations worked hand in hand with EPO and the Commission to shape European patent policies. Around the millennium no NGOs existed in Brussels that would address IP issues from an alternative perspective. European Digital Rights (EDRi) was not founded until 2002 and the Campaign for an Open Digital Environment (CODE) was initiated in 2004 as a reaction to the proposed European Intellectual Property Rights Enforcement Directive (COM 2003) by the US NGO IP Justice. FFII filled this gap and it could draw on an interested community of computer programmers and academics who had started to discuss these issues in the 1990s. In the mid to late 1990s a number of associations were founded to promote the development and dissemination of open source software. They provided an infrastructure of websites, discussion fora and mailing lists for people interested in the idea of open source and open access. But there was little coordination and no unifying campaign or project. FFII was able to draw on this counter-expertise already developed in the F/OSS community and a handful of academics who did research on the societal consequences of the IP system (Sell 1989; Besen and Raskind 1991; Drahos 1995; Halbert 1997; Maskus 1998; May 1998; Benkler 1999).

4.5.2. Actor networks

Within this institutional setting the opponents of software patents created a dense collective action network centred around FFII. In this network the FFII was a facilitator but not a gatekeeper. Without FFII this political mobilization would not have been possible. They were the hub around which all other oppositional actors congregated. But one important element that accounts for the strength of the mobilization was that, despite FFII's centrality, many actors still sought their own means of access to the decision-makers. The many strong direct cooperation links to the European political parties visible in Figure 4.4 are an expression of the autonomous activities of many oppositional actors.[16]

---

[16] In the complete network visible in Figure 4.2 the pro actors are connected through twenty-four distinct direct links to the MEPs whereas the contra actors have established more than twice that number of direct cooperation relationships (fifty-one).

The opponents of software patents were also densely connected among each other so that the oppositional network remains completely connected even if one were to remove the three core actors.

Taken together these elements characterize the network as a polycentric collective action network which is typical of civil society networks (Baldassarri and Diani 2007). It brought together several partly independent mobilizations for which FFII played an important coordinating role without exerting central command and control. The network is an informal network that was created and developed during the conflict. Existing civil society organizations (CSOs) played only a minor role in the mobilization, as did social movement organizations (SMOs) like Attac who joined the protest but remained marginal in the oppositional network.

4.5.3. Frames

The kit that held the network together was a shared set of beliefs and solidarity. The opponents constructed a clear story line, that innovation in the IT sector depended mainly on small firms and individual programmers whose livelihood (or business model) would be threatened by the directive. Software patents would have a negative effect on innovation in the IT sector and should therefore not be allowed in Europe. This core story was embedded in anti-monopoly and pro-democracy arguments. It contained a clear call for action ('Stop software patents!') and a strong motivational element ('Defend our livelihood!'), and thus provided a viable base for a collective identity of the activists involved in the mobilization.

Taken together it becomes clear that in the software patents conflict a social movement surfaced that questioned the logic of the current IP system. But despite the breadth of the mobilization, it stayed largely restricted to the very concrete aim of getting rid of software patents in Europe. After this issue is – for the time being – removed from the political stage with the EP's rejection of the directive, it remains to be seen whether this movement will continue beyond its single-issue focus.

Currently no mobilization of similar size is visible any more. But the activist networks still exist and continue to work below the surface of publicly visible mobilizations. In all social movements visible protest is but the tip of the iceberg. How big this iceberg is in the case of IP issues in Europe, I am not able to judge. But the sprouting of Pirate Parties, the continuing activity of FFII and several other NGOs which were founded in the software patent conflict and a number of mobilizations on the national level about digital rights and in the similarly successful campaign against the Anti-Counterfeiting Trade Agreement (ACTA) show that at least something still is there below the surface of publicly visible protest.

4.6.   Software patents and the knowledge society

Which are now the more general cleavages that were created in the software patents conflict? On the surface the conflict about software patents in Europe was a conflict about a single EU directive that immediately affected the business models of the actors involved in the conflict. But a careful analysis reveals that below this surface on a more abstract level the conflict can be interpreted as a conflict about one core mechanism that structures the knowledge society – the mode of innovation.

The discourse network analysis shows this most clearly: all actors – those in favour and those against software patents – framed the conflict as a conflict about innovation and transfer of knowledge. This was the most contentious core frame that both sides tried to hegemonize. In this conflict two clearly distinguishable models of innovation stood against each other, a model of *industrial innovation* against a model of *open innovation*.

The model that I call *industrial innovation* was advanced by the European Commission, the large industry associations and the IT firms that formed the pro-software-patents network as depicted in Figure 4.5. The core assumption of this model is that innovation is located (mainly) in large-scale industrial units. This means that innovation is seen as the result of organized efforts of economic actors who spend significant resources to produce innovative knowledge that can be used in industrial production processes. Innovation is produced directly in firms' research and development units, the production process can be outsourced to specialized research and innovation providers, innovation can be bought through licensing or direct IP purchases or via mergers and acquisitions, or it can be produced in public–private partnerships with universities and other public research institutions. To protect the investments, innovation and the knowledge on which it is based has to be guarded and privatized. Innovation policies therefore have to provide mechanisms that protect secrecy and non-disclosure of innovative knowledge and – more important – to restrict the use of innovative knowledge to those authorized by its producer, even if the knowledge is in principle publicly available. The core paradigms of the industrial innovation model thus are differential access and propertization of knowledge.

The current IP system, and especially the patent system, are designed to fulfil this mission.

The alternative model of *open innovation* that was advanced by the opponents of the software patent directive starts from a very different assumption. In this model it is assumed that innovation is essentially a dispersed and distributed process without centralized control. Innovation is seen as mainly incremental. The production of innovation is not restricted to large-scale facilities, although it is recognized that basic research will usually depend on large specialized institutions, and thus is located at universities and other specialized research institutions. The core principle is general access to knowledge and information, because only under this premise can future innovation productively build on existing knowledge. Within the open innovation paradigm actors have a strong interest in a legal framework that supports the creation of a knowledge commons that is freely accessible for everyone. The open innovation framework that has been advanced by the actors involved in the software patents conflict is not opposed to intellectual property as such. Several core actors have argued that they strongly support copyrights but oppose patents in the area of computer software. The reason for this is that open innovation depends on the availability of theoretical knowledge, on access to the abstract principles and ideas on which innovation builds. The final code in which the software is programmed may be protected, but the idea of which the code is only one possible incarnation has to remain accessible. The open innovation model can accommodate proprietary and open source software. The latter can be seen as a more radical version of the open innovation ideas, adding the aspect of cooperative distributed networks in which innovation is produced. But it should not be forgotten that the open source model relies nevertheless in its GPL on a functioning copyright system, even if the system is only used to prohibit the privatization of commons knowledge.

The actors involved in the conflict are all representatives of what Castells has called 'networked labour' (Castells 2000: 18). The conflict thus did not address the cleavage between networked and switched-off labour. Instead the conflict was about a core mechanism that governs the creation of knowledge and thus the reproduction of the knowledge society. Picking up on Castells' network metaphor, the conflict represents opposing attempts to control, or program, the network.

The conflict addressed thus a central pillar of the knowledge society and it was driven by a social movement, a network of actors, connected by dense informal cooperation relationships, engaged in a conflict against a clearly defined opponent and united by a collective identity. Today, six years after the end of the conflict, no conflictual mobilization is visible any more in public. But below the surface a number of organizations and informal networks of activists have survived. FFII still exists as a transnational NGO in Brussels with eighteen national chapters. Several of those organizations and individual activists who participated in the software patents conflict have more recently been involved in a campaign against the Anti-Counterfeiting Trade Agreement (ACTA), in campaigns against data-retention laws in several EU member states and against so-called 'three-strikes' laws. The latter threaten internet users who are exchanging copyright-protected works without the consent of the rights-holder with a graduated response, ranging from warning letters to suspending internet access (Pfanner 2009). As in other social movements NGOs provide 'abeyance structures' (Taylor 1989) for activists after a mobilization wave has abated. In the case of politics of intellectual property in Europe all signs suggest that we are currently witnessing only the beginning of a longer wave of mobilization in which abeyance structures from one mobilization become springboards for future mobilizations.

5   Access to medicines

On a global level, the broadest and most prominent conflict about intellectual property rights was certainly the conflict about access to (essential) medicines. In essence it was, and still is, a conflict about the effects of patents for pharmaceutical products on access to drugs for patients living in countries of the global South. It was fuelled, in particular, by the issue of access to HIV/AIDS medication.

As in the previous chapter, the aim of the following discussion is to analyse how the access to medicines conflict is embedded in more general conflict lines of the knowledge society. Parallel to the software patents case I will thus start with a discussion of the context in which the conflict took place (5.1) and a description of the main developments (5.2). In section 5.3 an analysis of the actor networks, coalitions and mobilizations follows. Then, the actors' interpretation of the conflict lines present in the access to medicines campaign are the focus of an analysis of the actors' framing strategies (5.4). The chapter closes with a summary of the conflict (5.5), and a discussion of the meaning this conflict has for more general conflicts of the knowledge society (5.6). The empirical analysis of this chapter is based on an evaluation of primary documents published online and offline by actors involved in the conflict, actor websites and mailing lists, and interviews with select activists (Interviews 26, 29, 30, 31, 32, 33, 34).

5.1.   The context of the conflict about access to medicines

The coordinates for this conflict were set by the dual dynamics of an accelerating rate of HIV infections in a number of developing countries in Africa, Asia and South America and a ratcheting up of IP protection that culminated in the 1995 TRIPS agreement.

Table 5.1 shows the development of HIV infections and AIDS deaths in Europe and sub-Saharan Africa between 1990 and 2007. In both regions the number of people living with AIDS has grown significantly in this period. In Europe the estimated number of people with an HIV

Table 5.1 *Development of HIV infections and deaths 1990–2007*

		1990	2000	2007
Western and	Infected	331,100	587,200	733,500
Central Europe	Deaths	13,500 (4.08%)	9,000 (1.53%)	9,000 (1.23%)
Sub-Saharan	Infected	4,560,200	17,934,800	20,510,400
Africa	Deaths	151,300 (3.32%)	1,065,400 (5.94%)	1,362,300 (6.64%)

Note: Estimated number of people living with HIV and AIDS deaths in adults and children by region. Numbers in parentheses give rate of AIDS deaths among infected. *Source: 2008 Report on the Global AIDS Epidemic*, UNAIDS/WHO, July 2008 (UNAIDS 2008).

infection more than doubled from 331 thousand to 733 thousand. In sub-Saharan Africa the number more than quadrupled from 4.5 million to over 20 million. But while these numbers already show the severity of the AIDS crisis in Africa, the full dimension of the problem only becomes visible by taking into account the death toll in both regions. Between 1990 and 2007 the death rate in Europe falls in absolute as well as in relative numbers. Over the same time in sub-Saharan Africa the death rate grows both absolutely and relatively. In 2007 in sub-Saharan Africa more than 6.6 per cent of the 20 million people living with AIDS died from the disease while in Europe only 1.2 per cent of the people infected with HIV died from AIDS-related illnesses. The main reason for the declining number of AIDS deaths in Europe is advances in the medical treatment of AIDS that led to a steadily decreasing morbidity and mortality rate. For many patients in the global North, in the twenty-first century AIDS has been converted from a deadly illness to a manageable chronic disease (Osborn 2008).

But for most patients in the global South this is not yet the case. By the end of the 1990s about one-third of the world's population did not have access to essential medicines, and often even no access to primary health care. One reason for this is that essential drugs are simply unaffordable for many people in the world's poor countries. WHO Director-General Gro Harlem Brundtland described the discrepancy between the North and the South as follows: 'In developed countries, ... [a] course of antibiotics to cure pneumonia can be bought for the equivalent of two or three hours' wages. One-year treatment for HIV infection costs the equivalent of four to six months' salary. And the majority of drug costs are reimbursed. In developing countries, ... [a] full course of antibiotics to cure a common pneumonia may cost one month's wages. In many countries, one year of HIV treatment – if it were purchased – would consume the equivalent of 30 years' income. And the majority of households must buy their medicines with money from their own pockets' (Brundtland 1999: 68 f.). As a result, despite the development of highly active antiretroviral therapies (HAART), for many people in Africa, Asia and South America AIDS is still an illness with a very high mortality rate. The treatment that is able, if not to cure then at least to keep the illness at bay, is not available for most of them. By 2000 fewer than 100,000 patients in sub-Saharan Africa were receiving antiretroviral medication (UNAIDS 2008). This is the epidemiological backdrop against which several NGOs started a campaign for access to essential medicines in the late 1990s.

The second thread of this conflict goes back to the Uruguay Round of world trade negotiations. The Uruguay Round of multilateral trade negotiations started in 1986 and ended nine years later with the transformation of the General Agreement on Tariffs and Trade (GATT) into the World Trade Organization (WTO). One part of the negotiations was a multilateral agreement on Trade-Related Aspects of Intellectual Property Rights (TRIPS) that was included in the final WTO treaty and came into force on 1 January 1995. TRIPS marked an important change in international IP politics as it shifted responsibility for IP issues from WIPO and other UN agencies to the WTO. All TRIPS member states are required to guarantee in their national legislation a number of minimum standards of IP protection, among them a minimum copyright term of fifty years after the death of the author, a minimum patent term of twenty years (Article 12) and a clause that patents must be granted in all 'fields of technology' (Articles 27–33).

Unlike with the older international treaties relating to intellectual property rights – the Paris and Berne Conventions – where UN member states could choose whether to accede to the treaties or not, accession to TRIPS is mandatory for all WTO member states, which as of this writing comprises 153 states, responsible – according to the WTO – for 97 per cent of world trade (WTO 2010).[1] Before TRIPS, states had considerable flexibility in drafting IP laws according to their local requirements. The coverage of the then existing international treaties was more limited – the Berne Convention applied only to 'literary and artistic works' without explicitly mentioning computer programs – and less prescriptive – the Paris Convention did not contain any concrete

---

[1] In comparison the Berne Convention for the Protection of Literary and Artistic Works dating originally from 1886 had 84 members in 1990, among them the USA which had joined only in 1989. The Paris Convention for the Protection of Industrial Property (dating back to 1883) had 98 members in 1990.

formulations on patentable subject matter or protection terms. Before TRIPS, most developing and many developed countries had significantly lower standards than those required in the agreement (Deere 2009: 8).

TRIPS was the project of a powerful lobby group of US, European and Japanese business interests who successfully seized the opportunity to make IP protection a part of the global free trade agenda. Several authors have reconstructed and analysed this political process (Drahos 1995, 2005; Sell 1995, 2002b, 2003; Ryan 1998; Correa 2000; Matthews 2002; Drezner 2007), emphasizing that the discursive coupling of trade and intellectual property together with the strategy of the countries of the global North to shift fora and to pursue IP issues not any longer within the UN framework but within the GATT negotiations were responsible for the industry's success. TRIPS was an enormous success for the industry lobbyists who had pushed for it since the mid 1980s. But its existence also galvanized a coalition of civil society actors which had been engaged for a long time around various issues of health, civil rights and development but had until then not come together with a shared mobilization or campaign.

The TRIPS agreement brought fundamental normative and substantial changes to the global IP regime (Sell and Prakash 2004). Especially in the area of patents it prescribes that 'any inventions, whether products or processes, in all fields of technology, provided that they are new, involve an inventive step and are capable of industrial application' (Article 27.1) shall be patentable under the treaty. For many countries this meant far-reaching changes to their patent legislations, and in the field of pharmaceutical patents it foreclosed the option of process patents that some developing countries, notably India, had chosen until then.

The Indian case is instructive since it shows how a country with an emerging economy had shaped its IP laws according to its development needs, and was quite successful in establishing a thriving pharmaceutical industry. Under the Indian patent law from 1972, product patents for medicines were abolished with the consequence that a drug itself as a chemical entity was no longer patentable, only the production process in which the pharmaceutical can be produced. The patent term was also reduced from sixteen to a maximum of seven years (Koshy 1995; George 2009). Taking into account that in the pharmaceutical production process the actual synthesization of the active ingredient is usually not overly complex, process patents thus allow competitors to analyse the chemical composition of pharmaceuticals available on the market, and then develop an alternative process to produce a bioequivalent drug with the same bioavailability. This was an intended effect of the legal framework that, together with regulatory restrictions for foreign pharmaceutical companies, allowed India to develop a large domestic pharmaceutical industry that produces mainly generic versions of established drugs. Within two decades India became the 'pharmacy of the developing world' (Médecins Sans Frontières 2007). With this policy, India essentially followed the Swiss example, where process patents for chemical compounds were only introduced in 1907 after considerable pressure from the USA and Germany, and where pharmaceutical product patents have only existed since 1977 – after the Swiss pharmaceutical industry had established their leading position in the world market (May and Sell 2006: 113; Boldrin and Levine 2008: 216).

TRIPS eliminated this option. Instead all countries are now required to introduce product patents in all fields of technology, including pharmaceuticals, and to guarantee a twenty-year minimum patent term. The full effect of TRIPS on global IP protection was not immediately felt because developing countries were granted a grace period of up to ten years, but since 2005 all member states have been obliged to implement the rules laid out in the treaty. This is the global IP backdrop to the access to essential medicines campaign.

The context of the access to medicines conflict was thus an emerging humanitarian crisis in countries of the developing world under conditions of a fundamental internationalization and expansion of intellectual property rights regimes. The economic and political weakness of the countries most affected by the AIDS epidemic and the internationalization of intellectual property rights regimes limited the viability of local or national strategies to address the humanitarian problem. Similar to the multi-level approach of the industry lobbyists that led to the TRIPS agreement, an oppositional international or multi-level strategy was needed to address the consequences of TRIPS, and a collective actor had to be established to implement such a strategy.

5.2.   From TRIPS to Doha

One of the first NGOs working on the issue of patents and drug prices was the US-based Taxpayer Asset Project, an NGO founded by US political activist and later presidential candidate Ralph Nader, for which James Love from 1990 onwards started to look into government funding for drug development, drug prices and pharmaceutical patents. The Taxpayer Asset Project, which in 1995 changed its name to Consumer Project on Technology (CPTech) and today operates under the name Knowledge Ecology International (KEI), started in the mid 1990s a cooperation with Health Action International (HAI), a network of more than 150 health, development and consumer organizations from the North and the South (Interview 29). HAI and its German member organization BUKO Pharma-Kampagne organized a seminar in 1996 in Bielefeld, Germany, where the issue of access to medicines was discussed for the first time in a broader civil society context. Until then, health NGOs active in developing countries were more concerned about drug quality and the issue that pharmaceutical companies were selling in the countries of the South drugs of inferior quality and pharmaceuticals that they were forced to withdraw in the northern hemisphere for health reasons (Schaaber 2006). Key speakers at this first meeting in Bielefeld were James Love from CPTech and Kumariah Balasubramaniam from the HAI Regional Office for Asia and the Pacific. They directed the participants' attention to the problem of monopoly prices for patented essential medicines in the developing world (Health Action International 1997). Balasubramaniam, who became a key activist in the access to medicines campaign, predicted that the implementation of the TRIPS agreement would lead to higher drug prices and severely limit governments' options to drive down drug prices by allowing generic competition. This would further exacerbate the problem that in poor countries often only a small proportion of the population had access to essential medicines (Balasubramaniam 1997).

Several developing countries' governments were well aware of the possible health implications of the TRIPS agreement and tried to incorporate the remaining flexibilities into their national IP legislation. The options that the TRIPS agreement still left open in Articles 30 and 31 are compulsory licences, parallel imports and early working exceptions (so-called 'Bolar exceptions'). With a compulsory licence a government can allow a third party to produce a patented good without the consent of the patent owner. Under TRIPS a compulsory licence may be granted for a limited time in an emergency situation, for public non-commercial use and under a number of other restricted circumstances. Parallel imports allow the acquisition of patented goods in a foreign country at lower prices, and a Bolar exception allows a firm to gain marketing approval for a generic version of a patented drug before the patent expires (Correa 2002). Compulsory licences are the strongest flexibility, as they allow the production of a generic version of a patented drug at drastically lower prices.

In the late 1990s several parallel conflict lines developed within the broader conflict about access to medicines. When in 1997 Thailand and South Africa drafted laws to incorporate the TRIPS flexibilities in their national legislation they were confronted with massive pressure from the United States. Thailand quickly abandoned their plans but South Africa adopted the Medicines and Related Substances Control Amendment Act in December 1997. The law was immediately challenged before the High Court by the South African Pharmaceutical Manufacturers' Association (PMA) and thirty-nine pharmaceutical companies for allegedly being against the constitution (Sell 2002a; Cameron and Berger 2005).

Around the same time a number of developing countries, supported by an NGO network, put a resolution on the agenda of the 1998 World Health Assembly (WHA) in which WHO member states were urged 'to ensure that public health rather than commercial interests have primacy in pharmaceutical and health policies and to review their options under the Agreement on Trade Related Aspects of Intellectual Property Rights to safeguard access to essential drugs' (World Health Organization 1998). Here again, pharmaceutical industry associations, especially Pharmaceutical Research and Manufacturers of America (PhRMA) and the International Federation of Pharmaceutical Manufacturers & Associations (IFPMA), strongly lobbied northern countries' governments to oppose this resolution. During the negotiations the US delegation and their European allies initially prevailed over the delegations of several sub-Saharan African countries and managed to postpone a decision and relegate the resolution to an ad hoc committee (Sell 2002a: 504 ff.).[2] A watered down resolution was adopted one year later at the WHA in 1999. It no longer contained the controversial formulation that public health should have primacy over commercial interest and instead asked member states 'to ensure that public health interests are paramount in pharmaceutical and health policies [and] to explore and review their options under relevant international agreements, including trade agreements, to safeguard access to essential drugs' (World Health Assembly 1999).

In the meantime the NGO coalition had gained an important ally. In September 1999 Médecins Sans Frontières (MSF), an international humanitarian aid organization that mainly provides emergency medical assistance in developing countries, joined the coalition and started its own campaign.[3] MSF's specific advantage was that it already had a high level of public visibility in countries of the North, combined with an even higher level of moral credibility. The medical professionals

---

[2] A very interesting insight into the US delegation's perspective gives a declassified cable from the US mission in Geneva to the US Department of State (DOC_NUMBER: 1998GENEVA03470), available at www.cptech.org/ip/health/who/confidential.rtf (accessed 21 November 2012).

[3] www.msfaccess.org/.

working with MSF often provide medical aid in war-torn countries or after natural disasters and had been awarded the Nobel Peace Prize in 1999. In its capacity of providing medical aid in developing countries, MSF also is one large buyer of essential medicines and was therefore immediately affected by increasing drug prices.

Together with CPTech and HAI they organized in 1999 and 2000 several meetings and conferences that brought together activists and academics from the North and the South and also included representatives from the pharmaceutical industry, national governments, WHO and WTO (Williams 1999). The meetings served several goals. One purpose was capacity-building among the NGOs and developing countries' representatives. They also served to coordinate NGO activities at various levels and develop a targeted strategy to promote the use of compulsory licences as a core measure to enable access to essential medicines. One of the largest meetings was a conference in Amsterdam in November 1999, immediately prior to the WTO's Seattle ministerial conference at which 350 NGO representatives from fifty countries participated ('t Hoen 2002). In their *Amsterdam Statement* the NGOs demanded that the WTO establish a Standing Working Group on Access to Medicines that should review TRIPS IP rules relating to access to medicines and facilitate the use of TRIPS flexibilities (Health Action International, Médecins Sans Frontières, and Consumer Project on Technology 1999).

Between 1999 and 2001 more and more organizations joined the network. CPTech brought in the US AIDS activist groups ACT UP and Health Global Access Project (Health GAP), in Geneva the Quaker United Nations Office (QUNO) played an important role as well as the southern intergovernmental organization and think-tank South Centre. The Third World Network (TWN), an international advocacy network on development issues, became involved and in 2001 another prominent NGO, Oxfam International, also joined the mobilization and started its own *Cut the Costs* campaign[4] aimed at bringing down drug prices in developing countries ('t Hoen 2002; Mayne 2002; Munoz Tellez 2006).

The NGOs in the campaign for access to medicines employed a broad range of action forms to try to influence policy-makers. They provided expertise to developing countries' administrations and governments to help them to better understand the consequences of the TRIPS agreement and the possible options that still remained. They

---

[4] http://web.archive.org/web/20010320143402/www.oxfam.org.uk/cutthecost/ (accessed 21 November 2012).

participated in expert groups in northern countries to counter the position of industry lobbyists. They organized meetings and conferences to coordinate the campaign, published information material, and intervened in several ways on the national and international level in the political process. During the 1999 US presidential campaign activists from ACT UP disrupted rallies of the presidential candidate and at that time US Vice President Al Gore and demanded that the US government should cease threats of trade sanctions against South Africa and other developing nations, which were attempting to provide access to essential AIDS medications through legal measures for compulsory licensing and parallel importing (ACT UP Philadelphia 1999). They argued that the high price of ARVs would allow only (mostly white) affluent South Africans to receive AIDS treatment and that the US trade policy would effectively lead to a form of medical apartheid in South Africa, an argument that resonated well with the US Congressional Black Caucus (Sell and Prakash 2004: 165). The result of this campaign was a remarkable policy-shift in which the Clinton administration substantially changed its position. In the Executive Order 13155 US President Clinton decreed that the USA should stop its practice of pressuring sub-Saharan African countries not to make use of the TRIPS flexibilities and instead recognized their right to use them to combat AIDS.

The biggest success of the mobilization was the *Doha Declaration on TRIPS and Public Health* at the WTO ministerial meeting in November 2001 in which the member states declare 'the TRIPS Agreement does not and should not prevent Members from taking measures to protect public health. Accordingly, while reiterating our commitment to the TRIPS Agreement, we affirm that the Agreement can and should be interpreted and implemented in a manner supportive of WTO Members' right to protect public health and, in particular, to promote access to medicines for all' (WTO 2001). They furthermore clarify that HIV/AIDS, tuberculosis, malaria and other epidemics can represent a national emergency and therefore entitle governments to grant compulsory licences and use the other TRIPS flexibilities.

The Doha Declaration also recognized the problem that in Article 31(f) TRIPS allows compulsory licences predominantly for the supply of the domestic market, which leaves many developing countries out in the cold as they lack the pharmaceutical production facilities to produce the needed medication. In the declaration the TRIPS council was instructed to find a workable solution for this problem within one year. Because the US Trade Representative (USTR) repeatedly blocked a decision (Drezner 2007: 198) it took the WTO members more than one and a half years to agree on a mechanism to solve this so-called

'Paragraph 6 problem'. The negotiations showed a continuing deep rift between developing countries on one side and the USA and Europe on the other. While the Africa Group, joined by Brazil, Cuba, Dominican Republic, Ecuador, Honduras, India, Indonesia, Jamaica, Malaysia, Sri Lanka and Thailand, favoured a solution that would automatically allow the production of a generic version of a drug for which a country has granted a compulsory licence, the USA and Europe tried to limit the scope of the Doha Declaration, and the NGOs tried to push for a solution with minimal administrative requirements ('t Hoen 2009).

The agreement on the *Implementation of Paragraph 6 of the Doha Declaration on the TRIPS Agreement and public health* (WTO 2003) that was reached in the WTO General Council on 30 August 2003 (often referred to as the 'August 30 Decision' or the 'Paragraph 6 Agreement') had the form of a temporary waiver of Article 31(f) of the TRIPS agreement. It was transformed in December 2005 into a permanent amendment to TRIPS (WTO 2005). The solution de facto narrows the scope of the Doha Declaration and installs a highly complex rule-set that many NGOs dismiss as unworkable (Cameron and Berger 2005; Médecins Sans Frontières 2006). So far it has only been used once by the Canadian generic manufacturer Apotex to make shipments of AIDS medicines to Rwanda (Tsai 2009; Saez 2010).

Overall this quick overview offers a glimpse into the complex web of interrelated conflicts that concurrently take place in multiple arenas. Susan Sell has characterized the constellation as a cat and mouse game (Sell 2010a), but it is not quite clear whether this game will end in the traditional way where the cat (the IP maximalists) in the end always catches the mouse (the access coalition) or whether the constellation resembles more the setting in the Tom and Jerry movies where the mouse always escapes – not without inflicting significant harm on the cat. So far wins and losses are only temporary. The NGO success that the WTO acknowledged the primacy of public health concerns in the Doha Declaration has largely vanished in its implementation where the resourceful countries of the North prevailed over the South. As Drahos has pointed out, the developing countries did not have a post-negotiation implementation strategy to realize the gains of the Doha Declaration (Drahos 2007: 24). Instead they were dragged into another negotiation round where technicalities dominated the agenda. Meanwhile the US administration shifted their focus from intergovernmental to bi- and multilateral fora and attempted to get selected developing countries to sign free trade agreements (FTAs) with TRIPS-plus clauses that further inhibit their possibilities to grant compulsory licences. Authors disagree whether the current state is still a victory for the developing countries or already another one for the IP maximalists from the countries of the North (Drahos 2007; Drezner 2007; Muzaka 2009). And the constellation becomes even more complicated as new arenas are opened where new policy instruments are developed that greatly affect IP policies in the area of public health.

5.2.1. Prize funds and an R&D Treaty

One such new arena is the activities around prize funds and patent pools. In a parallel process that has received much less public attention some of the NGOs, in particular CPTech/Knowledge Ecology International and MSF, have lobbied the WHO and other international organizations for the introduction of alternative research and development financing mechanisms. As early as 2001 they started to propose ideas for a Research and Development Treaty,[5] an international framework that would establish requirements and incentives to invest in areas of medical research and development that have been neglected in the current system, which incentivizes the most profitable and not the most needed medical innovations. Ideas were put forward for the introduction of prize funds as an alternative or a complement to the existing patent system, or for patent pools which would collect biomedical patents and make them available under a general public licence.

In contrast to patents that are post-hoc innovation reward mechanisms incentivizing innovation in the most profitable areas, prize funds are better suited to steer the direction of innovation according to predefined needs. In economic research they are seen as equally or even more effective than patents under certain circumstances (Wright 1983). Patent pools would keep the current IP system untouched but establish a medical commons of publicly available patents similar to the General Public License (GPL) for open source software or the Creative Commons licence for artistic and scientific works (see section 6.4).

While no R&D treaty has been adopted so far, some of the ideas that have been developed in the course of its discussion have found their way into several programmes that have been established internationally between 2005 and 2010. UNITAID, the international facility for the purchase of drugs against HIV/AIDS, malaria and tuberculosis, has set up a voluntary patent pool for medicines in 2008, aimed at increasing access to newer antiretroviral medicines and encouraging

[5] www.cptech.org/workingdrafts/rndtreaty4.pdf (accessed 21 November 2012).

the development of adapted formulations (e.g. heat stable or single-dosage) suitable for the needs of people living in developing countries. The WHO adopted at its fifty-ninth World Health Assembly a resolution establishing an Intergovernmental Working Group (IGWG) to develop a global strategy plan to promote needs-driven essential health research and development relevant to diseases that disproportionately affect developing countries (World Health Assembly 2006), and two years later established an expert working group (EWG) to develop concrete recommendations. After the EWG's results were deemed to be unsatisfactory by many developing countries and criticized by NGOs for being biased towards an industry perspective, a new consultative expert working group on research and development financing and coordination was created at the 2009 WHA to redo the work of the previous expert working group (Mara 2010).

5.2.2. Regional mobilizations

Below the level of international organizations success and failure are even harder to determine, as for each side gains in one area are often accompanied by losses in others. What can be said with certainty is that the access to medicines campaign had substantial effects on the price level for AIDS medication. Between 1999 and 2009 the price for an HIV triple-combination therapy fell from US\$10,439 per person per year to US\$67 (see Figure 5.1). This decline to less than 1 per cent of the original price was the double result of political mobilization and generic competition.

While this price decrease is impressive it does not on its own solve the problem of access to medicines. Depending on national IP laws, the lowest price may not be available in all countries, and even if available, US\$67 per year may still be unaffordable for large parts of the population who live on an average income of less than US\$1 per day. Also, in the longer run, for many patients the first-line treatment will become less effective due to increasing resistance. But second- and third-line antiretroviral drugs have mostly been developed after the new patent legislations came into force in the developing countries with large pharmaceutical production capacities, and therefore generic alternatives will not be available or much harder to get. A sustainable solution that will guarantee access to essential medicines for people in the developing world is therefore still not in sight.

Apart from lowering the general price level of antiretroviral drugs, mobilizations for access to medicines were successful at the national level in several conflicts.

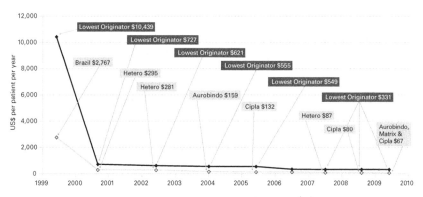

Figure 5.1 Generic competition and drug prices for HIV triple therapy.

Note: Sample of ARV triple-combination: stavudine (d4T) + lamivudine (3TC) + nevirapine (NVP). Lowest world prices per patient per year.
Source: Médecins Sans Frontières (2010).

In *South Africa* in April 2001 the Pharmaceutical Manufacturers' Association (PMA) and thirty-nine international pharmaceutical companies withdrew their lawsuit[6] against the South African government after local activists from the Treatment Action Campaign (TAC), international NGOs and AIDS activists from the North had accused them of putting profits before people and denying patients in AIDS-struck sub-Saharan Africa access to life-saving drugs (McGreal 2001; Barnard 2002; Berger 2002; Mayne 2002; Ford et al. 2004; Olesen 2006). In their lawsuit from 1998 the pharmaceutical companies –backed politically by the USTR – had claimed that the South African 'Medicines and Related Substances Control Amendment Act No 90 of 1997', which included several measures to bring down drug prices, would be unconstitutional and violate South Africa's obligations under the TRIPS agreement. The Medicines Act introduced a preference system for generic substitution of off-patent medicines, allowed parallel importation of patented brand-name drugs, and established a pricing committee to oversee drug prices – measures that are common practice in the USA and several EU member states, and that have not been legally challenged by the pharmaceutical industry in those countries.

---

[6] Case 4183/98: Pharmaceutical company lawsuit (forty-two applicants) against the Government of South Africa (ten respondents); www.cptech.org/ip/health/sa/pharmasuit.html (accessed 11 October 2010).

The civil society mobilization against this court case took place at several levels simultaneously: as mentioned above, US activists from ACT UP protested at rallies of the democratic presidential candidate Al Gore and MSF initiated a petition that collected 250,000 signatures (Interview 29). In South Africa a petition was published that was signed by 250 NGOs from 35 countries, and on the opening day of the trial activists organized parallel demonstrations in 30 cities across the world. Also the European Parliament and several national parliaments urged the companies to withdraw from the case ('t Hoen 2002; Forman 2008). For the pharmaceutical industry the trial developed into a public relations disaster in which they were portrayed as greedy corporations unwilling to provide affordable medication for poor people dying of AIDS. Their withdrawal from the case on 19 April was a success for the civil society mobilization and it encouraged developing countries to make use of the flexibilities granted under the TRIPS agreement.

In *Thailand* access to antiretroviral drugs had been a contentious issue since the mid 1990s. At that time people affected by the illness started to create local People Living with HIV/AIDS (PLWHA) peer support groups and in 1997 forged the nationwide Thai Network for People living with HIV/AIDS (TPN+), which in 2009 comprised 1,000 groups with over 100,000 members (Limpananont et al. 2009). In 1999, together with MSF and the Thai AIDS ACCESS foundation, they collected 50,000 signatures that allowed them under the 1997 Thai constitution to introduce a proposal for legislation in the parliament calling for universal health coverage – the so-called 30-baht universal health-care scheme (Krikorian 2009: 37). AIDS activists also campaigned for generic competition. In December 1999 they held a vigil in front of the Ministry of Public Health in support of the Thai Government Pharmaceutical Organization's (GPO) request for a compulsory licence for ddI, a reverse transcriptase inhibitor used in combination therapy against HIV (Ford et al. 2004; Limpananont et al. 2009). But the Thai government shied away from such a step in light of massive pressure from the pharmaceutical industry and the USA, which warned the Thai government that such a step might cause a trade dispute 'which is what we have always told them would happen if the compulsary [sic] licensing clause should be invoked'.[7]

But the political campaign for universal health care was very successful and resulted in the passage of the National Health Security Act of 2002

---

[7] Cable from Richard E. Hecklinger, at that time US ambassador to Thailand, writing to the Secretary of State and others, available at: http://lists.essential.org/pipermail/ip-health/2003-March/004424.html (accessed 15 September 2010).

that provides universal health care for about three-quarters of the Thai population. A side effect of this legislation was that it created significant financial pressure on the National Health Security Office (NHSO) due to high drug prices for antiretroviral drugs. Under these circumstances the option of compulsory licences was more seriously considered by the administration. At the same time the negotiations for a free trade agreement (FTA) between the USA and Thailand, in which the USA wanted to include TRIPS-plus IP provisions, produced the paradoxical effect of mobilizing and unifying Thai civil society organizations. In January 2006 10,000 people protested against the FTA in Chiang Mai, about a third of them members of PLWHA groups demanding compulsory licences to guarantee access to life-saving drugs (Krikorian 2009).

A very peculiar constellation led in the following years to a reversal of the Thai government's position and, as a consequence, to the granting of three compulsory licences between November 2006 and January 2007. In her analysis of the Thai case Gaëlle Krikorian (2009) highlights that this development was facilitated by the military coup after Prime Minister Thaksin's resignation in April 2006. The newly appointed Public Health Minister Mongkol Na Songkhla, who was sympathetic to the AIDS activists' cause and had first-hand experience of the problems of providing access to essential drugs from working as a rural doctor in the 1970s, was able to act with fewer constraints and more authority than his predecessors. Shortly after his appointment he announced the granting of a compulsory licence for the two HIV drugs Efavirenz and Kaletra (lopinavir/ritonavir), and Plavix, a drug for heart-disease patients.

Despite the pressure from the USTR that – on the request of the Pharmaceutical Research and Manufacturers of America (PhRMA) – has put Thailand on the 301 Priority Watch List, the compulsory licences are still in effect in 2010 (Pratruangkrai 2009).

Civil society groups were also active on issues of access to medicines in *India* and *Brazil*, the two most important producer countries for generic drugs for the developing world.

In *India* a coalition of AIDS activists, public health groups, NGOs and individuals lobbied for an amendment of the patent law to prevent the ever-greening of drug patents by requiring new forms of existing drugs to be more efficient in order to be patentable. This demand was realized in the 2005 amendment of section 3(d) of the 1970 Patent Act (George 2009: 130). Civil society groups also used the option of stakeholder opposition provided in the Indian patent law to oppose a patent claim from Novartis for its cancer drug Gleevec, and organized a 'Boycott Novartis' campaign to increase the political pressure.

In *Brazil* civil society groups have been strongly involved in public health policies since the 1980s and have considerably shaped the current public health system, which is anchored in a constitutional guarantee of universal health care. The reason for the democratic structure of the Brazilian health sector and the close cooperation between administration and civil society lies in the history of the struggle against the military dictatorship between 1964 and 1985 in which many 'sanitaristas', progressive health professionals, were actively involved. In the transition to democracy in the mid to late 1980s they occupied important positions in the political and administrative system, leading to the establishment of the Unified Health System (Sistema Único de Saúde (SUS)) in 1988, which guarantees free comprehensive health care to the entire population (Galvão 2005: 1112; Eimer and Lütz 2010: 141). Leading AIDS activists had also been active in the struggle against the military regime, giving their cause additional weight after democracy was re-established in Brazil (Galvão 2005).

While Brazil reintroduced pharmaceutical product patents to avoid US trade sanctions in 1991, the sanitaristas and other civil society actors successfully pressured the government to effectively implement the flexibilities allowed under TRIPS. The cornerstone of the resulting reforms was the establishment of the National Agency of Sanitary Surveillance (Agência Nacional de Vigilância Sanitária (ANVISA)) in 1999 (Flynn and Andrade de Oliveira 2009). This autonomous agency linked to the Ministry of Health has to give its 'prior consent' to any pharmaceutical patent application that is approved by the National Institute for Industrial Property (Instituto Nacional da Propriedade Industrial (INPI)). It is effectively a powerful veto player involved in the patent granting process with different preferences from the industry and IP professionals, curbing patent ever-greening and strengthening Brazil's compulsory licensing policies (Shadlen 2009a; Eimer and Lütz 2010).

Given the close cooperation between health administration and civil society organizations, access to medicines activists in Brazil were able to focus on public awareness campaigns about the social impact of intellectual property trade agreements, monitoring international fora that discuss the topic of intellectual property and access to medicines, organizing solidarity campaigns with NGOs in Thailand and India to support them in their legal battles against Abbott and Novartis, and providing expertise in South–South cooperations (Reis, Terto and Pimenta 2009).

During the access to medicines conflict a collective actor emerges. A network of local and transnational NGOs, engaged individuals, government officials from some countries of the global South and other actors was formed in the late 1990s. This network brought various issues together and connected mobilizations at various levels. Most of the actors who participated in the access to medicines mobilizations could already look back on a long history of engagement in public health issues, international solidarity work, or both. What is remarkable about the mobilization is that it connected local protests, like the demonstrations in Thailand against the US-Thailand free trade agreement and for compulsory licences for HIV/AIDS drugs, transnational protest campaigns, like the one against pharma lobbyists in South Africa, and lobby politics at international organizations, like the work for the WTO Doha Declaration.

How did the activists manage to coordinate their activities in this complex multi-level setting? How were they able to unite a diverse and heterogeneous group of collective and individual actors in a single campaign that received a high level of publicity all around the world? These questions will be addressed in the next two sections, in which I will take a closer look at the network of actors and their framing strategies through which they generated a shared interpretation of the problem, the configuration of actors, and the intervention strategies to solve the problem.

5.3. The network of actors

The access to medicines conflict was a worldwide conflict, and therefore the range of actors involved is extremely broad. Participants in the conflict were international organizations, national governments and administrations, international and national industry associations and individual firms from the pharmaceutical sector, transnational and local NGOs, patient groups, and academics. A much broader study would be necessary to disentangle the complex web of interactions between all these actors. I will limit my discussion here to the core actors and coalitions that have been identified in previous research and by actors involved in the conflict (Mayne 2002; Sell 2002a; Ford 2004; Sell and Prakash 2004; Munoz Tellez 2006; Kapczynski 2008; Yu 2008; 't Hoen 2009; Krikorian 2009; Eimer and Lütz 2010). This analysis is thus less formalized than the corresponding analysis of the actor networks in the chapter about the software patents conflict – although I use data from the most important mailing list (ip-health) of the access to medicines actors to identify core actors among the non-governmental actors within the access to medicines campaign.

5.3.1.   International organizations

International organizations were important fora and actors for the access to medicines conflict. Because TRIPS provided the legal framework for the conflict the WTO necessarily played a central role. Within the UN system those most prominently involved were the World Health Organization (WHO), the World Intellectual Property Organization (WIPO) and later the United Nations Conference on Trade and Development (UNCTAD).

WIPO, the UN organization that oversees the Paris and Berne Conventions and several other international IP treaties, is an obvious candidate. The WHO became involved in IP issues when it realized the possible consequences of the new international IP regime for the availability of affordable medicines in the world's poor countries (Helfer 2004: 42). And UNCTAD gained importance through its cooperation with the Geneva-based International Centre for Trade and Sustainable Development (ICTSD) as an alternative source for expertise with a strong focus on development goals for the developing countries.

The creation of the *WTO* installed a powerful new player in the field of intellectual property. Under the old GATT framework IP played only a marginal role, but with the TRIPS agreement the countries of the global North installed a binding and enforceable compulsory minimum standard that applies to all WTO member states. TRIPS meant a significant expansion of the scope of intellectual property rights and permanently changed the global framework of IP governance (Sell 2002b: 173).

While TRIPS was for all sides the core point of reference in the access to medicines conflict, the WTO as an organization played at most an ambivalent role in the conflict. Contrary to the expectation that the availability of the robust dispute settlement mechanism would lead to a flood of WTO disputes from developed against developing countries (cf. Reichman 2003: 125), an assessment of the so far fifteen years of the agreement reveals a more ambivalent picture.

In his stock-taking study Joost Pauwelyn points out that between 1995 and 2010 only 27 out of 402 WTO disputes were TRIPS-related, and only 9 of those ended before a panel, meaning that in the remaining 18 cases the parties reached a mutual agreement outside the dispute settlement mechanism (Pauwelyn 2010). The two most recent cases not yet covered by his study are complaints by India and Brazil against the EU for its seizure of legitimate generic medicines while they were in transit in the EU. This brings the total number of TRIPS-related WTO conflicts to 29. Less than one-third (9) of the TRIPS cases were disputes

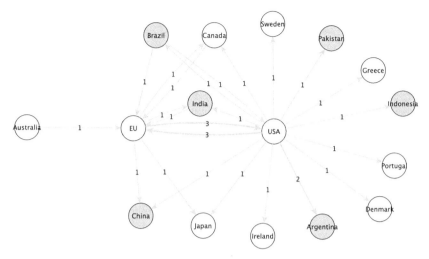

Figure 5.2 WTO TRIPS disputes between 1995 and 2010, N =29.

Note: Arrows are between complainant and targeted country,
developing countries are highlighted, numbers indicate the number
of disputes between the respective countries.
Data source: www.wto.org/english/tratop_e/dispu_e/dispu_
agreements_index_e.htm?id=A26.

brought by OECD against developing countries. Ten cases were disputes
between the USA and the EU or its member states, and no case was filed
between developing countries. Figure 5.2 illustrates the structure of the
TRIPS disputes since 1995. It shows clearly that the most active complainant was the USA with 17, followed by the EU with 7 complaints. It
also shows that most disputes happened between countries of the global
North, and especially between the USA and the EU.

On a substantive level the rulings of the Panels and the Appellate
Body were neither especially hard-line nor restrictive (Pauwelyn 2010:
401). So at least until now it can be said that the WTO did not engage
in rule-setting by providing, for example, very broad interpretations of
TRIPS obligations. Pauwelyn attributes this relative reluctance on the
one hand to the fact that TRIPS – unlike other WTO agreements – is
an instance of 'positive integration', meaning that member states have
to establish norms and institutions to comply with the minimum standards set up by the agreement, whereas other agreements usually are
instances of negative integration that force member states to abolish tariffs or preferential treatment. On the other hand he attributes the lack
of dispute settlement activities especially against developing countries

to the access to medicines mobilization that shifted public opinion to an IP sceptical position (Pauwelyn 2010: 427). This interpretation is corroborated by the fact that the only two cases that address pharmaceutical patents after 2001 are the complaints by Brazil and India in which they try to weaken patent protection for medicines. Before 2001 pharmaceutical patents were addressed in eight of the twenty-three cases filed until then, always with the aim to strengthen IP protection.

With a dispute settlement mechanism that did not lead to the expected IP maximalist policies the WTO became a rather ambivalent actor in the access to medicines conflict. Then, with the Doha Declaration emphasizing the flexibilities of its rules for IP protection, the WTO even became an important venue for IP sceptical positions voiced by Brazil, India, South Africa and a number of other developing countries.

The *WHO* became involved in the access to medicines conflict because the new TRIPS rules directly affected the availability of essential medicines in developing countries. The trustful cooperation between health NGOs and national health administrations in some developing countries had built a base on which in 1998, before the annual World Health Assembly (WHA), Zimbabwe's Minister of Health approached activists from Health Action International (HAI) and the Consumer Project on Technology (CPTech) to draft a resolution for the WHO's 'Revised Drug Strategy' (Sell 2002a: 504). As mentioned above, the resulting resolution that claimed primacy of health interests over intellectual property was approved by the WHO Executive Board (World Health Organization 1998), but then was delayed after the intervention of the USA and only adopted in a less critical form at the following WHA in 1999 (World Health Assembly 1999). But the USA and like-minded industrialized countries were only able to change the wording of the resolution and not to block it completely.

The fundamentally sceptical position towards the benefits of strong intellectual property rights became manifest in several resolutions and WHO activities in the following years, especially the creation of the Commission on Intellectual Property Rights, Innovation and Public Health at the fifty-sixth WHA in 2003 that delivered its report three years later, emphasizing once more that developing countries 'should provide in their legislation for the use of compulsory licensing provisions, consistent with the TRIPS agreement, as one means to facilitate access to cheaper medicines through import or local production' (CIPIH 2006: 120), should encourage generic market entry, prevent anti-competitive patenting practices, and refrain from agreeing to TRIPS-plus provision in bilateral trade agreements.

The WHO provided an important forum to foster collaboration among countries of the South and between developing countries and NGOs. The organization's mission to provide access to health care especially in the countries of the South makes it a forum much more conducive to normative public interest arguments than, for example, the WTO. But since the organization has no power over the relevant IP treaties it is restricted to providing guidance and expertise on how to explore existing flexibilities.

Another UN forum that was used by developing countries and NGOs is *UNCTAD*, the UN organization responsible for trade, investment and development issues. The focus here was less on resolutions and public statements than on capacity-building and counter-expertise. A manifestation of this is the 2001 initiated 'UNCTAD-ICTSD Project on IPRs and Sustainable Development',[8] a long-term cooperation between UNCTAD and the Geneva-based NGO ICTSD – a think-tank with strong commitment to sustainable development and with an outspoken IP sceptical position (Interview 32). This cooperation has produced a large number of issue-specific policy papers and a comprehensive resource book providing developing countries with expertise in how to make maximal use of the flexibilities allowed under TRIPS, 'highlighting the areas in which the treaty leaves lee-way to Members for the pursuit of their own policy objectives' (UNCTAD-ICTSD 2005: xi).

WIPO, the UN organization genuinely in charge of intellectual property rights, came into the conflict only at a relatively late stage. The reason for this lies in its diminished influence after important parts of the world IP system came under the aegis of the WTO (CIPR 2002: 157). But while WIPO may have been temporarily sidelined as an important political forum for IP politics, its role as a provider of technical expertise increased after TRIPS, with more and more countries having to adapt their legislation to the standards set in the agreement (May 2007: 35). Around the turn of the millennium several developing countries with a more critical position towards IP protection realized how important WIPO's role in implementing the TRIPS agreement was, and refocused their attention at the organization. From 2001 onwards Brazil and the African Group started to push the organization towards a more development-friendly position (Deere 2009: 131). These attempts culminated in the 2004 call for a WIPO Development Agenda, which was adopted in the WIPO General Assembly in 2007. The Development Agenda is a set of forty-five recommendations aimed at strengthening

[8] See: www.iprsonline.org/.

the development dimension of the organization's activities by providing member states with expertise in implementing TRIPS flexibilities according to the country's specific needs instead of promoting a maximalist one-size-fits-all approach (Interviews 30 and 33). Whether and to which extent it will yield material consequences remains still to be seen.

5.3.2. Nation-states

Several national governments and administrative bodies were involved in the access to medicines conflict. The coalitions here are not very surprising. On the one hand industrialized countries, notably the *USA*, the *EU*, its member states, *Switzerland* and *Japan*, were proponents of strong patent protection. In the Thai case the USA, the EU, France and Switzerland tried to exert pressure on the Thai government to refrain from using compulsory licences (Krikorian 2009: 33). In one of the few North–South TRIPS trade disputes the USA accused Brazil of violating TRIPS provisions in its patent law by allowing compulsory licences after three years if a patent holder does not produce the patented good locally and does not provide evidence that local production is not reasonable. The USA only withdrew their complaint after massive protests by NGOs ('t Hoen 2009: 22). The USA and Italy blocked the resolution claiming primacy of public health interest over intellectual property rights at the WHA in 1998. Likewise the USA and Switzerland opposed the Doha Declaration, claiming that patents would not be a barrier to access to medicines (Sell 2002a: 516).

Within the US administration the US Trade Representative (USTR) plays a special role as a leading proponent of an IP maximalist position. This is the result of a legal-institutional development in the 1970s and 1980s that expanded the USTR's power and autonomy and increased private sector influence on the institution (Sell 2010b). Its most prominent and notorious policy instrument is the annual 'Special 301 Report', which lists the countries that are accused of not providing 'adequate and effective' protection of US intellectual property rights. The main information input source for the list are complaints by firms and industry associations, among them the International Intellectual Property Alliance (IIPA), which was specifically founded in 1984 to promote copyright interests at the USTR (Sell 2010b: 772). Since 1989 India and Brazil have been put on the Special 301 Priority Watch List or the Watch List in almost every year,[9] Thailand has been put on one of the lists in every year except 1991 and South Africa was put on the list after it introduced its Medicines Act in 1997, but was removed in 2000 after strong political protests.

Among the OECD countries *Canada* stands out as the first OECD country to make use of the WTO's Paragraph 6 Solution, the temporary waiver allowing the production and export of medicines, for which a developing country's government has issued a compulsory licence, but where the country does not have the production capacities to manufacture the medicine ('t Hoen 2009: 37). Apart from Canada only a handful of other countries (Norway, China, India and South Korea) have adapted their legislation to implement the flexibility in their national laws, but so far only Canada has actually used this option to allow the export of the HIV/AIDS drug Apo-TriAvir, by the Canadian generic pharmaceutical manufacturer Apotex, to Rwanda (Tsai 2009). It may come as no surprise that all the countries who offer this legal option are currently on the USTR's Special 301 Watch List.

Occasionally there was limited disagreement within the northern countries' government institutions. The European Parliament in March 2001 adopted a resolution in which it expressed its solidarity with the South African government and called on the pharmaceutical companies to withdraw from the case (EP 2001). The German Minister of Development and the Dutch Minister of Development Cooperation also issued public statements urging the pharmaceutical companies to withdraw ('t Hoen 2001a). But these were isolated incidents that did not reflect the EU Commission's or the Dutch or German governments' position.

Brazil, India, Thailand, South Africa and *Rwanda* were the developing countries that played an important role in the conflict. India and Brazil are the countries with the largest generic drug manufacturing capacities in the developing world. Brazil especially played a very active role in changing IP political priorities and strengthening the development aspect in several fora (Interview 32). It tried in the early 1960s to make the worldwide IP system more favourable for developing countries (Menescal 2005) – but without success. Forty years later, together with Argentina, it was coordinating the efforts of the so-called 'Friends of Development Group' at the WIPO to establish the WIPO Development Agenda.

---

[9] India has been on the Priority Watch List every year except 1991, Brazil was on the Priority Watch List in 1989–93, 1995 and 2002–6, and on the Watch List in 1996–7, 1999–2001 and 2007–10.

South Africa and Thailand were core countries in which the conflict about compulsory licensing was played out. And Rwanda is the only country that so far has used the option to grant a compulsory licence for drugs which cannot be produced within the country but have to be manufactured in a foreign country and then imported for domestic use.

5.3.3. Corporate actors

The pharmaceutical industry played a core role in the creation of the TRIPS agreement. Pfizer, Merck and the US pharmaceutical industry association PhRMA were among the most active in pushing for the introduction of IP issues into the Uruguay trade round (Sell 2002a). In the access to medicines conflict it was again the US, European and international pharmaceutical industry trade associations – PhRMA, the European Federation of Pharmaceutical Industries and Associations (EFPIA), the International Federation of Pharmaceutical Manufacturers & Associations (IFPMA) – and many of the world's top twenty pharmaceutical companies that were pushing for stronger patent protection and fighting attempts to prioritize public health concerns over intellectual property rights. Bristol-Myers Squibb (BMS) and Abbott led the campaign in Thailand, and GlaxoSmithKline, BMS, Merck, Novartis, Eli Lilly, Wyeth, Roche, Schering, Boehringer-Ingelheim and Bayer were among the companies that sued the South African government after it had passed its Medicines Act. PhRMA regularly submits complaints about developing countries' laws that use TRIPS flexibilities to promote access to medicines with the result that these countries consequently show up on the Special 301 Watch List. Overall the pharmaceutical companies and their industry associations have very actively intervened and tried to influence the access to medicines conflict in their favour. They used various means ranging from behind-closed-doors lobbying to public relations campaigns to litigation. They tried to exert influence via powerful government actors like the USTR or the European Commission, and – under pressure – offered developing countries' administrations significant price reductions to avoid measures that would limit or weaken their intellectual property rights.

The price reductions in particular were often a direct response to the generic competition that has lowered drug prices dramatically for some core HIV/AIDS medication during the past twenty years. It is notable that neither the producers of these medicines – especially the Indian manufacturers Cipla and Hetero – nor the US and European industry associations of the generic pharmaceutical sector, the Generic

Pharmaceutical Association (GphA) and the European Generic Medicines Association (EGA), played a vocal role in the conflict. Cipla cooperated with MSF in a public-relations coup that generated world-wide attention, when it offered to sell its triple combination AIDS drug in developing countries for less than a tenth of the price the brand-name equivalent would cost in the USA (Médecins Sans Frontières and Cipla 2001), but it did not intervene on a political level in the conflict. EGA has published several documents on its website in which it welcomes the Doha Declaration, but no lobbying efforts were visible in relation to the access to medicines campaign. Unlike their brand-name counterparts the generic medicines sector did not develop a concerted strategy to intervene in the global conflict about intellectual property rights.

5.3.4. NGOs and civil society actors

The driving force behind the access to medicines conflict was a coalition of NGOs that came together in the late 1990s and remained in its core relatively constant. The literature (Sell 2002a; Ford 2004; Ford et al. 2004; Munoz Tellez 2006; Matthews 2007; Kapczynski 2008; 't Hoen 2009; Clapham and Robinson 2009) as well as my interviewees (Interviews 26, 29, 31, 32 and 33) mention a handful of core NGOs that played a central role in the conflict. These are the US NGO Consumer Project on Technology (CPTech), the international network of health, development, and consumer organizations Health Action International (HAI), the British NGO Oxfam, US and French chapters of the gay AIDS activist network ACT UP, the South African Treatment Action Campaign (TAC) and the international humanitarian aid organization Médecins Sans Frontières (MSF).

A similar group appears in a network analysis of the core mailing list of the NGO network. For this analysis, which is visualized in Figure 5.3, all posts on the 'ip-health' mailing list between January 2000 and December 2005 were analysed and a count was made of how many posts an organization or individual had contributed to the discussion. The size of the nodes represents the number of postings to the list by the respective organization. This gives an impression of how active an organization was. The figure also illustrates how early an organization joined the network, and how long and continuously it participated, by adjusting the shade of the node to the duration of participation.

The network shows CPTech, which runs the mailing list, as the most active actor, followed by Health GAP, MSF, Essential Action, the Canadian HIV/AIDS Legal Network, ACT UP Philadelphia, FIAR, ACT UP Paris, TAC, TWN, HAI, Oxfam, and a number of

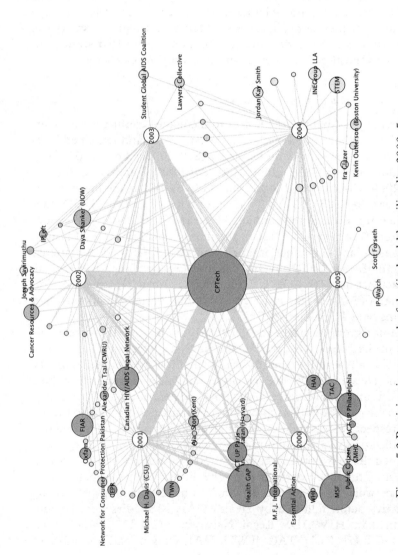

Figure 5.3 Participation network of the 'ip-health' mailing list 2000–5.
Note: Nodes are shaded according to participation duration, darker shades mean longer participation; node size *s* represents posting frequency *fp*, edge size represents participation frequency *ft* for the given year. Nodes with less than six postings (outdegree <6) are ignored.

individual academics. Most of the organizations that joined the network in December 1999 stayed onboard until 2005, the year in which the temporary waiver in paragraph 6 of the Doha Declaration was transformed into a permanent waiver for developing countries.

Since many of these groups are themselves umbrella organizations with many members (e.g. HAI, Health GAP, TWN), or organizations with regional units in many countries (e.g. Oxfam, MSF), the actual network of NGOs involved in the access to medicines conflict is significantly larger. It includes organizations and individuals from the North and the South but is clearly dominated by NGOs based in the USA and Europe. While the problems were most pressing in developing countries it was NGOs based in OECD countries that provided much of the expertise and ultimately shaped the conflict about access to medicines.

But the mobilization for access to medicines was not limited to this transnational advocacy network (Keck and Sikkink 1998). It also involved intensive grassroots mobilization of people living with HIV/AIDS in developing countries and large-scale protests that were supported by local unions (e.g. South Africa) or groups mobilizing against neoliberal economic globalization (e.g. Thailand).

5.3.5. Opposing coalitions

Overall the network of actors shows a strong North–South polarization with regard to nation-states and corporate actors. The countries pushing for stronger IP protection and less flexibilities are, without exception, industrialized countries from the global North. Countries in favour of more flexibilities and a primacy of public health concerns over private economic interests all come from the global South, with the emerging economies Brazil, India and South Africa playing a leading role. The pharmaceutical companies most actively opposing public health flexibilities are transnational corporations based in the USA and Europe. Among the thirty-nine companies that sued the South African government for its Medicines Act were only two South African firms. The rest were transnationals based in the USA, Germany, the UK, Switzerland, France, Denmark and Belgium or local subsidiaries of transnational firms from these countries ('t Hoen 2001b). None of the OECD countries with firms involved in the South African court case provides legal mechanisms to implement the Doha Paragraph 6 Solution.

The top international pharmaceutical companies worked closely together, as individual firms and within their national, regional and international industry associations. No company from an OECD country voiced a critical position about the TRIPS provisions. Especially close contacts existed between the pharmaceutical industry and the US administration where the amendments to Section 301 of the Trade Agreements Act of 1979 secure private-sector influence in the USTR (Fisher and Steinhardt 1982; Sell 2002b, 2010b).

In the international organizations that had been dominated by the USA, Europe, Japan and Canada in the 1980 and 1990s, developing countries appeared increasingly as self-conscious actors. They had formed coalitions to better withstand the US and European carrot-and-stick policy of combining market access offers with trade sanction threats, which had led many developing countries to agree to TRIPS – sometimes in full knowledge that their economies would not profit from stronger intellectual property rights (Drahos 2002). The Doha Declaration, the 1999 WHA resolution on the WHO's Revised Drug Strategy, the creation of the WHO Commission on Intellectual Property Rights, Innovation and Public Health and the WIPO Development Agenda are results of the new cooperation among developing countries. Admittedly the extent of the developing countries' gains can be doubted, and some authors see the Doha Paragraph 6 Solution already again as a loss for the developing countries (Drahos 2007: 14). But the current situation is clearly at least characterized by a stalemate between proponents and critics of stronger intellectual property rights, in which no side is able to substantially change the framework of IP regulation within the international organizations. The developing countries have effectively blocked attempts to further strengthen intellectual property rights in the negotiations for a WIPO Substantive Patent Law Treaty (SPLT) (New 2005), and the USA and Europe have watered down WHO resolutions on the primacy of public health over IP and effectively limited the scope of the WTO Doha Declaration. The result of this stalemate is that the USA and Europe have increasingly resorted to bi- and plurilateral settings where they are in a stronger negotiating position. TRIPS-plus intellectual property rights have been routinely included in free trade agreements between the USA or Europe and developing countries (Correa 2006), and the attempt to create a third international organization in charge of intellectual property rights within the framework of the Anti-Counterfeiting Trade Agreement (ACTA) is another example of a forum switching strategy similar to the creation of TRIPS.

NGOs and academics were the only actor group that did not replicate the North–South divide. On the contrary, the access to medicines mobilization is characterized by a very close cooperation between northern and southern NGOs and individual activists. While funding for the network came to a significant degree from US-based foundations, such as the Ford or Rockefeller Foundations, the NGO network from the beginning included organizations from developing and developed countries and several international NGOs (INGOs) with chapters in Europe, the USA, Asia, Africa and South America. Protest mobilizations that included mass demonstrations took place in the North and the South, but within the whole conflict they remained sporadic and did not develop into a genuine transnational social movement dynamic.

The oppositional network fits very well Keck and Sikkink's characterization of a transnational advocacy network that 'includes those relevant actors working internationally on an issue, who are bound together by shared values, a common discourse, and dense exchanges of information and services' (Keck and Sikkink 1998: 2). But the analytical separation between advocacy network and social movement is weak. Many mobilizations, like the abolitionists who fought against slavery in the eighteenth and nineteenth centuries, have alternatively been called advocacy networks (Keck and Sikkink 1998) or social movements (McAdam, Tarrow and Tilly 2001). And the access to medicines mobilization certainly also fits della Porta and Diani's definition of a social movement as a social process in which actors engaged in collective action are involved in conflictual interactions with clearly identified opponents, linked by dense informal networks, and sharing a distinct collective identity (della Porta and Diani 2006: 20).

A notable element in the oppositional network was the involvement of a number of concerned academics from universities in the USA, Canada, the UK, Australia and South Africa – mostly from medical and law schools. Some of them were involved as core activists, some participated occasionally in the movement debates or provided expertise on specific issues.

The network of actors thus had the form of two non-overlapping networks consisting on the one side of the world's largest pharmaceutical companies and government representatives from core OECD countries, and on the other hand international and national NGOs and advocacy organizations, local social movements, consumer groups, churches, trade unions, foundations, academics and representatives of several developing countries' governments. Figure 5.4 gives a rough illustration of the main actors involved in these networks.

The pro IP coalition had almost limitless financial resources at their disposal and were able to exert significant political and economic pressure. The access to medicines coalition had much more limited financial resources, but was able to finance several international conferences and meetings to discuss and coordinate the campaign. Several NGOs had full-time staff devoted to the issue, and MSF and Oxfam

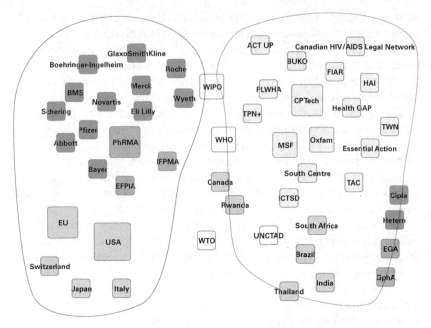

Figure 5.4 Actor coalitions in the access to medicines conflict.

Note: Core actors of the pro IP (left) and the access to medicines coalitions (right). Box size indicates centrality of the actor in the conflict, shade represents actor type (corporation: dark grey; industry association: mid grey; nation-state: pale grey; NGO: off white; international organization: white).

especially invested some of their funds in the international publicity campaign.

The conflict substantially addresses the main international framework that regulates intellectual property rights. By questioning the foundations of the dominant assumption that strong intellectual property rights are in the interest of all trading partners in the global economy, and that they would foster development in the countries of the South, the conflict has produced repercussions beyond the immediate issue of access to medicines. The mobilization addresses on a more general normative level the balance between economic and social foundations of intellectual property rights – whether social welfare should be seen as a secondary effect of economic prosperity driven by intellectual property rights, or whether social welfare should be considered in its own right as a possible limiting condition for intellectual property rights. Moreover, the conflict touches upon the power balance between countries of the global North and South. Especially for some emerging economies the conflict offered a chance to forge a more stable coalition of countries from the South to counter the hegemony of the North in the international organizations.

As in the case of software patents in Europe, we see the emergence of a dense informal cooperation network and a strong polarization between the camps. Another similarity is that command over resources is not the only and possibly not the decisive factor to explain when and why the two collective action networks were able to influence policies in their favour. Susan Sell has shown that in the formation of the TRIPS agreement successful framing was a key factor, to first raise awareness about the importance of IPRs among US, European and Japanese business organizations, and then to unite them in their lobbying efforts (Sell 2002b, 2003). The TRIPS negotiations did not receive much publicity at the time. But the access to medicines conflict was and still is fought more publicly. And therefore framing strategies play an even more pivotal role. Which framing strategies the participants of the conflict developed, how they interpreted the problem, which solutions they offered and which forms of action they advocated will be the focus of the next section.

5.4.   Framing the issue

The political process that led to TRIPS is an excellent example of a power game, in which resource-rich private actors, with support from the powerful governments of industrialized countries, were able to install a global IP regime requiring all WTO member countries to adopt strong national systems of IP protection. But resources alone cannot explain how TRIPS came into existence. In her analysis of the genesis of the agreement Susan Sell has argued that the establishment of an interpretive frame that defined intellectual property as a trade issue was another important element to explain the lobbying success of the industry coalition pushing for TRIPS (Sell 1989, 1995, 2003). According to her it 'is difficult to overestimate' the influence of Jacques Gorlin, adviser to the US Advisory Committee for Trade Negotiations (ACTN) and the private Intellectual Property Committee (IPC) (Sell 2003: 49). Gorlin's achievement was to develop a coherent argumentation framing intellectual property rights as a (free) trade issue (Gorlin 1985) – an inherently contradictory task, since intellectual property rights are by definition monopolies granted by the state for a designated period of time, and therefore intrinsically contradict the idea of free market competition. Building on Gorlin's argumentation, the business network was able to establish on the discursive level the notion of a causal relationship between patents, free trade and economic growth that Sell and Prakash summarize with the formula 'patents = free trade + investment = economic growth' (Sell and Prakash 2004: 145).

In the analysis of the software patents conflict in Europe (Chapter 4) I have shown that framing an issue the right way may sometimes be the key to success that outweighs or at least counters resource-based power (see also Haunss and Kohlmorgen 2009; Leifeld and Haunss 2012). Sell argues in a similar vein when she shows how, during the negotiations of the new WIPO copyright treaties, many of the same resource-rich and powerful actors that had lobbied for TRIPS were not able to advance their maximalist position. As a result of an intervention by a well-organized group of opponents who successfully reframed IP as an issue of 'fair use', the current WIPO copyright treaties emphasize a much more balanced approach between authors' rights and public interests (Sell 2003: 26).

In the access to medicines campaign the NGO network was faced with the task of challenging the notion established in the TRIPS negotiations that strong intellectual property rights would have beneficial welfare effects. In the following section (5.4.1) I will analyse the framing conflict that developed between the NGO network and a number of developing countries on one side and the pharmaceutical industry and some OECD countries on the other. The analysis is based on thirty documents published by core actors involved in the conflict (see Appendix 1 for a list of the documents). These documents were coded in a qualitative content analysis (Kelle, Prein and Bird 1995; Titscher et al. 2000) in which passages were identified that represent the actors' diagnostic, prognostic and motivational frames (Snow and Benford 1988). The coding was done using the qualitative data analysis package RQDA (Huang 2010). Based on this coding it is possible to identify the master frames of each of the two camps. I followed here Gerhards and Rucht's methodological approach to analyse mesomobilization processes, i.e. mobilization and negotiation processes among groups mobilizing in a common campaign (Gerhards and Rucht 1992). Similar to their study my main interest was to identify elements of the collective action frames that help the actors of a heterogeneous network to develop a common interpretation and action strategy.

5.4.1.   Public health versus IP – framing access to medicines

The background for the framing strategies employed by the actors involved in the conflict was the dramatic spread of the AIDS epidemic in sub-Saharan Africa and southeast Asia. The establishment of the Joint United Nations Programme on HIV/AIDS (UNAIDS) in 1994 is certainly an expression of the growing global awareness of the scope of the problem, but awareness of the problem does not necessarily mean that guaranteeing access to medicines was seen as the main priority to combat the epidemic. Many national and international programmes focused strongly on prevention, and only after the success of antiretroviral therapies became obvious in Europe and the USA did more and more actors begin to see the lack of access to medicines as a major hindrance for all attempts to prevent the further spread of the illness.

So when the access to medicines campaign started in the late 1990s, at least in the international health community many actors quickly agreed that improving access to medicines was critical to address the problem. The notion that 'one-third of the world's population has no guaranteed access to essential drugs' (World Health Organization 1998: 1) was not questioned by any party of the conflict. This basic diagnostic frame that defined the problem as a problem of access was shared by all relevant actors. But apart from that, interpretations of the reasons for this lack of access and the necessary steps to solve the problem varied widely.

The NGO coalition developed an overarching master frame that I propose to call *primacy of health frame* whereas the pharmaceutical industry advanced an *IP is good for health frame*. The latter was sometimes promoted in a less radical version as a *balance frame* that advocates strong intellectual property rights with some public health checks and balances. The two camps' frames can be summarized as follows:

The *primacy of health frame* was developed and used by the transnational NGO network. The various organizations did set different priorities and not always included all elements of the diagnostic and/or prognostic frame, but they agreed on the core assumption that high prices were the main problem and that economic interest should not rule public health. The patent system was identified as the main problem that 'was making drugs unaffordable for many people throughout the developing world and, on the other hand, it was doing little, if anything, to promote the research and development of drugs for diseases that only affect the poor' (Ford 2004: 138 f.). Based on the qualitative content analysis of the actors' own documents, the core elements of the primacy of health frame are:

(1) The problem is that millions of people have no access to essential medicines.
(2) The main reason for this lack of access is that the prices of those drugs are much too high in the developing world.

(3) The cause of these high prices is a market failure: drug production is driven by profit margins and not by public health needs. Intellectual property rights aggravate the problem by prohibiting competition, and trade liberalization forces developing countries to introduce and/or strengthen these intellectual property rights that are detrimental to public health.

(4) The problems can only be solved if public health concerns are given primacy over private economic interests.

(5) To solve the access problem developing countries should use compulsory licences, promote generic competition and allow parallel imports. More generally, developing countries should make use of the TRIPS flexibilities. The transition period should be extended and a moratorium should prevent developed countries from using the dispute settlement mechanism against TRIPS violations in relation to access to medicines.

(6) To address the problem more comprehensively the TRIPS agreement should be reformed and northern countries should refrain from including TRIPS-plus clauses in bilateral or regional trade agreements.

(7) Alternative mechanisms should be introduced to strengthen research and development of drugs for the needs of developing countries (Neglected Diseases Act, Medical Patent Pool) and additional financial resources should be provided to help developing countries to cope with the problem.

The first three points represent the diagnostic frame of the access to medicines coalition. In points four to seven the actors present their prognostic frame that tells them what to do. The motivational framing relies on the urgency of the health problem. This is most explicit in the more radical interpretation of some NGOs, which framed the problem not just as an access problem but as a problem of 'millions dying from preventable diseases' (TWN and Oxfam). There also existed a more radical version of the diagnostic part of the primacy of health frame, in which pharmaceutical companies were accused of 'murder' (TAC) by not providing life-saving drugs, or of supporting 'medical apartheid' (ACT UP) by taking the South African government to court because of its Medicines Act.

The primacy of health frame was also present in several WHO and UNCTAD-ICTSD publications, although the official WHO resolutions always included a statement on the merits of intellectual property rights for public health and refrained from stating a clear public health primacy. Developing countries involved in the conflict also subscribed to this frame, but also usually expressed their support for intellectual property rights in general.

The primacy of health frame was linked to several other frames, notably to a general development frame and (to a lesser extent and later in the campaign) to a human rights frame. The development frame questions the merits of strong intellectual property rights for development and had already left its mark on the TRIPS agreement where Article 7 states that intellectual property rights should contribute to the promotion of technological innovation and to the transfer and dissemination of technology.

This frame-bridging – the linking of issues in a common argumentation (Snow et al. 1986) – between the primacy of health and the development frame was essential to unify the developing countries, arguing that, for them, strong intellectual property rights would not bring a sustainable solution to their public health problems. Also, in a separate policy process many of the same countries and NGOs that were behind the access to medicines campaign were also advancing the WIPO Development Agenda that was discursively anchored in the development frame.

The link between human rights and health is most prominent in the WHO constitution stating that 'the enjoyment of the highest attainable standard of health is one of the fundamental rights of every human being', and one could argue that the assumption that every human has a right to health was a fundamental presupposition on which the campaign was based. Nevertheless, only relatively few statements from actors involved in the access to medicines conflict contain explicit references to a (human) right to health. The link between health and human rights was present in the arguments of some of the NGOs (notably TWN and Oxfam), and played an important role in the mobilizations in Brazil and Thailand against the backdrop of promises of universal health coverage, but more often the claims for access to medicines were made without an explicit reference to a right to health.

The *IP is good for health frame* was used by the pharmaceutical industry and the USTR. Its core message is that public health concerns should not have precedence over intellectual property rights, or, in other words, that intellectual property rights and public health concerns should at least be equally weighted in health policies. Again, based on the qualitative content analysis of the relevant documents, the following elements that together make up the frame can be identified:

(1) Insufficient access to essential medicines is a serious problem in many developing countries.

(2) The main reasons for this lack of access is a deficient health-care infrastructure in these countries, and poverty is the main reason for the deplorable state of the infrastructure.

(3) The solution for the infrastructure problem is economic development, and strong intellectual property rights are a precondition for technology transfer, foreign direct investment and more generally the development of industrial capacity.

(4) Intellectual property rights furthermore spur research and development for new drugs.

(5) Until the infrastructure problem is solved, philanthropic measures like drug donations and tiered pricing are the options of choice to reduce the burden on developing countries.

(6) Patent pools and alternative drug financing mechanisms like the Global Fund can also help to solve the access problem.

(7) TRIPS flexibilities strike a balance between intellectual property rights and public health; more far-reaching measures, especially parallel imports of medicines, are counterproductive.

The first two points contain the diagnostic framing of the coalition in favour of strong intellectual property rights, and the points three to seven their prognostic framing. A clear motivational framing could not be identified, but this is not very surprising since those actors acted from a dominant position and relied mainly on interventions in formalized institutional processes.

The USA and the pharmaceutical industry were the most radical proponents of the IP is good for health frame and consistently denied any negative effects of intellectual property rights. The WTO in its Doha Declaration and later also the EU took a less extreme position and conceded that patents may lead to high prices. The more radical actors in the pro IP coalition, notably the USTR, PhRMA, IFPMA and some individual pharmaceutical companies, linked the IP is good for health frame with piracy and counterfeiting, claiming that compulsory licences would be 'theft of the patented intellectual property' (PhRMA 2007) and that weaker intellectual property rights would lead to the flooding of the health-care system with counterfeit products (USTR 2010). The EU supported substantially the position of the pharmaceutical industry and the USA, but placed more emphasis on the need for a 'balanced approach' (Lamy 2004).[10]

Comparing the framing strategies of the two coalitions, one can immediately see that they disagree both in their diagnostic and their

---

[10] The documents referenced in this paragraph are listed in Appendix 1.

Table 5.2 *Issue positions in the access to medicines conflict*

Issue	Access coalition	Pro IP coalition
Core problem	Market failure	Lack of infrastructure
Patents	Restrict access to medicines	IPRs are good for health
Innovation	Alternative mechanisms	Intellectual property rights
Health	Primacy	Importance
Generics	Are critically important	Are important
Flexibilities	Should be extended	Are sufficient
Compulsory licences	Mechanism of choice	Last resort
Parallel imports	Should be allowed	Should be avoided
Prices	Generic competition	Tiered pricing
Additional funds	Private and from developed countries	Private and from developed countries
Medical R&D	Needs-driven	Incentive-driven

Note: The positions have been identified in the qualitative content analysis of the 30 core documents of the main actors involved in the conflict. A list of the documents is available in Appendix 1.

prognostic framing. While both sides start from the same fundamental problem description, they deeply disagree about the reasons for the lack of access to essential medicines and about possible solutions to the problem. Table 5.2 summarizes the conflicting issue positions of the two camps. One can easily see the fundamental disagreement in most issues and the relatively narrow area of possible compromise where the two sides agreed or at least had reconcilable positions.

While the two coalitions disagree on almost all counts they do address the same issues. They engage with the other side's arguments although little development is visible in the more than ten years of the conflict. The only area where both sides agree is that additional funds to combat the current health problems are necessary and that they should be provided by developed countries and the private sector. But of course this agreement was greatly facilitated by the entry of the Bill and Melinda Gates Foundation (BMGF) into international health politics. Today the private foundation is, after the USA, the second largest donor in the area of international health and has made funds available for public health programmes in the developing world on a scale hitherto unknown (McCoy et al. 2009).

The second relatively uncontroversial issue is the role of the generic industry. Both sides agree that generic firms should play an important role in the provision of essential drugs, but this has not prevented the

USTR from pressuring developing countries not to implement Bolar exceptions or to strengthen data exclusivity in their IP laws to impede market entry of generic products.

The main difference ultimately lies in a diverging interpretation of the relative or absolute value of intellectual property rights. The NGO and developing country coalition argues that intellectual property rights have only a derived value and therefore have to be judged by their welfare effects for the whole society. Consequently they therefore may be limited or even (temporarily) abolished if they impede the realization of health or other societal goals. The pro IP coalition essentially tries to defend the status intellectual property rights have received with the TRIPS agreement, where they are not protected as derived rights but as rights in themselves that only have to account for other rights at their margins.

The access coalition's perspective of only derivative intellectual property rights is mirrored in their framing strategy that builds on the value-laden juxtaposition of IP versus health. Their argument builds not so much on an intrinsic criticism of the current IP system but fundamentally questions the value of IP in the area of health. This value conflict resonated well with the general public. The argument that the health of people living in the developing world should be more important than the profits of a handful of northern transnational companies was taken up in many news reports. As Thomas Olesen (2006) has pointed out, this general normative argument was in the South African case combined with a portrayal of people suffering from HIV/AIDS as innocent victims upon whom bodily harm was inflicted. In her account of Oxfam's motivations to join the access campaign, Ruth Mayne furthermore highlights the strong injustice framing present in the campaign: 'This issue lent itself particularly well to popular campaigning, as it provided a powerful human illustration of how unjust global trade rules work against people in poor countries' (Mayne 2002: 247). Injustice and bodily harm against innocent victims have been identified in the literature on advocacy networks and social movements as two of the strongest mobilization frames to unite actors behind a common goal (Snow et al. 1986; Gamson 1995; Keck and Sikkink 1998).

The frame of the pro IP camp oscillates between denying the relevance of patents for the lack of access to essential medicines, offering tiered pricing as the solution for unaffordable medicines, and underlining the importance of IP for health and development.

The principal strength of the primacy of health frame is that it was able to unite a broad variety of actors. The access to medicines campaign has brought together international development and health

NGOs, AIDS activists, patients, academics, civil liberties groups, generic pharmaceutical companies and developing countries' governments to question current global IP policies. Many of them had until then never addressed IP issues nor realized how seriously they would affect their interests.

While the material success of the access coalition may be questionable, their discursive success in framing IP as a health issue cannot be denied. The Doha Declaration and several WHO resolutions acknowledge that the relationship between intellectual property rights and health is not only beneficial. The mobilization has forced the pro IP coalition to legitimize intellectual property rights on the grounds of their societal benefits. Through their mobilization the access coalition has replaced the neoliberal free market perspective that property – whether material or immaterial – would be a value in itself by the notion that, like its material counterpart, intellectual property comes with the obligation to contribute to the common good, a notion more compatible with ideas of a social market economy.

5.5.   Context, actors and frames of the access to medicines conflict

The access to medicines conflict was – and to some extent still is – a truly global conflict that addresses core elements of the international system of intellectual property rights. Its multi-level and multi-arena nature makes it more complex than the software patents conflict presented in the previous chapter. But despite this complexity, core elements can be identified in terms of its context, actors and framing

The political and institutional *context* of the conflicts is characterized by a strong North–South cleavage. The stark differences in economic capacity and wealth between the countries of the global North and the global South are the foundation on which the conflict developed. The AIDS crisis has amplified the realization that an individual's fundamental life chances depend heavily on the region he or she lives in. Contracting HIV in Western Europe or the USA today is a major nuisance that requires constant medical treatment with antiretroviral drugs, contracting HIV in sub-Saharan Africa still means a very high probability of imminent death. The conflict thus is in line with the re-actualization of the North–South conflict after the end of the Cold War. It is remarkable in that it facilitated the formation of a southern coalition led by the newly industrializing countries Brazil, South Africa and India.

The system of international organizations, in particular the WTO, WHO and WIPO, provides the main arenas for the conflict. But it also involved several local policy conflicts in which local actor constellations and power structures influenced the dynamics of the contentious inter-actions. The structural framework in which the conflict takes place is thus composed of the international legal system, the institutional bar-gaining structures of the international institutions and the local imple-mentation of international rules. As in the software patents case, the conflict about access to medicines is thus mainly located at the inter-national, not the national, level. This is in line with the expectations from theories of the knowledge society that nation-states will gradually lose their central role at the expense of transnational institutions and networks. But on the other hand locality in terms of structural loca-tion within the global North and South is reaffirmed, contradicting the notions of a declining importance of physical place and space.

The *network of actors* only partially reflects the multi-level structure of the conflict. On one side are the big pharmaceutical companies, their industry associations and northern countries' governments led by the USA. The access coalition is composed of international and national NGOs, several southern governments, a number of social movement organizations (SMOs) and some individual activists, of which most are based in academic institutions. Only the oppositional coalition involves to a relevant degree local actors that are able to act independ-ently from their international allies. Interestingly international organ-izations appear not only as arenas but also as actors in the conflict. In this capacity both WIPO and WHO were receptive for the access coalition's claims and – especially in the case of WHO – also provided some support. Again, similar to the software patents conflict, with the oppositional actor network a new collective actor emerges that is trans-national, united by a distinct collective action frame, and that did not play a role in the area of IP politics before the access to medicines con-flict started.

At the discursive level two clearly distinguishable opposing *frames* have been employed that I have labelled *primacy of health* versus *IP is good for health*. I have detailed above how these two frames differ in almost every aspect. On a meta-level that is not explicitly addressed in the framing, these frames contain strong assumptions about the appropriate governance of knowledge in the field of health. The pri-macy of health frame is essentially an argumentation for *socio-political* governance structures. This means the access coalition, which uses this frame, argues that the granting of intellectual property rights in the field of health should depend on the health benefits such temporary monopolies provide, and that decisions about the availability and scope of intellectual property rights should be made in a political process that involves all parties that are affected by such a decision – and include in particular health-care institutions and patients.

The IP is good for health frame used by the pharmaceutical industry and northern governments is essentially a *techno-economic* frame. The argumentation here is that the availability and scope of intellectual property rights should be primarily governed by economic considerations, so that monetary incentives create the base for technical advances that will then benefit patients all over the world.

5.6. Access to medicines – a conflict of the knowledge society

The actors involved in the access to medicines conflict have invested significant resources – financial, labour and time – in a struggle that has now lasted more than fifteen years. The persistence of the conflict is certainly an expression of the sheer value of the global pharmaceutical market and the profits it generates for the pharmaceutical industry. But the intractability of the conflict is also an expression of an underlying conflict structure that addresses two pillars of the knowledge society: like the software patents conflict, access to medicines is also a conflict about the mode of innovation. Only this time the conflict is not about the production of innovation but about the governance of innovation.

Overall the industrial innovation model that locates the capability for innovation in large-scale industrial production complexes and in specialized research institutions is not questioned by either side of the conflict. The dissent is about the rules that govern the institutional framework within which innovation is produced. The IP maximalist camp argues that these rules should in essence follow a *techno-economic logic*, that is, they should maximize the economic incentives for technological innovation. The access coalition on the other side argues for a normatively guided political framework in which innovation should not primarily follow technological feasibility but be guided by *social welfare concerns* and in which political decisions and not private investment define the course of innovation.

The conflict about access to medicines has furthermore a *redistributive component*. At stake is a system that guarantees a basic standard of human existence (health) for everyone. The access to medicines conflict thus contains traces of a more general conflict between neoliberal and welfare-state conceptions. Ultimately the conflict revolves around the question whether the creation of property should come with strings attached or not. The proponents of a socio-political frame argue that by analogy with the material world, intellectual property should also entail obligations on the part of property owners ('Eigentum verpflichtet'). This argumentation emphasizes the aspect that intellectual property rights should be seen as privileges granted in exchange for the creation of knowledge goods from which the public should benefit.

The most recent developments around the creation of prize funds and patent pools highlight a third dimension of the conflict: in the shadow of the stalemate between the two camps, ideas for the creation of a commons or a public domain of medical knowledge are gaining ground. The conflict thus contributes to the wider debate about alternatives to the ex-post monetary incentive of intellectual property rights for the creation of knowledge goods, by advocating alternative mechanisms which may fulfil at the international level a similar function to tax-financed public research funding in universities and other research institutions at the national level. Patent pools and prize funds transcend the traditionally national provision of public goods. But other aspects of the conflict reaffirm the importance of place and territory.

The strong North–South polarization of the access to medicines conflict contradicts a notion present more or less explicitly in all theories of the knowledge society: that, compared to industrial societies, power in the knowledge society would be based less on territorial entities. While Castells concedes the possibility of switched-off regions, the bipolar structure of the access to medicines conflict does not fit well with the notion that in the network society the space of flows would take precedence over the space of places (Castells 2000).

In the conflict two kinds of transnational networks appeared: on the one side the transnational industry network of pharmaceutical companies and their trade associations, on the other side the transnational network of NGOs, SMOs, engaged individual activists and various other actors. The first network is transnational, but in a limited sense. Its core members all come from a handful of highly developed countries of the global North. It has well-established cooperation relationships with the relevant government officials in the world's most powerful countries. The other network is truly transnational in a global sense and comprises actors from all regions of the world. It has also established cooperation relationships with government actors, but only with those of less powerful countries.

Compared to the software patents conflict, the social welfare aspect was much more prominent – on the local level as a demand for a right to health, and on the global level as a demand to revise the IP framework to enable economic development. Unlike the software patents conflict, the access to medicines mobilization was dominated by established NGOs with a long history of development and health politics. But the broad coalition was only possible once these NGOs started to address issues outside their core policy fields, and only after they integrated the crucial issue of the governance of intellectual property rights into their conceptual framework. Only by addressing the problem of access to medicines as a problem of the changing property system in the knowledge society were they able to construct a master frame to which all parties of the heterogeneous collective action network could subscribe.

6   Pirates and commoners

The conflicts about software patents in Europe and about access to medicines involved tens or even hundreds of thousands of activists staging demonstrations, signing petitions, lobbying decision-makers and amassing alternative expertise. They were the first two major mobilizations which questioned a core pillar of the knowledge economy – the international system of intellectual property rights. Many other initiatives, protests and mobilizations have addressed issues related to the production of knowledge, its economic use and valorization, and the rules that govern access to knowledge. Student protests have mobilized about learning and teaching conditions and about access to tertiary education. The 'University of the People' – a not-for-profit project – aims to provide access to tuition-free online education for people without access to a functioning higher-education system (University of the People 2011). Some social movements have addressed intellectual property as one issue among others in their mobilizations: the transnational peasants' movement 'La Via Campesina' has campaigned for farmers' rights to reuse a part of their crop as seeds, a traditional right that has become endangered by the TRIPS requirement for countries to adopt protection of plant varieties through patents or other means (CIPR 2002: 3; Desmarais 2007). The German branch of the alter-globalization network Attac has a working group that deals with IP issues and globalization (Bödeker, Moldenhauer and Rubbel 2005). These and other examples indicate that a variety of actors are becoming aware of the relevance of intellectual property rights for their respective policy field.

Among these mobilizations two stick out and merit more detailed attention: the creation of Pirate Parties and the mobilization around Creative Commons. The Pirate Parties are an important case because they have helped to bring IP issues closer to the centre of the parliamentary system. Their electoral campaigns not only provided them with two elected representatives in the European Parliament, but also forced other parties to position themselves in relation to the issues raised by the Pirate Parties. The importance of Creative Commons is not primarily reflected in the number of activists engaged in the project, but in the remarkable adoption rate of its alternative licence by millions of internet users, who have in a very short time already created a sizable pool of creative works that are free to use for everyone. Together with the conflict about software patents in Europe and the access to medicines campaign, the four cases are the most relevant contentious mobilizations that address the rules that govern the creation and use of knowledge in the knowledge society.

Compared to the other two conflicts, and reflecting the fact that the mobilizations of the Pirate Parties and Creative Commons involved a much smaller number of activists, the following two case studies will be shorter and less detailed. But the analysis will nevertheless address the same underlying questions about the contexts in which the mobilizations have developed, the configuration of actors and their framing strategies. The goal is to show which conflict lines are their point of departure, whether or not the mobilizations entail the creation of new collective actors, how the actors interpret their actions in a broader interpretive framework and, thus, how these mobilizations relate to more general conflicts in the knowledge society.

6.1.   The rise of Pirate Parties

In the struggle over unauthorized copying of copyright-protected software, music and other digital goods, industry associations have customarily labelled those who they accused of unauthorized copying as 'pirates'. The term was already frequently used in the debates about the unauthorized copying of sheet music in the nineteenth century (Johns 2002), and every new technology like tape recorders, photocopying machines or VCRs, which made the copying of books, music, films or software easier, led to a new wave of condemnation of piracy (Halbert 1997; Lessig 2004; Boyle 2008). But the figure of the pirate, which was meant to condemn the act of copyright infringement, carries with it an ambivalence that subverts the intention of the anti-piracy discourse. The pirate, as depicted in numerous (children's) books and Hollywood movies, is often not a villain but a rebel, who fights against unjust rule and lives the life of an adventurer.

6.1.1.   The Swedish Piratpartiet

It is thus not surprising that in 2003 a group of Swedish internet activists adopted the piracy symbolism and founded Piratbyrån (The

Bureau of Piracy), a website to coordinate their activities, publish texts reflecting on copyright, file-sharing and digital culture, and offer tutorials on how to use peer-to-peer file-sharing programs to distribute and download digital content on the internet.[1] A few months later, in November 2003, several Piratbyrån activists founded the BitTorrent tracker site 'The Pirate Bay' (Fleischer and Torsson 2006), which took advantage of the Swedish law that at that time allowed the downloading of copyrighted files and only criminalized the uploading of these files.[2] Owing to its rapid growth, The Pirate Bay was soon organizationally separated from Piratbyrån, but the two organizations nevertheless remained closely connected since the people running The Pirate Bay continued to be involved in Piratbyrån (Miegel and Olsson 2008). Gottfrid Svartholm, one of the administrators of The Pirate Bay, characterized the relationship between the two organizations in an interview in the following way: 'Piratbyrån does the political stuff – rallies, petitions, lobbying, etc., but also publishes a lot on the practical, moral and philosophical issues of file sharing. ... [The Pirate Bay's] goal is to help people exchange information, much of which happens to be copyrighted' (Ingram 2005).

The Pirate Bay was immediately anathema to the music and film industry, which at that time had filed a number of high-profile lawsuits against developers of peer-to-peer software programs and individual users of file-sharing networks in the USA (Li 2009: 288). The Pirate Bay was vigorously attacked by the music and film industry, which several times tried unsuccessfully to take the website offline, until they finally succeeded in filing a suit against the founders of The Pirate Bay, Peter Sunde, Fredrik Neij and Gottfrid Svartholm, and against Carl Lundström who had financially supported the website and provided webspace and internet connectivity. The trial ended in April 2009 with the conviction of all four defendants, but did not stop the website from being online and growing (the internet traffic analysis site Alexa

---

[1] In 2009 Piratbyrån received the Prix Ars Electronica for striving 'to educate the general public by presenting a broad, citizen-centered view of the facts & circumstances beyond the narrow views of lobbying associations' on issues of copyright, intellectual property, and the sharing of information and cultural artefacts (http://new.aec.at/prix/en/gewinner/2009/#digital-communities, accessed 20 May 2011).

[2] A BitTorrent tracker is a website that hosts torrent files that contain meta-data about the files that are offered for download by individual internet users based on the BitTorrent peer-to-peer file-sharing protocol. The website thus does not store any potentially copyright infringing files, but offers the necessary information that client programs need to find the files in the distributed peer-to-peer network (see http://en.wikipedia.org/wiki/BitTorrent_%28protocol%29).

ranked The Pirate Bay in 2008 at position 120 among all internet sites worldwide; by 2011 it was the top 90th website).

The enormous popularity of The Pirate Bay among internet users and the relentless attempts of the content industry to take the site off-line and sue the site operators for copyright infringement generated a lot of media attention for the issues of file-sharing and intellectual property rights. This created a conducive climate for a third pirate-branded organization in Sweden, the Piratpartiet (Pirate Party).

The Swedish Pirate Party was founded in January 2006 by a group around Rickard Falkvinge, who became the party's first leader. In less than twenty-four hours the party collected more than the 2,000 signatures that were necessary to register with the Swedish Election Authority to participate in the Swedish general election scheduled for 17 September of the same year. The party's campaign goal is limited to a three-point agenda consisting of strengthening privacy protection, reforming the copyrights system to generally allow copying and sharing of copyrighted works for non-commercial purposes and abolishing the patent system (Piratpartiet 2008).

Initially only a modest number of people joined the party, allowing its membership to climb to a little less than 2,000 by the end of April. But then the Swedish police did the Pirate Party a big favour when on 31 May they seized the servers on which The Pirate Bay was running. This led to several demonstrations and a distributed denial of service (DDOS) attack on Swedish police servers (Libbenga 2006), and gained the Pirate Party almost 500 new members on the day of the raid and another 900 the following day; within a week the membership count tripled to more than 6,000 members, and then climbed steadily to 9,200 in the run-up to the election (see Figure 6.1).

In the Swedish election campaign the party received much press coverage and commentators agree that the party had a strong influence on the other parties' campaigning, leading to changes in the Swedish Green Party's (Miljöpartiet de Gröna), the Moderate Party's (Moderaterna) and the Left Party's (Vänsterpartiet) position on file-sharing (TankGirl 2006). In the Swedish election the pirates gained a mere 0.63 per cent of the votes, which was less than four times its membership count. In the following years party membership dropped to around 5,000, only rising again in the run-up to the European election in 2009. According to Marie Demker, the debate about the Swedish Signal Intelligence Act, which gives the Swedish National Defence Radio Establishment (FRA, Swedish Försvarets Radioanstalt) the right to intercept trans-border internet traffic, was another event that mobilized support for the Pirate Party (Demker 2011: 4), but this is not reflected in the membership

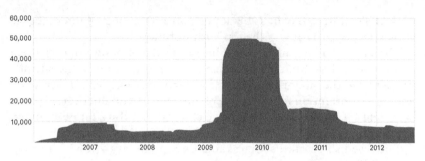

Figure 6.1 Membership development of the Swedish Piratpartiet (2006–12).

Source: http://data.piratpartiet.se/Charts/MemberCountHistory.aspx.

numbers. They started to rise once more only in the wake of the trial against The Pirate Bay. The prosecution of file-sharing bestowed the Piratpartiet with another push in media attention and skyrocketing membership numbers. The harsh sentencing in the Pirate Bay trial, in which the defendants were sentenced to one year in prison and a fine of SEK30 million (about €2.7 million), led to protests against the trial by more than a thousand people in Stockholm and to a tripling of the Swedish Pirate Party's membership within a month from 15,000 just before the verdict on 17 April to more than 45,000 one month later – making them the fourth largest Swedish party in terms of membership (Ernesto [pseud.] 2009).

The election to the European Parliament was a huge success for the Swedish Pirate Party. They gained 7.1 per cent of the Swedish vote, securing them their first parliamentary representation with two seats in the European Parliament filled by Christian Engström and Amelia Andersdotter.[3] But in the following national election in September 2010 they were not able to repeat this surprising result and gained only 0.65 per cent of the vote, bringing them down to almost exactly the result of the previous national election. Membership numbers plummeted as well. The majority of those who had joined the party after the trial against The Pirate Bay did not extend their one-year membership – in contrast to other parties, members of the Pirate Party have to actively

---

[3] Originally the Piratpartiet only gained one seat in the European election in 2009. With the Lisbon Treaty entering into force on 1 December 2009, the member countries' relative strengths in the parliament have changed, giving the Swedish Pirate Party a second mandate which Amelia Andersdotter was only able to fill two years later after all member states had finally ratified the treaty.

renew their membership each year – bringing the party again down to about 7,600 members in September 2012.

The idea of Pirate Parties quickly spread beyond the Swedish borders. Soon after the first Pirate Party was founded in Sweden, similar parties emerged in several other countries. The website of Pirate Parties International (PPI)[4] lists sixteen officially registered Pirate Parties and twenty-four countries with parties in formation. In most cases these parties are very small and only in Germany, the Czech Republic and Switzerland have they gained parliamentary seats in local or regional elections. I will take a closer look at the development in Germany because of all the Pirate Parties, the German Piratenpartei is by far the largest and most active.

6.1.2. The German Piratenpartei

The German Piratenpartei is, with more than 33,000 members in September 2012,[5] the largest Pirate Party in terms of membership, and also one of the oldest. It was founded on 10 September 2006, as a reaction to the criminalization of The Pirate Bay, and encouraged by the success of the Swedish pirates. While the Piratenpartei received some – often favourable – news coverage, its membership numbers grew only slowly to around a thousand in the time between its foundation and May 2009. At the European election on 7 June the Piratenpartei gained a surprising 0.9 per cent of the vote (229,464 votes), and by the end of the year the party was able to increase its membership to around 11,400. Christoph Bieber and Henning Bartels have argued that this rapid expansion was not so much fuelled by the relatively successful European election results but resulted mainly from the massive mobilization around privacy and internet censorship in the weeks immediately after the European election, the so-called #zensursula campaign, the e-petition to the German Bundestag against the proposed 'Zugangserschwerungsgesetz' (access restriction law),[6] and the campaign 'Freedom not Fear' (Freiheit statt Angst) against surveillance and internet censorship (Bartels 2009;

---

[4] According to its website (www.pp-international.net/about, accessed 21 November 2012), PPI is an NGO, founded in April 2010 in Brussels, with the aim of helping to establish, support, promote and maintain communication and cooperation between Pirate Parties around the world.

[5] Source: https://wiki.piratenpartei.de/Mitglieder (accessed 21 November 2012).

[6] https://epetitionen.bundestag.de/petitionen/_2009/_04/_22/Petition_3860.nc.html (accessed 21 November 2012).

Bieber 2011). The term #zensursula was used as a hash-tag to enable the search for messages related to this campaign in the internet short message service Twitter. The meme is assembled from the German word Zensur (censorship) and the first name of the then German Federal Minister for Family Affairs, Senior citizens, Women and Youth (Bundesfamilienministerin) Ursula von der Leyen, who was the leading protagonist of the Zugangserschwerungsgesetz, the law to restrict access to child-pornographic content in communication networks.

Although the German Pirate Party was not the initiator of any of these campaigns, members of the party were involved and publicly supported them, so that in the media these campaigns were often directly associated with the Piratenpartei. The #zensursula campaign and the e-petition both addressed the proposed law to restrict access to child-pornographic content in communication networks (Zugangserschwerungsgesetz). The law requires internet service providers (ISPs) to block traffic to websites with child-pornographic content if they are on a list maintained by the German federal criminal police office (BKA) and to record the user data (IP number and time) of those trying to access such sites. The opponents of the proposed law argued that instead of building a blocking infrastructure, which effectively is a complex internet surveillance infrastructure that can easily be augmented to block access to other unwanted content on the internet, resources should be focused on deleting child-pornographic sites – a procedure that would be more effective in combatting child pornography and less intrusive in terms of internet privacy (for a detailed discussion of the legislative process and the positions of the various actors see Meister 2011). The e-petition ended on 16 June with 134,015 signatures, making it the petition with the highest number of supporters until then. The #zensursula campaign culminated in demonstrations in seventeen cities under the slogan 'Löschen statt Sperren' (delete not block) on 20 June 2009, two days after the German Bundestag had adopted the controversial law.

The 'Freiheit statt Angst' campaign stood in the tradition of similar anti-surveillance and pro-privacy-protection campaigns of earlier years and addressed on a more general level the built-up of surveillance infrastructures in the physical (CCTV cameras) and virtual (access blocking, traffic monitoring, data retention) world and the growing disregard for privacy concerns by commercial and government actors. The campaign mobilized about 20,000 protesters to a demonstration in Berlin on 12 September (Krempl 2009). The protest received widespread media attention, and pictures with demonstrators waving the

Pirate Party's orange flags with the pirate ship logo were often used to represent the protest in the print and TV news.[7]

The Piratenpartei was one among many organizations involved in these mobilizations, but unlike the Greens and the Left Party who also supported the Freedom not Fear demonstration, the pirates were able to capitalize on these mobilizations. Two weeks later in the German general election on 27 September 2009, the Piratenpartei received 2 per cent (847,870) of the votes. In the ensuing state-level elections they were at first not able to reproduce this result, but in September 2011 they received an astonishing 8.9 per cent of the votes in the election to the Berlin state parliament (Abgeordnetenhaus). Since then the German Pirate Party has been able to produce similar results in every state election, with 7.4 per cent in Saarland (March 2012), 8.5 per cent in Schleswig-Holstein and 7.8 per cent in North Rhine-Westphalia (both May 2012), and is consistently ranked between 3 and 5 per cent in national election polls (for a more detailed discussion of the German Pirate Party, see Bieber and Leggewie 2012).

6.1.3.   Sailing on unstable seas

The development of the Swedish and the German Pirate Parties seems to follow different trajectories. Until 2011 the development of the two parties followed a similar pattern where membership numbers and electoral success strongly fluctuated and depended highly on the availability of mobilizing events that generate attention for the issues these parties address. The trial against The Pirate Bay and reform of the Swedish copyright law, and the debate about access restriction measures and the plans for far-reaching data-retention laws in Germany have provided temporary opportunities which the pirates were able to exploit. These events brought them media attention, party members and votes. More recently the Swedish Pirate Party has lost most of the members who joined the party in the wake of the trial against The Pirate Bay, although it still has more members than the smallest of the eight Swedish parties with parliamentary representation. Membership of the German pirates had been stagnating after the federal election in 2009 but then started to rise sharply after the successful state elections.

Reliable information about the demographic characteristics of the party members is only available for the Swedish Pirate Party, where the

---

[7] See e.g. www.spiegel.de/netzwelt/netzpolitik/0,1518,648623,00.html (accessed 24 May 2011) or www.tagesschau.de/inland/datenschutzdemonstration100.html (accessed 24 May 2011).

party website provides detailed information about the activists. The party members are mostly men in their twenties and thirties. In May 2011 only 12 per cent of party members were women and the median age of party members was 29 years, with the average age being 33. The German Pirate Party does not provide such detailed information and does deliberately not collect information on the gender of party members. The information that is available shows that the German pirates are even younger, with an average age of 29.[8] In Germany the next 'youngest' party with an average age of its members of 46 years is the Green Party (Niedermayer 2011). Obviously the concerns that the Pirate Parties address are predominantly shared by the younger generation of heavy internet users. In their age structure the Pirate Parties show strong similarities to the German Green Party at the time when they were founded in 1980, although the Greens had significantly more female members (Raschke 1993: 213).

At least until 2011 the Pirate Parties in Sweden and Germany have been more successful in mobilizing adherents than in mobilizing voters. This suggests that they may actually be more like social movement organizations (SMOs) than political parties, providing a platform for the organization of like-minded activists. While the fate of the Swedish Pirate Party as a political party seems to be gloomy, it is still too early to judge whether the German Pirate Party will be able to establish itself as a permanent and relevant player in the German party landscape. But it is clear – and recent research by Leonard Dobusch and Kirsten Gollatz corroborates this finding – that the links between protest mobilization and party remain strong, and that the development of the Pirate Parties and their recent electoral success can only be understood if one realizes that they belong to a cluster of IP-related social movements (Dobusch and Gollatz 2012: 27).

6.2.   Pirate frames

What do the Pirate Parties stand for? Which grievances do they address? Which frames do they offer in order to interpret the issues around which they mobilize? The following analysis is based on a qualitative content analysis of the party manifestos of the Swedish and German Pirate Parties. Both manifestos have been revised many times since

---

[8] Sources for the membership data: www.piratpartiet.se/partiet/medlemsstatistik-admin (accessed 21 November 2012) and http://wiki.piratenpartei.de/wiki//index.php?title= Datei:Durchschnittsalter.eps (accessed 21 November 2012); no detailed data about age composition or gender was available for the German Pirate Party.

2006, and both parties provide detailed information on their website about the nature of the changes.

6.2.1. *Sweden*

The Swedish Pirate Party's manifesto strongly reflects the conditions of its foundation. The 'Declaration of Principles (Princippprogram version 3.4)' is quite compact and contains only three main points (Piratpartiet 2010). It has been amended four times, broadening its scope a bit, without changing any of the core claims and frames.

The Piratpartiet's manifesto addresses the issues of (1) data protection and citizens' rights, (2) cultural production and copyright, and (3) patents and private monopolies. The pirates claim that the right to privacy is a fundamental right on which other basic human rights like the right to free speech, freedom of opinion, access to information, or cultural and personal development are built. Every person must have the right to anonymity and therefore the protection of postal secrets should be expanded to all forms of communication. For the Swedish Pirate Party privacy, anonymity and protection of personal data are necessary preconditions for a functioning democracy and should therefore be strongly protected. Recent laws (the data-retention directive) that allow the government to collect personal data should therefore be repealed. In programme revisions the claims that the democracy deficit of the European Union should be addressed, that citizens should have a right to unrestricted internet access, and that internet service providers (ISPs) must follow the principles of network neutrality – i.e. treat all internet traffic indiscriminately without blocking or limiting certain kinds of traffic (e.g. file-sharing) – have been added to the manifesto. The programme thus combines in its first chapter general claims about citizens' rights in the field of privacy with more specific claims about the governance of the information infrastructure, especially the internet.

The second point that is raised in the party manifesto is the issue of cultural production and copyrights. Here the pirates (historically not really correct – see Chapter 3) argue that copyrights were originally meant to protect authors but have developed into tools to restrict access to humankind's cultural heritage and favour commercial over public interest. They suggest a copyright reform with a drastically shorter protection period of five years from the date of publication, the right to share and copy works for non-profit use, and the banning of restriction management technologies (DRM, digital rights management). The core argument is that a better balance between private and public interest should be found to promote the creation of a cultural commons.

The claims in this section are very concrete and address the regulation of a specific policy field, the frames, on the other hand, refer to general principles like cultural diversity, balance and abundance.

The third section of the Swedish Pirate Party's manifesto deals with patents. The claims are here more radical than in the field of copyrights: the Pirate Party wants to (gradually) abolish patents because they stifle innovation and the creation of knowledge, and cause – in the case of pharmaceutical patents – preventable human deaths. The framing in this part combines the human tragedy argument with a utilitarian argumentation about patent inefficiency and with a normative argument that patents are, because they are monopolies, running against the ideals of free and fair markets. Instead of being enclosed by patents, research results (and public records) should be made available in open access repositories. In a recent revision of the party manifesto, a paragraph about trademarks was added to this section. The argument here is that the Pirate Party does not oppose the existence of trademarks as long as they serve to protect consumers from fake, low-quality copies and are not used to curb the freedom of expression.

In the closing remarks the party manifesto contains one more important claim, which was added in 2008 to the programme: while the work of the party is focused on parliamentary means, the pirates clearly formulate that they will not strive to be part of a government, but rather use parliament as a platform to advance the party's goals – an explicit claim about the oppositional character of the party, supporting the notion of the Piratpartiet being more an SMO than a traditional political party.

6.2.2. Germany

The original 2006 manifesto of the German Piratenpartei was similar to its Swedish counterpart, although a bit more extensive, containing claims about (1) the copyright system, (2) privacy and data protection, (3) the patent system, (4) transparency, (5) open access and (6) infrastructure monopolies. It was extended several times so that it now covers fifteen points (Piratenpartei 2010).

In the area of copyrights the German Pirate Party demanded that non-commercial copying and use of works should be allowed and actively encouraged. In their manifesto the Pirate Party recognizes authors' rights but wants to drastically reduce the protection period to facilitate the creation of a public domain of cultural goods. These claims are based on the arguments that access to knowledge is a necessary precondition for the social, technical and economic development of our society, that a balance between economic interests of creators and the public should be sought, leading to a copyright system that guarantees the sustainability of the public domain, and that the production of artificial scarcity through DRM systems is morally wrong.

The second chapter of the party manifesto contains claims about privacy and data protection. Here the pirates argue that privacy rights are the indispensable conditions of democracy. Every citizen has thus the right to anonymity, which should be guaranteed by expanding the legal protection of postal secrets to all forms of communication. As a consequence the Pirate Party does not support data retention and comprehensive video-surveillance. Instead the party demands an encompassing right of 'informational self-determination' (informationelle Selbstbestimmung) – a term established in the public discourse by the German Federal Constitutional Court in its ruling about the constitutionality of the census law in 1984 (Simitis 1984). Every citizen should always be able to know who stores which data about her/him and shall have a right to require correction or deletion of this data. Overall the Pirate Party argues for 'data parsimony' to reduce the amount of data stored about each individual. Privacy rights are framed by the Pirate Party as essential citizens' rights. Their protection is seen as an especially urgent issue in Germany because of its history of two dictatorships in the twentieth century. The technical possibility of data collection has to be actively curbed to prevent the development of a surveillance society.

The German Pirate Party's claims about the future of the patent system are less radical than those of their Swedish sister party. They argue that patents have become obstacles to innovation and that therefore the patent system has to be revised or replaced by a more adequate system. They strongly oppose the patentability of living organisms, genes and software, arguing that innovations in these fields are not inventions and patents in these areas constrict the development of a knowledge society. The dominant argumentative frame in this section is a free market frame that contradicts the granting of monopolies.

In the final three points of the original manifesto, the German Pirate Party demands that all administrative decision-making processes should be transparent and that all citizens should have the right to access all information on which administrative decisions are based. They claim that all publicly funded research, software and digital goods should be made available in open access repositories (in later versions the demand for open standards and open source software has been added to this section of the manifesto). And finally they oppose infrastructure monopolies in the area of telecommunication, arguing that monopolies restrict innovation and should be replaced by a decentralized structure that embraces the principle of network neutrality. This section was expanded and restructured in later versions of the manifesto, putting more emphasis on the aspect of citizens' participation in the digital world, adding the claim that access to digital communication is an essential precondition for participation in current societies, and therefore should never be restricted or cut off. Also added was the demand that no laws should require internet service providers (ISPs) to monitor their users, because the separation of powers authorizes only the courts and the police to conduct criminal prosecutions, which should not be privatized or replaced by indiscriminate content filtering and censorship.

The dominant frames in these sections are democracy and popular sovereignty frames, arguing that open access and open standards would enhance democratic participation while attempts to restrict the free flow of information would limit the possibility of free communication, which is the foundation of a functioning democracy.

Until November 2010 the manifesto underwent only minor revisions. At their party convention on 7 July 2009 in Hamburg, a section on education was added in which the pirates demand free access to primary, secondary and tertiary education and a democratization of the educational institutions. In 2010, at the party convention on 16 May in Bingen, a section entitled 'more democracy', in which the pirates state that democracy is the best possible form of government, that new technologies offer possibilities to enhance citizen participation, and that the freedom of individual representatives should be strengthened, was added as the first point of the manifesto.

In the run-up to several state-level elections in 2011 the pirates significantly expanded their programme at their party convention on 21 November 2010 in Chemnitz, adding chapters about securing basic needs and participation, gender and family, environment, whistle-blowing, the court system and information freedom laws. These additions were the subject of contentious debates within the party, in which one faction – among them the party leader Jens Seipenbusch – wanted to keep the party programme limited to the core issues of privacy, data protection and intellectual property rights whereas another faction wanted to expand the party's agenda to more policy fields (Laaff 2010). At the convention the latter faction succeeded, expanding the manifesto from nine to fifteen points, in which the party now demands a social security system that guarantees a basic income[9] for each citizen,

---

[9] After a heated debate the party manifesto deliberately avoids the term 'basic income' and instead talks about an 'income to secure existence' (Einkommen zur Existenzsicherung), which is conceptually the same.

a sustainable environmental policy, legal protection for whistle-blowers, and a gender and family policy that puts same-sex partnerships on a par with traditional marriage, allows individuals to freely choose a gender identity, expands the system of 'registered partnerships'[10] to more than two persons and secures full-time childcare facilities.

The resulting party manifesto is a mixed bag of demands that lacks a coherent framework and now contains claims on some issues (freedom of information, transparency, childcare) in the same or slightly different form in multiple sections. Most likely this programme will again be significantly altered at future party conventions.

The Swedish and German Pirate Parties' core claims and frames can be summarized as follows (see Table 6.1): they demand strong individual citizens' rights to protect personal data and public expression.[11] Their diagnostic framing stands in a liberal civil-rights tradition that emphasizes individual rights and sees civil rights as protective rights against state intrusion. In contrast to their liberal predecessors, they locate the main danger not in physical space but in the virtual realm. Where civil rights advocates of earlier periods have campaigned for freedom of expression in public places and print publications, the pirates are mainly concerned with the internet and communication technologies more generally. Their concern is not public gatherings and the possibility to build associations, but the unrestricted flow of data, and protection of and control over personal information.

In the field of cultural production and innovation their vision is strongly influenced by a market-liberal perspective that embraces the market as the superior productive and allocative mechanism. Here their core diagnostic frame is an anti-monopolistic free competition frame that identifies the inefficiencies and free market distorting effects of intellectual property rights as the main problem. These utilitarian arguments are sometimes accompanied by normative arguments where the parties refer to general human rights or historical precedents. The liberal argument is also prevalent in their prognostic frames where the pirates make claims about administrative or participatory reforms, and where they focus, again, on individual participation and the right to control administrations and governments.

Redistributive questions are not on the core policy agenda of the Pirate Parties. The latest changes to the German Pirate Party's manifesto have added some redistributive claims (basic income, provision of free

---

[10] Registered partnerships are under German law same-sex relationships that are in selected, but not all, aspects equal to traditional marriages.

[11] Dobusch and Gollatz show that these core claims are those most widely shared among other Pirate Parties as well (Dobusch and Gollatz 2012: 30).

Table 6.1 *The Pirate Parties' core claims and frames*

Policy field	Claim	Frame
Privacy	• Data protection • Right to anonymity • No surveillance	• Basic human/citizens' right • Precondition for democracy • Informational self-determination • History of dictatorships
Cultural production	• Restriction of copyrights (5 years) • Non-commercial copying and sharing • No DRM	• Public interest • Balance • Cultural diversity
Innovation	• Reform or abolish patents	• Inefficiency • Free (and fair) markets • Patents stifle innovation
Governance	• Transparency	• Citizen participation • Popular sovereignty

education and childcare), but so far not in a consistent way. The pirates can thus be seen as a form of knowledge society liberalism that has strong conceptual – although only few personal or institutional – links to the civil-rights liberalism of the second half of the twentieth century.

6.3.   Pirates in the knowledge society

The Pirate Parties address all three levels of conflict that were present in the theoretical literature on knowledge societies. They address the level of inclusion/exclusion and personal autonomy with their demands for civil rights in a digital world, they address the level of knowledge production in their demands on reforming and/or abolishing parts of the current intellectual property rights system, and they address the level of access to knowledge with their claims about free non-commercial copying and sharing and their emphasis on securing the richness of the public domain. The lynchpin of their programme is the protection of privacy and personal information, and here the pirates address a conflict that was not – or only marginally – present in the mobilizations about software patents and access to medicines.

In a paper about the Swedish Pirate Party, Marie Demker argues that the pirates would address a new cleavage of the knowledge society between knowledge and market in which the notion of knowledge as a tradable commodity would be opposed to the notion of knowledge as a collective process and shared resource (Demker 2011: 3). A closer look at the pirates' argumentation reveals that this is a false opposition. The Swedish and the German Pirate Parties are not opposed to the commodification of knowledge. On the contrary, the pirates are strong supporters of free market principles. They only oppose the monopolization of knowledge and demand the possibility of non-commercial use and access.

The more fundamental conflict line of the knowledge society that the pirates address is the one about personal rights in the digital realm. Data protection and the right to privacy and anonymity in the virtual world protect the integrity of the individual in cyberspace. The control over personalized digital data is a key power technology in the twenty-first century. Democratic and undemocratic states alike have extended their surveillance capacities and infrastructures from the great Chinese firewall to the collection of passenger data records and the monitoring of international bank transfers by the USA and Europe. The trend towards all-encompassing surveillance that David Lyon has analysed already in his 1994 book *The Electronic Eye* (Lyon 1994) has accelerated in the last two decades, and the expansion of the internet and ubiquitous internet use (at least in the countries of the global North) has created huge databases of personal information in the hands of private enterprises. The Pirate Parties are the most visible actor among a more diverse set of initiatives, associations, NGOs and individuals who have re-animated the privacy and data-protection discourse of the 1980s and adapted it to the requirements of the internet age. The German Chaos Computer Club (CCC) and the US Electronic Frontier Foundation (EFF) are only two examples of NGOs with similar policy agendas. The rapid spread of the idea of Pirate Parties from Sweden to currently forty countries was possible because of these pre-existing activist networks. Therefore the conflict is likely to persist, even if the pirates have only limited success in gaining parliamentary representation in most countries.

6.4. Creative Commons

In contrast to the other three cases that I have discussed so far, Creative Commons (CC) did not grow in the context of widespread contentious mobilizations. Creative Commons is an NGO, founded in 2001 as a US charitable corporation by – in their own words – '[c]yberlaw and intellectual property experts James Boyle, Michael Carroll, and Lawrence Lessig, MIT computer science professor Hal Abelson, lawyer-turned-documentary filmmaker-turned-cyberlaw expert Eric Saltzman, and public domain Web publisher Eric Eldred'.[12] It received initial support from the Berkman Center for Internet & Society at Harvard Law School, from Stanford Law School and its Center for Internet and Society. Creative Commons thus grew out of widespread discomfort with the current state of the intellectual property rights system among US legal scholars and other academics working in the field of internet and society. But while it did not start as a social movement, Leonhard Dobusch and Sigrid Quack (2008) have argued that it became part of a broader social movement in the course of its rapid growth and internationalization after its inception in the seclusion of US Ivy League law schools. Creative Commons does not rely on the collective action repertoire that is usually associated with contentious mobilizations – no demonstrations or other forms of confrontational protest, not even petitioning and similar non-disruptive acts of contention played a significant role. But because Creative Commons is challenging the norms on which the current IP system is built, it should nevertheless be seen as a conflictual mobilization.

The driving force behind Creative Commons was Lawrence Lessig, a US law professor who worked at Harvard Law School and Stanford Law School where he founded the Center for Internet and Society. In his book *Code and Other Laws of Cyberspace* (Lessig 1999), he presents a sceptical assessment of the often claimed 'freedom' of the internet and identifies the expansion of copyright in the digital realm as one source for restrictive regulation in favour of business interests and to the detriment of the freedom of ordinary internet users. He argues that the combination of strong intellectual property rights with technical access restrictions in trusted platform or digital rights management systems restricts the public's rights of fair use and tilts the balance heavily towards the side of rights-holders (1999: 135). In *The Future of Ideas* (Lessig 2001), he further develops his argumentation that a delicate balance between protection of creative works and general access to these works is necessary for innovation and creativity to flourish. Against the backdrop of an ongoing expansion of intellectual property

---

[12] http://wiki.creativecommons.org/FAQ#Who_started_Creative_Commons.3F (accessed 4 June 2011). A complete list of the participants of the inaugural meeting on 7 May 2001 can be found at http://cyber.law.harvard.edu/creativecommons/ (accessed 3 June 2011).

rights in depth and scope in the late twentieth century, he claims that 'we need specific changes to reestablish a balance between control and creativity. Our aim should be a system of sufficient control to give artists enough incentive to produce, while leaving free as much as we can for others to build upon and create' (2001: 249).

In addition to his academic writings, his conviction that the direction of the current intellectual property rights policies is fundamentally wrong led him – together with his colleagues Charles Nesson and Jonathan Zittrain from the Berkman Center for Internet & Society – to challenge the constitutionality of the latest extension of the copyright term in the USA: the Sonny Bono Copyright Term Extension Act (Levy 2002). In the court case *Eldred* v. *Ashcroft* (2003), Lessig argued that the retroactive extension of the copyright term for already published works was against the constitutional provision of a *limited* copyright term, because such an extension would not generate an incentive for creators of artistic works but instead limit the sources from which creators of future works might draw (Jones 2004). The case was finally dismissed in January 2003 by the Supreme Court, which maintained that the copyright extension did not contradict the constitution, especially since the EU had also a similar protection term of seventy years plus the life of the author. Against this backdrop Creative Commons developed as an alternative attempt to create and secure a rich public domain of artistic works and cultural productions – and this attempt turned out to be very successful.

While the *Eldred* case made its way through the courts a group of legal scholars, law students and internet experts interested in IP issues founded an organization that was first called 'Copyright's Commons' and then changed its name to Creative Commons, whose aim was to promote the availability of works of literature, art, music and film (Bollier 2008: 95). Fuelled by the public controversy over the peer-to-peer file-sharing service Napster that had to shut down after it lost a court case against the lobbying association of the US music industry, Recording Industry Association of America (RIAA), the Creative Commons project gained momentum, but its contours were still rather vague before the inaugural meeting in May 2001 (Creative Commons 2001a). The original idea was to create an online repository that would be a digital 'conservancy, like a land trust, where people can get access to content in the public domain that otherwise wouldn't be there' (Lessig, cited in Levy 2002). In a preparatory paper for the meeting, Chris Babbitt summarizes the state of the debate, discussing how Creative Commons might compete with other websites offering digital content, whether donated works should be screened for quality, and how the donated content might be effectively searched (Creative Commons 2001b). The idea of the Creative Commons thus started as a plan for an online repository of works that would be free to use, where the creative works would stand in the centre and where the licence would only secure the public domain status of these works (for a more detailed history of CC see Bollier 2008).

But at the meeting in May 2001 concerns about the sustainability of such a repository and the possible legal risks associated with it prevailed, and when the first version of the Creative Commons licence was issued in December 2002 the focus of the project had changed. Instead of offering a repository for public domain works, the main goal was now to provide a set of copyright licences and a web-based interface to attach these licences to digital works so that these works could be reliably identified and searched over the internet.

The concept of a 'copyleft' licence, that is a licence that effectively reverses the working of the established copyrights system by granting public access instead of reserving all rights, was modelled on the 'GNU General Public License' (GPL) which had been developed to distribute open source software. The GPL developed out of an initiative by a handful of software programmers to create an operating system that can be freely distributed to everyone and where the underlying program code is openly available and modifiable for everyone (provided he or she has the necessary know-how). It has developed into a serious business model on which large parts of the internet software infrastructure is built (Grassmuck 2002; Lutterbeck, Bärwolff and Gehring 2008).

The core idea is that the source, the human-readable program code, should be openly available, so that every programmer can use the existing code to build new programs or add new functionality to existing software. To guarantee that the freely available code could not be appropriated and thus privatized by a programmer who would try to protect his or her software based on the open source code via exclusive intellectual property rights, the pioneers of the open source movement had to develop a tool to make sure that such appropriation would be impossible. The tool that Richard Stallman developed for this purpose was the GNU General Public License, a so-called 'copyleft' licence that obliges every contributor to GPL-licensed software to make the source code of the new or enhanced software available and distribute the software also under GPL (Stallman 1999). The GPL thus effectively uses the existing copyright that automatically confers exclusive rights to the author (i.e. programmer) of new software against the intention of the copyright law, by requiring each author to relinquish all rights except the right to prohibit unauthorized modification – which in this case would be a modification that would remove the GPL from the work and withdraw the source code from public circulation (Mulgan, Salem and Steinberg 2005).[13]

But while the GPL offers only one version that guarantees public access to the code of the licensed and all derivative works, Creative Commons licences offer more flexibility with regard to the scope of rights that a creator of a work may choose to retain or forfeit. The current third version of the Creative Commons licence offers six licences that differ in terms of the freedom a user is granted (see Table 6.2) and a seventh licence that waives all rights and thus releases the work into the public domain. Each of these licences technically consists of three layers: a human-readable, a machine-readable and a lawyer-readable licence.

The first layer is meant to be understandable by ordinary people, to enable them to choose which licence they would like to use for their works and to allow the average internet user to understand under which conditions CC-licensed works from other authors can be used. This first layer is represented by a combination of symbols, indicating the permitted uses of the work. The second layer is realized by embedding meta-data into the digital files (texts, photos, audio and video files, etc.), allowing computers to identify the level of rights associated with the file. Search engines can then identify CC-licensed files in general and files that are available for specific uses in particular. The third layer is the legal code of the licence that guarantees that the licence will be valid before court. It is realized by either attaching the complete text of the licence to the work or by linking to the appropriate version of the licence on the Creative Commons website.

Early versions of the Creative Commons website still mentioned the creation of an 'intellectual property conservancy' as a second, more long-term goal,[14] but under the impression of the success of the licensing tool, this goal was eventually abandoned. It soon became clear that the internet offers already numerous places to store all kinds of content. What was missing was a tool to reliably declare this content as open for access and use under conditions less restrictive than with the existing copyright.

The success of the Creative Commons licences is impressive in several aspects. First, the success of Creative Commons manifests itself in the extraordinary growth of CC-licensed works. Figure 6.2 shows the

---

[13] www.gnu.org/licenses/gpl.html (accessed 15 May 2011).
[14] http://web.archive.org/web/20020610051523/http://creativecommons.org/aboutus/ (accessed 4 June 2011).

Table 6.2 *Creative Commons licences (version 3.0)*

Licence modules

 Attribution. All CC licences require that others who use the licensed work in any way must give credit to the creator of the licensed work.

 NonCommercial. Others may copy, distribute, display, perform, and (unless combined with NoDerivatives) modify and use the licensed work for any purpose other than commercially unless they get permission first.

 NoDerivatives. Others may copy, distribute, display and perform only original copies of the licensed work.

 ShareAlike. Others may copy, distribute, display, perform and modify the licensed work, as long as they distribute any modified work on the same terms.

Licences
The three optional components (attribution is always mandatory) can be combined to give six licences with decreasing freedom for the user:

- Attribution (CC-by)
- Attribution – ShareAlike (CC-by-SA)
- Attribution – NoDerivatives (CC-by-ND)
- Attribution – NonCommercial (CC-by-NC)
- Attribution – NonCommercial – ShareAlike (CC-by-NC-SA)
- Attribution – NonCommercial – NoDerivatives (CC-by-NC-ND)

In addition, since 2010, Creative Commons also offers a *CC0* licence under which the author waives all her/his rights and effectively donates the work without restrictions to the public domain. For uses beyond those granted in the specified licence, permission has to be granted by the creator of the work.

---

number of back-links to the licences on the creativecommons.org website as recorded by the Yahoo search engine. Participants in the Creative Commons project have automatically queried this data on a daily basis since May 2003, but strong fluctuations in this daily data indicate that the back-link count is very unreliable (Creative Commons 2011a). An annual aggregation of the data nevertheless gives a robust indication about the overall growth pattern: from the first licence in December 2002 it took about one year to reach the first million licensed works. In the next year the number of licensed works grew to about 7 million. In 2005 the number of CC-licensed works was still growing but at a lower rate until in 2006 a second phase of rapid expansion followed.

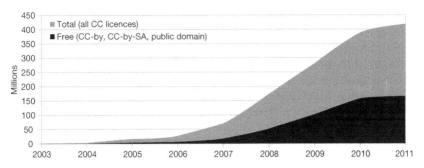

Figure 6.2 Creative Commons licence adoption 2003–11.

Source: http://labs.creativecommons.org/2011/06/27/
powerofopen-metrics/.

The data presented here may actually be a very conservative estima-
tion of CC licence adoption on the internet. A current Google search[15]
for web pages that contain the term 'http' – probably the most generic
term on the internet – lists about 576 million pages that are free to use
or share under a Creative Commons licence or otherwise marked as
being in the public domain. The solid growth trend is corroborated
if one looks at the number of photos with a CC licence, posted at the
popular image-sharing site Flickr. This site started to offer its users
the option to publish their photos under a CC licence from mid 2004
(Flickr 2004), and since then the Flickr data shows an almost linear
growth to about 184 million CC-licensed photos in May 2011.[16]

The growth of the general number of CC-licensed works in the first
years most likely reflects licence adoption among persons and organizations already sympathetic to the idea of a creative commons. After 2006
a second phase starts in which ordinary internet users are increasingly
switching to CC licences. This second phase was greatly facilitated by
the integration of CC licensing options into photo- and video-sharing
sites and into popular blogging software and portals. Even the incomplete data shows that Creative Commons have succeeded in establishing
their licences as an alternative standard that is now customarily used by
millions of internet users who are willing to share their creative works
much more freely than existing copyright laws expect them to do.

[15] www.google.com/search?q=http&hl=en&client=firefox-a&hs=vw3&rls=org.
mozilla%3Aen-US%3Aofficial&biw=1280&bih=869&num=10&lr=&ft=i&as_
rights=%28cc_publicdomain|cc_attribute|cc_sharealike|cc_noncommercial|cc_no
nderived%29&cr=&safe=images&tbs= (accessed 15 July 2011).
[16] The Flickr data is available at http://labs.creativecommons.org/metrics/sql-dumps/
(accessed 15 July 2011).

The second notable aspect of Creative Commons' success is that, as soon as the licence became operational, a process of rapid internationalization and transnationalization started in which like-minded activists from around the globe started to port the Creative Commons licence, which had originally been developed to conform to the US legal system. Each year between 2003 and 2007, between eight and twelve national versions of the licences were developed. According to the information on the Creative Commons website, in 2011 the licences have been ported to 54 jurisdictions, and another 36 are in the process of being ported.[17] More than 100 affiliates – this may be an informal group of a handful of like-minded activists or a formal organization with a large support network – exist in 70 countries.[18]

In their study of the development of Creative Commons, Leonhard Dobusch and Sigrid Quack show that 'transnationalization during the early period (2003–2005) was predominantly fueled by the absorption of critical open source and Internet lawyers from outside the US into the epistemic community' (Dobusch and Quack 2008: 21). Later NGOs and organizations with a focus on more general political, educational or social issues became more important in the licence porting process and the overall constituency of Creative Commons. Within a few years Creative Commons changed from a project of a small epistemic community to an important node in a broader current of social discontent with the state of the existing system of cultural production and intellectual property rights, which is sometimes called 'fee culture movement' (Lessig 2004; Berry and Moss 2008) or 'movement for a digital commons' (Stalder 2011).

The diversity of actors involved in the Creative Commons project augmented its reach and enhanced its impact, but it also brought some conflicts to the project. The conflict of interests between actors who saw Creative Commons mainly as a provider of licensing tools and actors who saw it as an advocacy organization for more democratic or free access to cultural goods was pragmatically solved by diversification: in November 2005 Creative Commons hived off the London-based iCommons as a separate entity responsible for the more political campaigning and as a coordinating and liaison organization with other projects with similar goals (Dobusch and Quack 2008: 29). Another spin-off is the semi-autonomous Creative Commons sub-project Science Commons, a project aimed at the scientific community and their specific needs of open access to scientific data and research results. With

[17] http://wiki.creativecommons.org/Jurisdiction_Database (accessed 3 June 2011).
[18] http://wiki.creativecommons.org/CC_Affiliate_Network (accessed 3 June 2011).

its core of committed legal scholars and lawyers, an institutional structure which rests on the two NGOs Creative Commons and iCommons, and its involvement in broader social movement processes, the Creative Commons project is a hybrid between epistemic community, NGO and social movement, combining elements of all three in a unique manner.

On a third level, the success of Creative Commons is reflected in the adoption of its licences by a growing number of high-profile actors. The Massachusetts Institute of Technology (MIT), Rice University, Stanford Law School and Sun Microsystems were among the first to adopt CC licences and gave them some additional credibility and publicity in the academic world and in the open source software community (Bollier 2008: 171). Cory Doctorow's move to release his novel *Down and Out in the Magic Kingdom* (2003) under a CC licence generated significant media attention, as did the founding of Magnatune in spring 2003, an independent record label that offers music licensed under a CC-by-NC-SA licence. The photo-sharing site Flickr, which started to offer an option to mark uploaded photos with a CC licence in 2004, was one of the early adopters among the big Web 2.0 websites. In January 2009 the Arabian news channel Al Jazeera was the first major news outlet to offer part of its video footage under a CC licence (Al Jazeera 2009), and in April 2012 the Word Bank announced its adoption of an open access strategy and, starting 1 July 2012, publication of their documents under a CC-by licence (World Bank 2012). The Wikimedia Foundation's move in May 2009 to publish all Wikipedia content under a CC-by-SA licence (Wikimedia Foundation 2009),[19] and the video-sharing site YouTube's decision in June 2011 to offer a CC licensing option for uploaded videos (Peterson 2011) further enhance the visibility of Creative Commons on the web.

In a time span of less than ten years Creative Commons' accomplishments are remarkable. It has established an alternative to the existing copyrights regime that builds on existing copyright laws but effectively turns them on their heads. It exploits the fact that the existing copyright regime automatically gives authors exclusive rights to their works. These rights have existed since the 1709 Statute of Anne but in the past 300 years authors usually had to resign most of their rights to publishers because only they had the technical means to distribute their

---

[19] Wikipedia content was originally licensed under a GNU Free Documentation License (GFDL), a copyleft licence that was originally developed to enable publication of documentation for open source software under similar terms as the software itself. The GFDL licence predates CC and was until 2007 incompatible with any of the CC licences. Since these incompatibility problems have been solved, GFDL-licensed works can now be distributed under a CC-by-SA 3.0 licence as well.

works in the form of books, sheet music, musical recordings, films, etc. The internet now offers the possibility to skip these intermediaries and distribute artistic and scientific works directly through its networked infrastructure.

Creative Commons has established its alternative legal code in an unprecedented instance of private international norm-setting. No national legislation so far has adopted Creative Commons licences in its national laws – although Russian President Medvedev proposed in June 2011 setting up a new flexible Creative Commons-like copyright scheme for the Russian-language part of the internet.[20] No legislative or executive body was involved in establishing this legal norm that nevertheless has been adopted by millions of people around the world, and that has already stood its test of legal validity in several court cases. This is possible because Creative Commons has drafted the licences in a way that relies on existing legal institutions to enforce their alternative norms, and because a critical mass of actors exists who are willing to contribute to the growing digital commons. These millions of users of the alternative licensing option are belying the utilitarian assumption that, without exclusive intellectual property rights, no incentive would exist to create digital common goods.

6.5.   The Creative Commons frame

How did Creative Commons convince individuals and organizations to support their alternative norms? In the following section I will analyse Creative Commons' framing strategies based on a qualitative content analysis of official documents published on their website. In its official documents and statements Creative Commons combines a very broad vision with a very focused and limited framing. The vision that functions as a motivational frame is 'realizing the full potential of the internet – universal access to research and education, full participation in culture – to drive a new era of development, growth, and productivity' (Creative Commons 2011b). The goal is nothing less than tearing down the barriers that keep people from accessing the wealth of knowledge and cultural goods and revolutionizing the base of economic growth and development. These bold aims are qualified in the sections about culture, education and science, and there the goals sound a bit less grandiose: increasing cultural creativity by expanding the body of freely available works and thus enhancing access to the stock of existing cultural production; making textbooks and lesson plans available

[20] http://en.rian.ru/society/20110602/164385846.html (accessed 8 June 2011).

to enhance digitally enabled education; and promoting open access to scientific data and the results of scientific research. This vision provides a motivational frame for the activists that is at the same time very broad and offers hooks for very concrete activities.

The diagnostic frame that is presented on the website is, in contrast, surprisingly modest. The problem that is said to be at the base of the proposed collective action is that the current copyright regime does not allow the realization of the internet's great potential to share all kinds of digital content at minimal costs without the restrictions of space and to act as a 'multiplier of cultural innovation' (Creative Commons 2011c). The core argument is that the internet – for the first time in human history – makes the vision of universal access a realistic possibility, but the existing legal framework inhibits the full realization of this potential. On its website CC carefully avoids attacking the current intellectual property rights regime. In his books Lawrence Lessig is much more outspoken. There he argues that the most powerful actors of the culture industry have successfully managed to influence the policy-making process with the result that current copyright laws and the fight against piracy will 'rid our culture of values that have been integral to our tradition from the start' – the rights that enabled creators 'to build freely upon their past, and protected creators and innovators from either state or private control' (Lessig 2004: 10), and that it is necessary to reclaim these rights in a movement for free culture.

The prognostic frame, which formulates what is to be done, matches well the modest diagnostic frame. To advance its goals Creative Commons develops and supports 'legal and technical infrastructure that maximizes digital creativity, sharing and innovation' (Creative Commons 2011b). It offers a set of tools that follow a 'some rights reserved' approach to copyright.

Two argumentative figures are used in these frames: first, creativity and abundance, and second, effectiveness and progress. The creativity and abundance argument is present in the vision of the internet as a plentiful source of knowledge and cultural diversity that, as Lessig writes, 'has unleashed an extraordinary possibility for many to participate in the process of building and cultivating a culture that reaches far beyond local boundaries' (Lessig 2004: 9). The effectiveness and progress argument complements this idealistic argument by providing a more prosaic justification for Creative Commons' activities. This argument is mainly used in the context of science and education when Creative Commons claims that scientific progress will be more effective and research will achieve better results if scientific data and the results of scientific research are made available in an open access regime, or that open educational resources will enhance the quality of education.

The combination of Creative Commons' diagnostic, prognostic and motivational framing leads to a very peculiar collective action frame. The framing, on the one hand, legitimizes Creative Commons' provision of infrastructure, tools and advocacy work. On the other hand, it is a frame that assigns agency to dispersed individual internet users who are enabled to participate in and contribute to the project of a digital commons. Whether individual users who license their works in increasing numbers under CC licences are motivated by Creative Commons' framing or not is unknown, but the choices the users make give some indication about their motives: in May 2011 more than half of the licences recorded by Yahoo are ShareAlike licences (CC-by-SA: 37 per cent, CC-by-NC-SA: 16 per cent), meaning that 53 per cent of the users want to make sure that derivative works based on the content they have provided will also remain firmly in the digital commons.

6.6.   Creative Commons and the conflicts in the knowledge society

Creative Commons addresses first of all the access/distribution level of conflicts in the knowledge society. With its licences it provides a tool that has the potential to fundamentally change the way knowledge, information and cultural productions can be accessed on the internet. It replaces the current model where access is in general only possible after asking permission and usually only after paying a fee for limited access, with a model where – at least for non-commercial purposes – access is generally granted and further use is less restricted. It is thus not very surprising that the business associations of the culture industry are less than enthusiastic about the project and its success. The US collecting society ASCAP (American Society of Composers, Authors and Publishers) has formulated this discontent in rather bold words, but they are not alone with their complaint that '[a]t this moment we are facing our biggest challenge ever. Many forces including Creative Commons, Public Knowledge, Electronic Frontier Foundation and technology companies with deep pockets are mobilizing to promote "Copyleft" in order to undermine our "Copyright." They say they are advocates of consumer rights, but the truth is these groups simply do not want to pay for the use of our music' (quoted in Wilson 2010).

Creative Commons addresses the core mechanisms that regulate how immaterial goods are distributed in the knowledge society. This upsets an institutional order that has been established in a long historical process. ASCAP is right when it identifies 'technology companies with deep pockets' as powerful allies of Creative Commons and other advocates of a digital commons. Internet firms like Google and Yahoo have adopted Creative Commons licences because they see a business model that is still compatible with the commodification of culture and propertization of knowledge, but relies less on restricting access through exclusive rights. Instead their business model is centred around providing access to a growing and unstructured mass of digital content – and in this they collide with the culture industry's established business model.

But the challenge of Creative Commons goes beyond offering an alternative business model. Its insistence on a permissive interpretation of non-commercial use of digital goods addresses conflicts located on the level of generation and production of knowledge. Creative Commons strengthens a countervailing discourse to the growing propertization of knowledge, by augmenting the realm of non-commercial – private, educational, scientific – use. If we follow James Boyle's metaphor that the current expansion of intellectual property rights is 'a second enclosure movement ... the enclosure of the intangible commons of the mind' (Boyle 2003: 37), then the various – and mostly unsuccessful – attempts to reform copyright laws in favour of open access and fair use and the initial approach of Creative Commons resemble the establishment of rights of way to guarantee access to fenced-off land for the limited purpose of crossing it. Clearly the 'owners' of these virtual lands made of digital knowledge goods are trying to fend off all claims for public access to those lands with all the means that they have at their disposal. And legislators are in most cases not willing to force them to grant access.

In this constellation Creative Commons offers a strategy that was not available for the citizens who fought in the physical realm against the first enclosure movement. Creative Commons, by helping to produce a growing source of digital goods which can be used with very few restrictions, offers the possibility to create new virtual land – without fences, and free to access for all. Doing this, it has helped to establish an alternative to the utilitarian intellectual property discourse by replacing the notion of scarcity with the idea of abundance, and by strengthening normative arguments about the necessity and value of unrestricted public goods.

7 Conclusion: new cleavages and new collective actors

At the outset of this book stood the claim that the software patents conflict, the access to medicines mobilization, the development of Pirate Parties and the massive adoption of Creative Commons licences share a common thread that unites them despite their obvious differences in terms of issues, protagonists, action forms and geography. On the one hand, they indicate the wide spectrum of contention about the practices and norms governing the creation and use of knowledge in current societies. On the other hand, they reveal a number of underlying conflicts that are characteristic of the knowledge society, and that are addressed in these conflicts from different perspectives, but in a consistent pattern.

In this final chapter I will first (7.1) systematically compare the four conflicts along the three dimensions that have guided the case studies – contexts, actors and frames. I will highlight along these three dimensions what unites and what separates the four conflicts at the most concrete level. In the next step (7.2) I will discuss which more general conflicts and meta-issues of the knowledge society these conflicts address. Based on this it will be possible to give the abstract model of conflict and change in the knowledge society a more substantial form, and identify the relationships between processes of social change and conflicts that embody the cleavages of the knowledge society. This conclusion closes (7.3) with some reflections about the possible collective actors that may or may not bring about social change in these conflicts of the knowledge society and their potential to establish an alternative to the current social order that is still a knowledge society, but one based on access and sharing and not on property and exclusion.

7.1. Patterns of difference and similarity

The common denominator of the four conflicts is that they all challenge the rules that determine how property in immaterial goods is created – how knowledge is propertized, and which rights-owners of intellectual property have to exclude others from accessing this knowledge. How this critique of the current economic order of the knowledge society has been developed in different circumstances and contexts, advanced in collective action networks, and framed to mobilize various constituencies will be compared across the four cases in the following pages.

7.1.1. Contexts

In the *software patents* case the starting point was the attempt to 'harmonize' the European IP system with the two major competing economies, the USA and Japan. 'Harmonization' in the eyes of the European Commission meant expanding the scope of patent protection in the field of computer software, in order to establish a sound legal basis for software patents in the European Union. These attempts were met with resistance from various actors without strong and established representation at the European level, who were not convinced that the possibility of software patents in Europe would put them in a better position in the global market. On the contrary, they claimed that software patents would be detrimental for their businesses and disadvantage small and medium-sized enterprises (SMEs), which – they claim – are the key drivers of innovation in Europe. In the conflict these oppositional actors formed a transnational network to fight the expansion of intellectual property rights. They intervened at various levels of the European multi-level governance system, but the main arena was the decision-making process of the European institutions – European Commission, Parliament and Council.

The *access to medicines* conflict was initially not a legislative process. Its starting point was the implementation of the new international IP framework which had come into effect with the signing of the WTO treaty and the accompanying TRIPS agreement at the end of the Uruguay trade round in April 1994. With the TRIPS agreement a small group of countries from the global North had established an international intellectual property rights system that with its substantial, mandatory minimum standards went far beyond the hitherto existing patchwork of IP treaties. The far-reaching effects of TRIPS were felt in many areas, but they fostered coordinated resistance especially in the field of health policies. A transnational network of NGOs was formed to fight the negative consequences of stronger intellectual property rights for access to essential medicines in developing countries. Local mobilizations joined the campaign, and support came from developing country governments which had already before TRIPS been vocal critics of stronger intellectual property rights (India, Brazil, Argentina). Support also came from secretariats of several international organizations such as WHO, UNCTAD and UNDP who have traditionally been seen as 'development friendly', but also from selected secretariats in WIPO whose policy agenda is usually determined by the countries of the global North (Deere 2009: 137). International organizations thus were actors and at the same time the main arena of the conflict, which was on the international level above all a conflict about the interpretation of the rules that govern use and ownership of and access to knowledge, but also – with the Doha Declaration and the WIPO Development Agenda – a conflict about the creation of alternative rules and norms. Several local protest mobilizations accompanied the conflict, addressing specific issues at the local level or targeting politicians or companies 'at home' to influence their behaviour at the international level.

The *Pirate Parties* represent a very different conflict dynamic. They bundle the dispersed criticism of inadequate data-protection measures and excessive intellectual property rights and channel diffuse discontent with policies that criminalize individual internet users for file-sharing into the project of a political party. The Pirate Parties have run for elections in several countries at the national, sub-national and European level with varying success. But as with the early Green parties, the electoral arena is for the pirates only one playing-field among others. They have been involved in various protest mobilizations against the criminalization of file-sharers and against data-retention laws and internet censorship. In Kitschelt's taxonomy the Pirate Parties, with their involvement in protest mobilizations and their commitment to direct-democratic participatory forms of organization, are clearly movement parties, even if they only partially fulfil his assumption of post-material orientation and neglect of economic issues (Kitschelt 1989: 64 ff.). While the Pirate Parties may not represent the economic interests of their constituencies, they do question the foundation of the property order in the knowledge society: the current international system of intellectual property rights.

Finally, *Creative Commons* developed out of discontent with the (US) intellectual property rights system and the realization that chances to influence the IP legislation or legal practice are minimal for critics of the current IP system. As a consequence, a group of legal scholars and internet activists created, in an unprecedented act of private international rule-setting, a set of alternative licences to foster unrestricted access to and sharing of digital works. The Creative Commons licences, which were quickly adopted by millions of internet users, challenge the rationale and some underlying assumptions of the existing copyrights regime by creating licences that enhance access and limit exclusivity instead of enhancing exclusivity and limiting access. Unlike the three other cases, Creative Commons is not a protest mobilization. It is not primarily aimed at the political decision-making process. Instead it enables individuals to circumvent some restrictions of the intellectual property rights system. The 'arena' of Creative Commons' intervention is the global virtual space of the internet. But at the same time it created a very real mobilization of committed individuals who transposed the set of licences to many national legislations, who propagated the ideas behind Creative Commons in various settings, and who integrated Creative Commons into a loose network of activists engaged in sub- and counter-cultural production and internet activism, such as the Berlin 'Wizards of OS' conferences of the F/OSS community, the Barcelona 'Free Culture Forum' meetings of free/libre culture activists and the US-based student organization 'Students for Free Culture'.[1]

With regard to their starting points and action contexts, three elements unite the four conflicts:

(1) They all question the existing intellectual property rights regime and with this the property order of the knowledge society. They thus rattle the foundations of the economic order of current knowledge societies. But while the activists in all four mobilizations agree on the inadequacy of the current IP system, it is much less clear whether they would agree on an alternative. Many opponents of software patents are in favour of strong copyrights. The core issue of the Pirate Parties – privacy and digital civil rights – are not or only marginally present in the other three conflicts.

(2) The second concordance is the profound transnationality of the four conflicts. In line with the notion that knowledge societies will be networked and globalized, none of the four conflicts remained restricted to the national realm. Even the Pirate Parties, which are necessarily linked to national elections, quickly developed a transnational network of linked mobilizations and transnational exchange.

(3) Finally, all four conflicts did not develop along the cleavages of the industrial age. In none of the conflicts is it possible to locate the conflicting parties along the labour–capital or left–right cleavage, nor did other conflict lines like religion, gender, urban/rural, environment, ethnicity or post-materialism play a relevant role. Only the North–South conflict played an important role in the access

---

[1] More information about the events and the respective supporting organizations is available at the following websites: www.wizards-of-os.org/, http://fcforum.net/, http://freeculture.org/.

to medicines conflict, although the oppositional network of actors comprised organizations from the North and the South.

7.1.2.   Actors

The transnational character of all four conflicts affects the organizational structure of the collective action networks of the actors involved in the conflicts. The mobilizations of the opponents of software patents and the advocates of access to medicines show many elements of classical social movement processes. Both have been conflictual mobilizations of actors connected through dense informal networks, united by a shared collective identity.

In the *software patents* conflict this was most pronounced. The collective action network here comprised SMEs, individuals, NGOs, social movement organizations (SMOs), members of the European Parliament, party representatives, business associations and a number of large transnational corporations. No formal organization existed that coordinated the activities of these diverse actors. Instead a set of shared convictions and interpretations expressed in a set of strongly integrated frames formed the kit that held this network together. What distinguishes this collective action network from most other social movements is the dominance of business actors, mostly from SMEs. Usually SMEs are not known to be able to coordinate effective collective action beyond the most local level. An explanation for the immensely successful mobilization in the software patents conflict may be sought in the idiosyncrasies of the software sector where collaboration is common, and where the use of collaborative tools like wikis or mailing lists is widespread. Coupled with some political awareness in parts of the F/OSS community, this has helped the SMEs to overcome their collective action problem. And the mobilization would certainly not have evolved the way it did without the relentless engagement of a handful of movement entrepreneurs, who invested their time and labour into the conflict.

In the collective action network of the *access to medicines* conflict, transnational NGOs and local SMOs in the fields of health and globalization played a much stronger role than in the software patents conflict, but the distinguishing attribute of this mobilization is certainly the involvement of developing country governments and select divisions of international organizations which actively participated in the network. The involvement of a high number of engaged academics from legal and medical schools in the USA, Canada, the UK, Australia and South Africa is another remarkable aspect of this mobilization.

The collective action networks of the *Pirate Parties* are, in contrast, characterized by the notable absence of pre-existing NGOs and organizations. The founding process of the Pirate Parties in Sweden and Germany was dominated by individuals with little or no previous political experience. Many leading figures in the Pirate Parties were IT professionals or individuals with some record of online engagement. This is a stark contrast to the early years of, for example, the German Green Party, where many core activists had a long history of libertarian or sectarian leftist politics (and some even in right-wing politics).

The distinctive feature of the collective action network of the *Creative Commons* mobilization is certainly, on the one hand, the dominance of legal scholars and other academics. During the transnational growth process they have been joined by activists with various backgrounds, but the strong roots in the US university system remain visible today, with four out of fourteen board members being professors at US universities. On the other hand, what is unique about the Creative Commons mobilization is its repercussions far beyond the activists' network. Its adoption by millions of internet users, its incorporation into major internet services like Wikipedia, Flickr and YouTube, its adoption in the world of academic publishing, are expressions of the establishment of alternative norms regulating the use of creative and knowledge goods on the internet. In this, Creative Commons resembles less a social movement wanting to change a policy by intervening in the policy-making process. It resembles more a counter-cultural movement whose aim is changing individual and collective behaviour.

All four collective action networks are at their cores composed of actors who have previously not played a relevant role in the field of IP policies. Patients, SMEs, IT professionals, critical academics, NGOs or social movements had until recently not even tried to influence the rules and norms that govern intellectual property rights. That such a broad group of actors has started to intervene in IP politics is remarkable in itself. It shows that societal actors are starting to realize the importance of IP issues in many areas of society. Their engagement takes the politicization of IP to another level, transforming it from an expert and stakeholder issue to a truly political issue with ramifications for ordinary citizens.

7.1.3. *Frames*

The four conflicts show some similarities in their contexts and collective action networks, but they differ markedly in their collective action frames. Obviously the conflicts were about different concrete issues, but the frames the actors used to identify the problem at hand and their proposed course of action also address different meta-issues. As I will argue further below (7.2), these meta-issues are from an analytical perspective often present in several conflicts, but in the activists' framing they are usually only addressed in one of the conflicts.

In the *software patents* conflict the opponents of software patents created a tightly bundled set of frames, centred around SMEs as drivers of innovation, and democratic control of the societal framework of rules and norms governing the process of innovation. Their core frame proposed a system of distributed innovation with democratic control over the basic conditions governing the creation and distribution of knowledge, which they juxtaposed to a model of centralized, corporate-driven innovation. The conflict about software patents in Europe was thus, on a more abstract level, a conflict about the desired mode of innovation in which a model of decentralized open innovation was positioned against a model of centralized industrial innovation.

In the *access to medicines* conflict the actors of the NGO network framed their actions as demands for the primacy of health over profits. They argued that economic gains for some actors should be balanced against the social costs of intellectual property rights, and that social and health concerns should be given priority. As in the software patents conflict, this socio-political frame demands political control over the conditions that shape the possibilities for the production and use of knowledge. The dynamics of knowledge creation and use should be governed by democratically legitimized actors and not by the invisible hand of the market.

The overarching frame that unites the *Pirate Parties'* demands connects privacy and civil rights. They argue that in the knowledge society civil rights have to be protected not only in the physical world but also in the virtual space, where each individual has to regain command over his or her data. These personal privacy rights should go hand in hand with information rights vis-à-vis corporate or institutional actors. To be able to exert democratic control, citizens have to be able to access the data that underlies institutional decision-making. The Pirate Parties' framing is essentially defensive. It calls for the protection of digital civil rights from state and corporate intrusion.

In contrast, *Creative Commons'* framing is proactive. In its core frame it presents a vision of abundance and universal access to cultural goods. By calling the structure that contains the freely accessible knowledge goods a 'commons', it highlights the fact that its existence depends on the continuing supply of these goods. Creating a commons does not just mean giving everybody access, even though in the digital world this would not diminish the goods and their usability. A knowledge commons depends on the continuing input of new cultural material, creative works, ideas and innovations. Otherwise it would become an archive or a museum. Creative Commons' success depends on its ability to secure this input, and so far, it has been very successful in this regard. The frame that underlines the need for contribution is sharing – providing goods without expecting payment, but with an at least implicit expectation of reciprocity.

Table 7.1 summarizes the three dimensions of contexts, collective action networks and frames of the four conflicts. All conflicts are driven by collective actors united by a shared collective identity. The level of contention differs from high in the software patents and access to medicines conflict to relatively low in the Creative Commons mobilization. The more contentious conflicts also have more concrete starting points, and thus clearly defined opponents against which the mobilization is directed. The four mobilizations interacted by influencing their respective framing and through actors and organizations engaged in more than one of the conflicts. The two US-based NGOs Electronic Frontier Foundation (EFF) and Consumer Project on Technology (CPTech; now Knowledge Ecology International, KEI) were involved in the software patents, access to medicines and Creative Commons mobilizations. The Federation of a Free Information Infrastructure (FFII) and the Free Software Foundation link the software patents conflict with the Pirate Parties. On a substantial level the Pirate Parties took up the criticism of software and business methods patents, and of the TRIPS agreement, formulated in the other campaigns; and inspired by the access to medicines conflict, Creative Commons created a developing nations licence.

All four mobilizations transcended the concrete policy issues which were their starting points, raising awareness about IP conflicts on a more abstract level. And because these conflicts address issues that touch upon more general conflicts in the knowledge society, a careful analysis of the conflict lines present in the empirical conflicts can qualify and sometimes contradict the assumptions about new social cleavages that would come with the knowledge society, present in the theories of the knowledge society elaborated by Daniel Bell, Nico Stehr and Manuel Castells. Which of their claims and assumptions have to be modified and which additional aspects have to be considered? In the following section I will discuss how the four empirical conflicts reveal a number of general conflict lines specific to the knowledge society. This will lead to a more theoretically founded understanding of the empirical conflicts and a more empirically founded theory of conflicts in the knowledge society.

Table 7.1 *Contexts, collective action networks and frames of the four conflicts*

Conflict	Context	Collective action network	Master frame
Software patents	*Starting point:* Introduction of software patents in Europe *Institutional context:* European Institutions	Transnational social movement *Core actors:* SMEs	Distributed open innovation and democratic control of knowledge-production framework
Access to medicines	*Starting point:* Implementation of TRIPS and AIDS epidemic *Institutional context:* International organizations and local mobilizations	Transnational social movement *Core actors:* NGOs	Primacy of health and political governance of access to and use of knowledge
Pirate Parties	*Starting point:* Criminalization of file-sharing and neglect of data protection *Institutional context:* National, sub-national, and European elections and privacy protests	Movement party *Core actors:* IT professionals	Digital civil rights and privacy
Creative Commons	*Starting point:* Second Enclosure *Institutional context:* Private international norm-setting	Hybrid of NGO, epistemic community, and transnational social movement *Core actors:* Academics	Abundance, access and sharing

7.2. Beyond policy conflicts – patterns of conflict and change in the knowledge society

The large transnational mobilizations that accompanied the four conflicts together with the diversity of the mobilized actors are an indicator that these conflicts address more general cleavages that are relevant for much wider constituencies than those immediately affected by the concrete problems from which the mobilizations started. This does not mean that the conflicts are 'really' about something else, but that these conflicts have a second dimension, beyond the respective concrete policy issue. Just as protests for women's rights to legal abortions have also been struggles for women's rights in general and against the patriarchal order of societies, the campaign for access to medicines is, beyond its aim to provide AIDS medication for poor people in developing countries, also a struggle about the limits of private appropriation of knowledge.

The more general social conflict lines in which the four concrete conflicts are embedded are (1) the mode of innovation, (2) the rules that govern access to knowledge and (3) the limits of anonymous markets.

7.2.1. Mode of innovation

The software patents conflict, the access to medicines mobilization and the Creative Commons project directly address the issue of the appropriate mode of innovation. Mode of innovation is the set of social mechanisms that determine how and where innovation is produced. In the industrial era industrialized mass production is accompanied by industrialized mass innovation – innovation that is concentrated in large industrial units, either in privately owned research labs or in public universities and research institutes. This centralized mass production of innovation is reflected in the patenting patterns in industrialized countries. In her empirical analysis of Australian and US patent ownership, Hazel Moir shows that the distribution of patents among patent owners follows a power law: a small number of firms are frequent patenters, owning several hundreds or even thousands of patents, while the large majority of firms (and a small number of individuals and non-profit organizations) each own only a small number of patents (Moir 2009). According to her study the USA and Australia show a similar structure, where the top 100 patentees own about one third of the patents. Current data from the US Patent and Trademark Office indicates that more recently this distribution has become even more skewed. In 2010 in the USA, the top 100 patentees received 38.2 per cent of all patent grants, whereas 29,229 patentees shared the remaining 61.8 per cent (US Patent and Trademark Office 2011). IBM, Samsung, Microsoft, Canon, Panasonic and Toshiba alone received more than 10 per cent of all patents. This does not tell anything about the value of the patents held by these firms, because the distribution of the value of patents is similarly skewed, with a high number of patents with little value and only a small number of high-value patents (Gambardella, Giuri and Mariani 2005; Troy and Werle 2008). But it indicates that the field of patent-protected innovation is strongly centralized and dominated by a small number of powerful corporations.

This centralized, industrial model of innovation is directly challenged in three of the conflicts and criticized in the Pirate Parties' manifestos. In the software patents conflict this challenge was most obvious. The opponents of software patents argued that the 'real' innovators of the European high-tech sector would not be the handful of large transnational corporations who make extensive use of the patent system, but the many thousands of small and medium-sized software and technology companies, who would suffer rather than profit from patent protection in the area of software.

In the access to medicines conflict the industrial innovation model was challenged from a different angle. The core criticism here was not so much that the big pharmaceutical companies would not be the 'real' innovators, but that the innovation they produce would be driven by the wrong incentives. The access coalition argued that in the area of medicines the aim of innovation should be providing drugs for those who need them the most. And because the current model directs innovation to the needs of those able to pay the most, public authorities should be able to intervene and redirect innovation processes and make existing drugs available according to human needs and not according to the patients' wallets.

Creative Commons – even though it is an initiative in the area of copyrights and not in the area of patents – poses a fundamental challenge to the centralized, industrial model of innovation. By offering tools to protect access to knowledge and cultural goods, it has greatly enhanced the visibility of dispersed and distributed innovation processes that build upon each other and make use of a growing pool of shared resources. The existence of millions of Creative Commons licensed works helps build a consciousness that the centralized, industrial mode of innovation is only one model among many, and that the rules that govern the production and use of knowledge should therefore not only account for this particular model.

The focus on political priorities in the access to medicines campaign and the strategy of the opponents of software patents to politicize the conflict furthermore challenge the industrial innovation model on another level. In both cases the social movement actors insisted that knowledge policies should not be shaped by business actors and the patent community, but by the people and/or accountable and democratically legitimized institutions.

As I have argued in Chapter 3, the writings of Bell and Stehr, and Castells suggest that the mode of innovation may indeed become a site of social conflict in the knowledge society. The empirical conflicts confirm this but they also show that the conflicts develop along a somewhat different trajectory than expected. In all three authors' writings the major transformation that lies behind the mode-of-innovation conflict is the transition from manufacturing to knowledge-based production. They argue that in this transition the old model of innovation that relies on enhancing productivity through automation and the use of more efficient machinery is replaced by innovation based on theoretical and scientific knowledge (Bell 1999: Ch. 1), and that the network enterprise will be superior to the old vertically integrated firm, because it is able to horizontally coordinate and delegate distributed innovation processes (Castells 2010a: Ch. 3).

In the four cases that I have discussed in this book, the conflict about the mode of innovation is not about tacit versus theoretical knowledge, manufacturing versus services, or vertical versus horizontal integration. The conflicts are about different forms of the network economy. Castells denounces the importance of SMEs as economic actors (Castells 2010a: 168), but in the software patents conflict economically independent but networked and interacting SMEs represent in the core sector of the knowledge economy an alternative to the horizontally integrated transnational network enterprise. And while the latter depends on centralized control over privatized knowledge, the alternative model works better with shared and accessible knowledge.

The notion that democratic control over the mechanisms that govern innovation is needed qualifies Stehr's and Bell's claim about the priority of theoretical knowledge. The conflicts show that the growing importance of theoretical knowledge does not automatically imply that the dynamic of knowledge creation is necessarily driven by a scientific logic. A large body of highly qualified scientists may be a necessary condition for development of a new drug. But the ultimate decision where their intellectual energy should be focused is taken not in the research but in the marketing department of a pharmaceutical firm. In the mobilization for access to medicines the demand now is that decisions about the development of knowledge should account for a third logic, the political logic of redistribution, welfare and representation.

7.2.2. Access to knowledge

The second meta-conflict that the empirical conflicts speak to is a conflict about general rules that govern access to knowledge. All four conflicts challenge the notion that privatization and propertization of knowledge are the economically most efficient and politically most desirable solutions to encourage innovation and creativity. In the software patents conflict, the open source business model is offered as an alternative to the closed, proprietary model of the large IT corporations. In the access to medicines conflict, compulsory licences are propagated as a tool to enforce better access, and alternative research financing models (prize funds, patent pools) are offered as measures to combat the propertization of knowledge on a more general level. The Pirate Parties demand drastically shorter protection periods for knowledge goods, broad exceptions to enable general access for private and non-commercial use, and – in the case of the Swedish Piratpartiet – even the complete abolishment of the patent system. And Creative Commons provides tools to enable access to knowledge and to broaden the pool of available non-proprietary knowledge goods.

The access to medicines conflict addresses the issue of access to knowledge on two levels. First, it challenges the general norms that allow patent holders to exclude others from using their propertized knowledge. Second, it addresses the specific problem of access to knowledge caused by the 'digital divide' (Norris 2001) between the affluent countries of the global North and the poor countries of the global South.

The Pirate Parties add two further aspects to the access issue. On a third level they demand limits to access rooted in individual privacy and personality rights. And fourthly they demand transparency and access to public records and to information held by authorities, to enable citizens to hold decision-makers accountable. While the pirates do not couch their demands in the terminology of access, from an analytical perspective data protection and privacy are nevertheless access issues. The overarching questions on all four levels are: Who should be able to access which knowledge and information? On which norms should the limits to access be based? and Who should be able to set these norms?

The four aspects describe in essence two sides of a coin. On the one side, the open access perspective asserts primacy of public over private interests, where public means the population at large and private means corporate, economic interests. This perspective questions the neoliberal assertion of private property as an essential precondition of freedom, and highlights the need for state intervention to balance inequalities and secure social standards. On the other side, the privacy perspective defends the primacy of the private in terms of personal integrity and autonomy against state and corporate control. This perspective highlights what Isaiah Berlin has called 'negative freedom' (Berlin 1959), the freedom from interference. Together these four aspects illustrate that the issue of access to knowledge goes beyond the question of private ownership and exclusive property rights. The question of access is ultimately a question of power – power of corporations and states – and its limits.

This aspect, that a central conflict line of the knowledge society is about controlling access to knowledge and that the core gatekeeping mechanism is the creation of intellectual property, has been largely neglected by the theorists of the knowledge society. Stehr briefly mentions intellectual property as an area of conflict dating back to the nineteenth century (Stehr 1994a: 256). But because he claims that knowledge would replace property as the defining characteristic of the society, he does not see major conflicts related to the issue of intellectual property. Neither in Castells' nor in Bell's account of the knowledge society does the control of access to knowledge by intellectual property rights play a significant role. And the aspect of regaining autonomy over one's own personal data is absent in all three theories. The three authors' ignorance of the conflict dimension embedded in the access to knowledge issue is not just an empirical oversight but a theoretical shortcoming. The access dimension of the conflicts that I have discussed in this book addresses the question of digital citizenship in its dimensions of individual freedom and social inclusion.

Privacy rights and demands for accountability and access to information on which administrative decision-making is based are contentious because they circumscribe an area of liberal freedoms in the virtual realm of the knowledge society. Like their counterparts in the material world they have to be won in struggles against authorities wishing to curb these rights.

The conflict about the limits of intellectual property rights and the rules and norms that govern access to knowledge is the knowledge society's pendant to the struggle about limits of individual and corporate property rights in the industrial age. In contrast to Castells' claim, that power, in the network society, will be based on controlling the network and the information flows (Castells 2000: 20), the structure of the empirical conflicts suggests that this is only one part of the picture. And the same is true for Bell's claim that skill and education are becoming new bases of power (Bell 1999: 358 ff.). The enormous expansion of intellectual property rights in terms of protected subject matter, protection length and geographical coverage shows that property has far from ceased to be an important base of power. Skill and education do not replace the old bases of power. Instead property is redefined to include knowledge and information, which are the preconditions for skill and education.

The struggles of the industrial age to limit power based on material property have led in some countries to more or less encompassing welfare systems and redistributive policies, limiting the rights and expanding the obligations of property owners. Their success depended to a significant extent on the strength of the workers' movements. In the conflicts about access to knowledge various actors rally for the establishment of similar limits to immaterial property rights, and their success will again likely depend on their ability to become a collective actor.

7.2.3.   The limits of anonymous markets

The third conflict line that the four mobilizations address is about the limits of anonymous markets. None of the actors involved in the conflicts question that anonymous markets are extremely efficient institutions to solve certain information and allocation problems. But the conflicts question the neoliberal assumption that anonymous markets are in general superior to social forms of organization. They question this assumption of superiority of market mechanisms on two levels: first, by contradicting the assumption that markets would lead to an optimal allocation of resources, and that economic incentives would most effectively solve the problem of market under-provision of public goods; and second, the conflicts contradict the idea that the production of goods would necessarily be driven by cost-benefit calculations.

The first claim is made most explicitly in the access to medicines conflict. The core argument of the access coalition was that market mechanisms may well spur innovation and lead to the production of the most profitable medications, but they will not necessarily lead to a sufficient provision of the most needed drugs to save human lives. For this, political governance is needed that imposes priorities based on normative considerations. The access to knowledge conflict is in this respect another iteration of the much older conflict between market liberalism and state intervention.

The second claim is more specific to the knowledge society. It undermines the idea that the rational, utility-maximizing actor would be the appropriate model to understand the mechanisms that lead to the creation of cultural and knowledge goods. As I have argued in Chapter 2, classical economic theory assumes that rational economic actors would have no incentive to produce knowledge goods. Their non-rivalrous nature would make it irrational for anyone to produce them because everyone would try to avoid the costs of producing them by free-riding on the goods produced by others. They therefore should either be provided by the state or additional incentives in the form of monopoly rights must be created to spur private production.

The success of Creative Commons and of open source software fundamentally challenges this assumption. Obviously the millions of internet users who have made the products of their creative activities freely available under Creative Commons licences did not need additional economic incentives to create cultural goods. And while one might object that the majority of these goods were created by individuals and never intended to generate profits, this is certainly not true for open source software, which is produced by large for-profit corporations like Google, IBM, Oracle, MySQL or even Microsoft, by SMEs, by individuals in their spare time or by academics as part of their research. The important insight is that knowledge goods are produced for a variety of reasons, and digitization and the internet have dramatically altered the conditions under which these various motives can become relevant.

To give one example: in the pre-internet age encyclopedias were produced by a small number of publishing houses which could afford to find thousands of experts for all subjects covered in the encyclopedia, pay them (usually small sums) for their contributions, employ a full-time editorial staff to verify and edit the contributions, finance the printing of a multi-volume work with many thousand pages, and organize distribution and sale of the final work. The motives behind publishing these works were economic. Wikipedia, on the other hand, is a collaborative online encyclopedia that several studies deem is comparable in quality to the established traditional encyclopedias (Hammwöhner et al. 2007). It now covers broader areas of knowledge than the traditional paper-based encyclopedias, and is the result of the contributions of thousands of volunteers, writing articles and correcting errors in this constantly evolving digital knowledge base. The collaborative project Wikipedia has become possible because many thousand contributors wanted to share their knowledge – without remuneration and even without symbolic acknowledgement – and because the technology enabled this kind of collaboration.

The internet offers the possibility to coordinate distributed collaboration on a previously unknown scale and with minimal costs. It enables peer production, that is 'effective, large-scale cooperative efforts' (Benkler 2006: 5), on a global scale and under conditions of abundance. In pre-knowledge societies innovation and the creation of knowledge was always hampered by conditions of scarcity. Education and expertise were limited to a small section of the population. Geographic distances and different languages made the exchange of information costly and slow. The transaction costs of creating knowledge were high. In the twenty-first century this scarcity is in some areas being replaced by abundance. Coupled with rapidly decreasing costs for transmitting, storing and acquiring information, this fundamentally alters the conditions for the creation of knowledge.

The Creative Commons project, but also the other conflicts with their claims about the importance of values and norms in the governance of innovation and knowledge, thus question the logic of the current IP system, which is based on the assumption of isolated, utility-maximizing economic actors. They highlight that innovation and the creation of knowledge and cultural goods is a social process. They do not deny that this process is driven by utilitarian incentives. But they claim that it is *also* driven by other incentive structures, and that these other incentives, based for example in the social norm of sharing, have already become significant in some areas, and should become dominant in other areas as well.

This conflict line adds another dimension to the theory of the knowledge society that neither Bell nor Stehr nor Castells addresses. Their theories of the knowledge society are all centred around core processes of change that affect first and foremost the economic order of societies, and then have wider effects in other sectors. The idea that knowledge production may be driven by other than economic reasons is present in Bell's and Stehr's writings, but only in the form of an internal logic of knowledge production. Bell describes the incessant branching of science (Bell 1999: Ch. 3), and Stehr stresses the self-reflexivity of theoretical knowledge (Stehr 1994a: Ch. 5). But what is missing is the idea put forward by Yochai Benkler, who provides a theoretical explanation for the rise of Wikipedia and other instances of peer production. He claims that in 'networked information economies' knowledge production is essentially a social process, driven to an important degree by social-norms-based decisions, and not only by utility-maximizing economic decisions (Benkler 2006: Ch. 3).

7.2.4.   Conflicts and change revisited

The general conflict lines, along which the four conflicts about software patents, access to medicines, Pirate Parties and Creative Commons have developed, are related to a number of processes of change. These processes of change have enabled or at least accelerated the development of conflicts along the lines mentioned above.

The most fundamental of these changes is the one that lies at the base of Manuel Castells' network society: the establishment of a *networking logic* that displaces the hierarchical organization of economic and social relations and permeates all aspects of current societies. Castells claims that power in the network society depends ultimately on the ability to program the network (Castells 2000: 22). Given the centrality of controlling the networking logic, it is no wonder that the conflicts are all related to this process of change.

The conflict about digital civil rights is an attempt to limit, on the one hand, the reach of the networking logic and to regain some space for personal privacy. On the other hand, it is a struggle for democratic control over dispersed decision-making structures where governance networks are replacing government institutions. In the other conflicts the collective actors strive to establish alternative networking logics of distributed innovation, and collaboration and sharing. These conflicts are not just consequences of processes of social change – the actors involved in these conflicts are also trying to change the processes of change while they are happening. They offer alternative versions of the knowledge society and not an alternative to the knowledge society.

This is most explicit with regard to the technological process of change – *digitization*. The digital revolution was clearly a necessary precondition for the development of current knowledge societies. Only in digital form can information in today's quantities be stored, transferred and processed in a global information network. This technological change is directly related to the changes in the property structure of the knowledge society – the increasing propertization of knowledge and other immaterial goods. The conflicts react to this technological change of digitization in general by embracing its possibilities. The attempts to foster a culture of sharing, to strengthen access to knowledge and to develop models of distributed open innovation all built on the potential of more egalitarian access to knowledge and information. Only in the conflict about digital civil rights does a cautionary perspective prevail that broaches the issue of surveillance and privacy.

The growing *propertization of knowledge* is, in contrast, unanimously attacked in the conflicts that I have analysed in this book. This process of change was certainly the immediate source of the conflicts about software patents and access to medicines in which the more general conflicts of the modes of innovation and access to knowledge have been addressed.

These processes of change and the general conflicts that lie behind the four contentious mobilizations about software patents, access to medicines, Pirate Parties and Creative Commons are connected in a complex web of relations. The three processes of change (establishment of a networking logic, digitization and propertization of knowledge) are each connected to multiple conflict lines. The growing propertization of knowledge structures the conflicts about the mode of innovation and about access to knowledge and creates a backdrop for the counter-movement to establish a culture of sharing. And in a similar way the other processes of change each influence the possibilities for action in multiple conflict settings. The processes of change are also connected with each other, so that for example the growing digitization strongly influences the conditions and possibilities for propertization of knowledge. And finally the conflicts are also interconnected, so that for example the conflict about a culture of sharing that questions the economic logic of knowledge generation is directly related to the conflicts about access to knowledge and the modes of innovation.

It should be noted though that the conflicts that can be seen in the four contentious mobilizations are not directly connected to a number of other processes of change that appear prominently in the theoretical literature on the knowledge society. None of the conflicts has resulted from the transition from manufacturing to service, the core process of change in Bell's (1999) description of the knowledge society. The transformation in the economy that Castells (2010a) associates with the displacement of the hierarchical industrial corporation by the network enterprise is also not at the root of the current most visible contentious mobilizations. The detachment of cultural production from local experience that Castells (2000) identifies as a major process of change in the cultural realm has also not yet become a source of conflictual action. And neither are the changes in gender relations and in women's roles in society and production that Castells identifies with the end of patriarchalism (1997: Ch 4) immediately reflected in the current conflicts.

This does not mean that these changes have happened without conflicts. It only means that these processes of change have not immediately influenced the trajectories of the most prominent contentious mobilizations which can clearly be identified as mobilizations about conflicts in the knowledge society so far.

What this rough sketch of the relationships between processes of change and conflicts in the knowledge society tells us, nevertheless, is that a new set of conflicts has emerged that is no longer firmly rooted in the cleavages of the industrial area. While the changes in the economic and occupational structure may still be addressed in a slightly modified framework of conflictual interaction developed in the industrial era, the conflicts that have been addressed in the contentious mobilizations discussed in this book seem to warrant new frameworks of interpretation and collective action. The unusual coalitions of actors, which not only are broadly transnational but also often comprise actors that are usually not present in social movement mobilizations, characterize all four conflicts and are an expression of this new conflict constellation. The analysis of the empirical conflicts thus reveals an area of contention that existing theories have largely ignored. But without accounting for these conflicts any understanding of the social dynamics of the knowledge society would be seriously flawed.

In the conflicts an alternative version of the knowledge society is proposed: a knowledge society in which knowledge remains the base for profit-driven economic activity, but in which this economic activity is not based on maximal exclusion but on social production based on shared knowledge resources. If this vision is to have any chance of becoming reality, it will need to be backed by a strong collective actor able to establish it as the hegemonic version of the knowledge society. Clearly no such collective actor exists today. But instead of ending with this pessimistic note, I will spend the remaining few pages of this book discussing whether the conflictual mobilizations that already exist today bear the traces of a social movement that may at some point become the agent of such an alternative version of the knowledge society.

7.3.   A movement in the making?

Throughout this book I have argued that the four mobilizations around software patents, access to medicines, Pirate Parties and Creative Commons overlap in several respects. They formulate similar criticisms of the current IP system, they show some similarities in their mobilization structures and some personal and organizational overlap between the mobilizations, and they develop partially along the same conflict lines, driven by the same processes of change in the knowledge society. These similarities have not escaped a number of activists involved in the four mobilizations, and in the early to mid 2000s some of them started to forge contacts and exchange ideas across the limits of the single mobilizations. As a result a mesomobilization started, that is a mobilization among 'groups and organizations that coordinate and integrate micromobilization groups' (Gerhards and Rucht 1992: 558).

The two focal points of this mesomobilization were the mobilization around the WIPO Development Agenda (see section 5.3.1) and the Information Society Project at Yale Law School. The first brought together developing country government officials, Geneva-based diplomats, Northern and Southern NGOs, and academics, who all share a broad policy goal of influencing the implementation of current and the framework for future IP treaties at the international level. It resulted in the formulation of a draft for an 'Access to Knowledge Treaty'[2] that can be seen as a more encompassing campaign platform against access restrictions, for users' rights and for open source models of innovation (Kapczynski 2008: 834).

The second focal point was the Information Society Project at Yale Law School, where in 2004 a number of eminent legal scholars – among them Yochai Benkler, Jack Balkin and Eddan Katz – started to bring together activists and researchers involved in various mobilizations around food and health, education and science, culture and media, and communication and infrastructure in a series of so far four conferences between 2006 and 2011 (Interview 25; Katz 2010: 279). During these and other meetings and conferences 'a diverse coalition of movements, political and economic actors, NGOs, scientists, and other academics have begun to coalesce around the idea, or the catchphrase, "access to knowledge" – A2K' (Benkler 2010: 217).

Key protagonists involved in this mesomobilization claim that what has developed there is a social movement – the access to knowledge movement that formulates in its demand for access a demand for distributive justice in the knowledge society (Krikorian and Kapczynski 2010). Gaëlle Krikorian sees the A2K mobilization as a 'common umbrella under which individuals and organizations could denounce inequalities and injustices related to intellectual property' (Krikorian 2010: 69). For her, A2K is not a mass movement engaged in street demonstrations or other forms of confrontational protest, but a 'movement of movements' (2010: 70) – a term that was originally coined for the global justice movement (e.g. della Porta and Mosca 2005).

But if a social movement is a social process in which actors engaged in collective action are involved in conflictual interactions with clearly identified opponents, linked by dense informal networks and sharing a distinct collective identity (della Porta and Diani 2006: 20), then the mesomobilization under the umbrella access to knowledge fulfils this definition only partially. The actual opponents vary according to the policy fields of the activists' main field of action, but they show some structural similarities across policy conflicts, in that the pro IP coalition is usually headed by business interests – usually transnational

---

[2] www.cptech.org/a2k/a2k_treaty_may9.pdf (accessed 27 July 2011).

corporations and local export-oriented firms (Shadlen 2009b) – and IP professionals, and supported by those parts of national administrations in charge of economic and trade policies. The mobilization is certainly characterized by dense informal networks among several hundred organizations and individual activists. What is missing is a shared master frame that would be an expression of a distinct and shared collective identity.

Amy Kapczynski argues that the A2K mobilization has started to develop a common language that integrates demands for the public domain, the commons, sharing, openness and access (Kapczynski 2010: 30). But she and Gaëlle Krikorian also acknowledge the still existing differences between the various actors and mobilizations. So far there is no agreement about how the demands of activists from the global South for better protection of traditional knowledge should be reconciled with the demand for open access and the public domain. And activists from the South also remind their Northern counterparts that free access to information alone will not solve the problem of inadequate educational systems that in many countries do not provide reliable primary education to the majority of the population – let alone secondary or tertiary (Kapczynski 2010: 45 ff.; Krikorian 2010: 83 ff.).

Based on the analysis of the mobilizations around software patents, access to medicines, the Pirate Parties and Creative Commons, I would also object that access to knowledge may be a too narrow frame to unite the demands for alternative modes of innovation, digital civil rights and the project of a culture of sharing. It highlights a specific aspect of the conflicts of the knowledge society but does not provide an overarching interpretation of the problem at hand and desired solution. Access to knowledge is not yet the pendant to ecology that would enable an 'environmentalism of the net' (Boyle 1997), that is, create a shared consciousness for a problem that is not collectively perceived as a problem until the term has been invented.

What is even more conspicuously missing is a pattern of sustained confrontation. Apart from the four contentious mobilizations that I have discussed in this book, there are a number of smaller campaigns in which activists fight the extension of intellectual property rights at the national level – as in the mobilization against data-retention laws in Germany or the three-strikes internet access blocking in France. There are lobbying campaigns to limit copyrights to enable better access for handicapped people, to strengthen fair use clauses or to create more extensive limitations for educational and scientific use of copyrighted works. The access to medicines conflict goes on, although with a less visible mobilization. And some protests – mostly in the form of petitions and public statements – have accompanied and exposed recent secretive negotiations for an Anti-Counterfeiting Trade Agreement (ACTA) and the Trans-Pacific Partnership Agreement, which would both substantially strengthen intellectual property rights through multilateral agreements focusing on stronger enforcement measures. The websites of the NGOs Knowledge Ecology International (keionline.org) and TransAtlantic Consumer Dialog (tacd-ip.org) and the Geneva-based IP critical news service Intellectual Property Watch (ip-watch.org) provide a pretty good overview of the variety of these conflicts and mobilizations that are often connected through individual actors or NGOs, bringing in knowledge and experience from earlier mobilizations. But most of these mobilizations involve only a handful of committed activists. They lack the mobilization strength found in the software patents and access to medicines conflict. They fail to mobilize large constituencies beyond the circle of activists already engaged in these issues.

So far there is thus no social movement of the knowledge society visible that would either deepen the conflicts addressed in this book by making them more salient and involving larger constituencies, or connect the conflict lines in a broader mobilization. But at the same time, the many small contentious mobilizations and the myriad of initiatives that spread the ideas of open access and sharing in the cultural, scientific, political and economic realm may still be the beginnings of such a movement. They certainly are expressions of a new class of conflicts, distinct to the knowledge society and developing along new cleavages not present in the industrial era.

References

ACT UP Philadelphia (1999), 'Al Gore's "Apartheid 2000" Campaign Comes to Philadelphia' [www.healthgap.org/press_releases/99/062899_AU_PR_GORE_PHILLY.html, accessed 19 August 2010].

Adam, Silke, and Hanspeter Kriesi (2007), 'The Network Approach', in: Paul A. Sabatier (ed.), *Theories of the Policy Process*, Boulder, CO: Westview Press, pp. 129–54.

Aglietta, Michel (2001), *A Theory of Capitalist Regulation: The US Experience*, London: Verso.

Aigrain, Philippe (2001), '11 Questions on Software Patentability Issues in Europe and the US' [http://paigrain.debatpublic.net/docs/elevenquestions, accessed 7 April 2010].

——— (2012), *Sharing: Culture and the Economy in the Internet Age*, Amsterdam University Press.

Al Jazeera (2009), 'Al Jazeera Announces Launch of Free Footage under Creative Commons License', *Al Jazeera* [http://cc.aljazeera.net/content/launch-press-release, accessed 7 June 2011].

Albers, Erik (2009), 'Der interinstitutionelle Konflikt um die EU-Richtlinie über die Patentierbarkeit computerimplementierter Erfindungen. Eine Prozess- und Konfliktanalyse der gescheiterten Richtlinie unter Verwendung der Vetospielertheorie Tsebelis' [http://kops.ub.uni-konstanz.de/volltexte/2010/9894/, accessed 28 April 2010].

Albert, Réka, Hawoong Jeong and Albert-László Barabási (2000), 'Error and Attack Tolerance of Complex Networks', *Nature* 406(6794): 378–82.

Andersen, Birgitte (2004), 'If "Intellectual Property Rights" is the Answer, what is the Question? Revisiting the Patent Controversies', *Economics of Innovation and New Technology* 13(5): 417.

Archibugi, Daniele, and Mario Pianta (1996), 'Innovation Surveys and Patents as Technology Indicators: The State of the Art', in: OECD (ed.), *Innovation, patents and technological strategies*, OECD Publishing, pp. 17–56.

Arrow, Kenneth J. (1962), 'Economic Welfare and the Allocation of Resources for Invention', in: National Bureau of Economic Research (ed.), *The Rate and Direction of Inventive Activity*, Princeton University Press, pp. 609–26.

Attac Deutschland (2003), 'Offener Brief von Attac an die deutschen Mitglieder des EP' [http://web.archive.org/web/20041221205231/www.attac.de/geig/mdep-brief.php, accessed 28 April 2010].

Bakels, Reinier, and P. Bernt Hugenholtz (2002), *The Patentability of Computer Programs. Discussion of European-Level Legislation in the Field of Patents for Software*, European Parliament, Directorate-General for Research [www.europarl.eu.int/hearings/20021107/juri/bakels_en.pdf, accessed 19 January 2009].

Balasubramaniam, Kumariah (1997), 'Heads-TNCs Win, Tails-South Loses or the GATT/WTO/TRIPs Agreement', in: Health Action International (ed.), *Power, Patents and Pills*, HAI-Europe.

Baldassarri, Delia, and Mario Diani (2007), 'The Integrative Power of Civic Networks', *American Journal of Sociology* 113(3): 735–80.

Ballardini, Rosa Maria (2008), 'Software Patents in Europe: The Technical Requirement Dilemma', *Journal of Intellectual Property Law Practice* 3(9): 563–75.

Banks, Martin (2005), 'The Lobbying Frenzy', *European Voice*, 7 July 2005 [www.spinwatch.org.uk/latest-news-mainmenu-10/159-eu-politics/1448-the-lobbying-frenzy, 18 accessed May 2010].

Barnard, David (2002), 'In the High Court of South Africa, Case No. 4138/98: The Global Politics of Access to Low-Cost AIDS Drugs in Poor Countries', *Kennedy Institute of Ethics Journal* 12(2): 159–74.

Barroso, José Manuel (2005), 'Letter to J. Morell Fontelles. Subject: Proposal for a Directive on the Patentability of Computer-Implemented Inventions COD/2002/0047' [http://eupat.ffii.org/papers/barroso0502/barroso0502.pdf, accessed 5 May 2010].

Bartels, Henning (2009), *Die Piratenpartei: Entstehung, Forderungen und Perspektiven der Bewegung*, Berlin: Contumax.

Beck, Ulrich (1986), *Risikogesellschaft. Auf dem Weg in eine andere Moderne*, Frankfurt: Suhrkamp.

Beckedahl, Markus (2003), 'Eine ungewöhnliche Lobbyaktion. Brüsseler Erlebnisse in der letzten Augustwoche 2003', *FIfF-Kommunikation* 4/2003: 42–3.

Beemiller, Richard M., and George K. Downey (2001), 'Gross State Product by Industry, 1992–99', *Survey of Current Business* 81(August): 159–72.

Bell, Daniel (1960), *The End of Ideology. On the Exhaustion of Political Ideas in the Fifties*, Glencoe, IL: Free Press.

(1976), 'Welcome to the Post-Industrial Society', *Physics Today* 28(2): 46.

(1999), *The Coming of Post-Industrial Society: A Venture in Social Forecasting*, Special Anniversary Edition with a new Foreword by the Author. New York: Basic Books. [First published 1973.]

Benford, Robert D., and David A. Snow (2000), 'Framing Processes and Social Movements: An Overview and Assessment', *Annual Review of Sociology* 26(1): 611–39.

Benkler, Yochai (1999), 'Free as the Air to Common Use: First Amendment Constraints on Enclosure of the Public Domain', *New York University Law Review* 74: 354–446.

(2006), *The Wealth of Networks: How Social Production Transforms Markets and Freedom*, New Haven, CT: Yale University Press.

(2010), 'The Idea of Access to Knowledge and the Information Commons. Long-Term Trends and Basic Elements', in: Gaëlle Krikorian and Amy

Kapczynski (eds.), *Access to Knowledge in the Age of Intellectual Property*, Cambridge, MA: Zone Books, pp. 217–36.

Bentham, Jeremy (1843), 'A Manual of Political Economy', in: John Bowring (ed.), *The Collected Works of Jeremy Bentham*, Edinburgh: W. Tait, pp. 32–84.

Berger, Jonathan Michael (2002), 'Litigation Strategies to Gain Access to Treatment for HIV/AIDS: The Case of South Africa's Treatment Action Campaign', *Wisconsin International Law Journal* 20(3): 595–610.

Berlin, Isaiah (1959), *Two Concepts of Liberty. An Inaugural Lecture Delivered before the University of Oxford on 31 Oct. 1958*, Oxford: Clarendon Press.

Berry, David M., and Giles Moss, eds. (2008), *Libre Culture. Meditations on Free Culture*, Winnipeg: Pygmalion Books.

Besen, Stanley M., and Leo J. Raskind (1991), 'An Introduction to the Law and Economics of Intellectual Property', *Journal of Economic Perspectives* 5(1): 3–27.

Bessen, James, and Michael J. Meurer (2008), *Patent Failure: How Judges, Bureaucrats, and Lawyers Put Innovators at Risk*, Princeton University Press.

Bieber, Christoph (2011), 'Wahlkampf als Onlinespiel? Die Piratenpartei als Innovationsträgerin im Bundestagswahlkampf 2009', in: Martin Eifert and Martin Hoffmann-Riehm (eds.), *Innovation, Recht, öffentliche Kommunikation*, Baden-Baden: Nomos, pp. 233–54.

Bieber, Christoph, and Claus Leggewie, eds. (2012), *Unter Piraten: Erkundungen in einer neuen politischen Arena*, Bielefeld: Transcript.

Biesenbender, Jan, and Katharina Holzinger (2009), 'Who has Power in the EU? A New Approach to the Analysis of Decision-Making Procedures', paper presented at *Reform processes and policy change: How do veto players determine decision-making in modern democracies*, Mannheim, 14 May 2009.

Biliouri, Daphne (1999), 'Environmental NGOs in Brussels: How Powerful are Their Lobbying Activities?', *Environmental Politics* 8(2): 173–82.

BITKOM (2003), 'Stellungnahme zur Entschließung des Europäischen Parlaments vom 25. September 2003 zur Richtlinie über die Patentierbarkeit computerimplementierter Erfindungen', Berlin: BITKOM [https://www.mcert.de/files/documents/Stellungnahme_Beschluss_EP_zu_CII_7.11.2003.pdf, accessed 25 November 2008].

Blackburn, McKinley L. (1989), 'Interpreting the Magnitude of Changes in Measures of Income Inequality', *Journal of Econometrics* 42(1): 21–5.

Bleich, Holger (2010), 'Die Abmahn-Industrie', *c't – Magazin für Computertechnik*, 2010, pp. 154–7.

Blind, Knut et al. (2001), *Mikro- und makroökonomische Implikationen der Patentierbarkeit von Softwareinnovationen geistige Eigentumsrechte in der Informationstechnologie im Spannungsfeld von Wettbewerb und Innovation*, Forschungsprojekt im Auftrage des Bundesministeriums für Wirtschaft und Technologie (Forschungsauftrag 36/00); Endbericht [www.bmwi.de/Redaktion/Inhalte/Downloads/mikro-und-makrooekonomische-implikationen-der-patentierbarkeit-von-softwareinnovationen-Softwarepatentstudie,property=pdf.pdf, accessed 19 January 2009].

Blind, Knut, Jakob Edler and Michael Friedewald (2003), *Geistige Eigentumsrechte in der Informationsgesellschaft: Eine Analyse der Rolle gewerblicher Schutzrechte bei Gründung und Markteintritt sowie für die Innovations- und Wettbewerbsfähigkeit von Softwareunternehmen anhand unternehmens- und softwaretypenbezogener Fallstudien*, Karlsruhe: Fraunhofer-Institut für Systemtechnik und Innovationsforschung (ISI) im Auftrag des Bundesministeriums für Wirtschaft und Arbeit (Projekt 31/02), Endbericht [www.bmwi.de/Redaktion/Inhalte/Downloads/br-geistige-eigentumsrechte-in-der-informationsgesellschaft-lang-de,property=pdf.pdf, accessed 19 January 2009].

'Blood and Oil' (2000), *The Economist*, 4 March 2000, p. 68.

Bödeker, Sebastian, Oliver Moldenhauer and Benedikt Rubbel (2005), *Wissensallmende. Gegen die Privatisierung des Wissens der Welt durch "geistige Eigentumsrechte"*, Hamburg: VSA.

Boldrin, Michele, and David K. Levine (2008), *Against Intellectual Monopoly*, New York: Cambridge University Press.

Bollier, David (2008), *Viral Spiral. How the Commoners Built a Digital Republic of Their Own*, New York: The New Press.

Bouwen, Pieter (2002), 'Corporate Lobbying in the European Union: The Logic of Access', *Journal of European Public Policy* 9(3): 365–90.

(2004), 'Exchanging Access Goods for Access: A Comparative Study of Business Lobbying in the European Union Institutions', *European Journal of Political Research* 43: 337–69.

Boyle, James (1997), 'A Politics Of Intellectual Property: Environmentalism for the Net?', *Duke Law Journal* 47(1): 87–116.

(2003), 'The Second Enclosure Movement and the Construction of the Public Domain', *Law and Contemporary Problems* 66(1&2): 33–74.

(2008), *The Public Domain: Enclosing the Commons of the Mind*, New Haven, CT: Yale University Press.

Brandes, Ulrik et al. (1999), 'Explorations into the Visualization of Policy Networks', *Journal of Theoretical Politics* 11(1): 75–106.

Brenni, Claudio (2010), *The Anti-Counterfeiting Trade Agreement (ACTA): A New Obstacle to Human Rights?*, 3D Information note 10, June 2010, Geneva: 3D.

Britt, Ronda (2010), *Universities Report $55 Billion in Science and Engineering R&D Spending for FY 2009*, InfoBrief SRS NSF 10–329, Arlington, VA: National Science Foundation [www.nsf.gov/statistics/infbrief/nsf10329/nsf10329.pdf, accessed 6 July 2011].

Brundtland, Gro Harlem (1999), 'Speech of the WHO Director-General Dr Gro Harlem Brundtland', in: Germán Velásquez and Pascale Boulet (eds.), *Globalization and Access to Drugs: Implications of the WTO/TRIPS Agreement*, Geneva: World Health Organization, pp. 67–73.

BSA (2005), 'Vote on CII Directive Sends Mixed Signals – BSA Urges European Parliament to Vote for Innovation and Growth' [w3.bsa.org/eupolicy/press/newsreleases/Vote-on-CII-Directive-Sends-Mixed-Signals.cfm, accessed 17 November 2008].

Budapest Open Access Initiative (2002), 'Budapest Open Access Initiative' [www.soros.org/openaccess/g/read.shtml, accessed 6 July 2011].

Buechler, Steven M. (1995), 'New Social Movement Theories', *The Sociological Quarterly* 36(3): 441–64.

Burns, Charlotte (2004), 'Codecision and the European Commission: A Study of Declining Influence', *Journal of European Public Policy* 11(1): 1–18.

Buzek, Jerzy et al. (2004), *Motion for a Resolution tabled by Jerzy Buzek, Adam Gierek, Tomas Zatloukal, Jan Marinus Wiersma, Marco Pannella, Zuzana Roithová, Georgs Andrejevs, Janusz Onyszkiewicz, Toomas Hendrik Ilves pursuant to Rule 55(4) of the Rules of Procedure on the patentability of computer-implemented inventions (0092/2002 – C5 0082/2002 – 2002/0047(COD))*, Brussels: European Parliament [http://people.ffii.org/~jmaebe/reso/resolution_55_4.pdf, accessed 5 May 2010].

Cameron, Edwin, and Jonathan Berger (2005), 'Patents and Public Health: Principle, Politics and Paradox', *Proceedings of the British Academy* 131: 331–69.

Carrington, Peter J., John Scott and Stanley Wasserman, eds. (2005), *Models and methods in social network analysis*, Cambridge University Press.

Castells, Manuel (1997), *The Power of Identity*, Oxford: Blackwell.

(1998), *End of Millennium*, Oxford: Blackwell.

(2000), 'Materials for an Exploratory Theory of the Network Society', *British Journal of Sociology* 51(1): 5–24.

(2004), *The Power of Identity*, 2nd edn, Oxford: Blackwell.

(2010a), *The Rise of the Network Society*, 2nd edn with a new preface. Oxford: Blackwell. [First published 1996.]

(2010b), *End of Millennium*, 2nd edn with a new preface. Oxford: Blackwell.

CIPIH (2006), *Public Health, Innovation and Intellectual Property Rights: Report of the Commission on Intellectual Property Rights, Innovation and Public Health*, Geneva: World Health Organization [www.who.int/entity/intellectualproperty/documents/thereport/ENPublicHealthReport.pdf, accessed 13 October 2010].

CIPR (2002), *Integrating Intellectual Property Rights and Development Policy. Report of the Commission on Intellectual Property Rights*, London.

Clapham, Andrew, and Mary Robinson, eds. (2009), *Realizing the Right to Health*, Zurich: rüffer & rub.

COM (1997), *Promoting Innovation through Patents. Green Paper on the Community Patent and the Patent System in Europe*, COM(1997) 314 final, Brussels: Commission of the European Communities [http://europa.eu/documents/comm/green_papers/pdf/com97_314_en.pdf, accessed 28 November 2008].

(1999), *Promoting Innovation through Patents – The Follow-Up to the Green Paper on the Community Patent and the Patent System in Europe*, COM(99) 42 final, Brussels: Commission of the European Communities [http://ec.europa.eu/internal_market/indprop/docs/patent/docs/8682_en.pdf, accessed 5 April 2010].

(2000a), *Proposal for a Council Regulation on the Community Patent*, COM(2000) 412 final, Brussels: Commission of the European Communities [http://eur-lex.europa.eu/LexUriServ/LexUriServ.do?uri=COM:2000:0412:FIN:EN:PDF, accessed 1 April 2010].

(2000b), *The Patentability of Computer-Implemented Inventions. Consultation Paper by the Services of the Directorate General for the Internal Market*, Brussels: Commission of the European Communities [http://ec.europa. eu/internal_market/indprop/docs/comp/soft_en.pdf, accessed 5 April 2010].

(2000c), *Report from the Commission to the Council, the European Parliament and the Economic and Social Committee on the Implementation and Effects of Directive 91/250/EEC on the Legal Protection of Computer Programs*, COM(2000) 0199, Brussels: Commission of the European Communities.

(2002), *Proposal for a Directive of the European Parliament and of the Council on the Patentability of Computer-Implemented Inventions*, COM(2002) 92, Brussels: Commission of the European Communities [http://eur-lex. europa.eu/LexUriServ/site/en/com/2002/com2002_0092en01.pdf, accessed 8 April 2010].

(2003), *Proposal for a Directive of the European Parliament and of the Council on Measures and Procedures to Ensure the Enforcement of Intellectual Property Rights*, COM(2003) 46 final, Brussels: Commission of the European Communities [http://eur-lex.europa.eu/LexUriServ/LexUriServ.do?uri= COM:2003:0046:FIN:EN:PDF, accessed 4 October 2006].

Comte, Auguste (1875), *System of Positive Polity*, London: Longmans, Green and Co.

Correa, Carlos M. (2000), *Intellectual Property Rights, the WTO and Developing Countries. The TRIPS Agreement and Policy Options*, London: Zed Books.

(2002), 'Public Health and Intellectual Property Rights', *Global Social Policy* 2(3): 261–78.

(2006), 'Implications of Bilateral Free Trade Agreements on Access to Medicines', *Bulletin of the World Health Organization* 84(5): 399–404.

COUNCIL (2009), *Press Releases – 2982nd Council meeting Competitiveness (Internal Market, Industry and Research) Brussels, 3–4 December 2009*, 17076/09 (Presse 365), Brussels: Council of the European Union [http:// europa.eu/rapid/pressReleasesAction.do?reference=PRES/09/365&forma t=HTML&aged=0&lg=en&guiLanguage=en, accessed 1 April 2010].

Council General Secretariat (2003), *Proposal for a Directive of the European Parliament and of the Council on the Patentability of Computer-Implemented Inventions – Examination of the Amendments Proposed by the European Parliament at First Reading Procedure*, 13955/03, Council of the European Union [http://register.consilium.europa.eu/pdf/en/03/st13/st13955.en03. pdf, accessed 30 March 2010].

(2004), *Proposal for a Directive of the European Parliament and of the Council on the Patentability of Computer-Implemented Inventions – Political Agreement on the Council's Common Position*, 9713/04, Brussels: Council of the European Union [http://register.consilium.europa.eu/pdf/en/04/st09/st09713.en04. pdf, accessed 5 May 2010].

(2010), *Guide to the Ordinary Legislative Procedure*, Luxembourg: Publications Office of the European Union.

Creative Commons (2001a), 'Creative Commons Inaugural Meeting – May 7, 2001' [http://cyber.law.harvard.edu/creativecommons/, accessed 2 June 2011].

(2001b), 'Executive Summary of Issues Facing Creative Commons' [http://cyber.law.harvard.edu/creativecommons/exec.html, accessed 2 June 2011].

(2011a), *The Power of Open*, Creative Commons.

(2011b), 'Creative Commons – About', *Creative Commons* [http://creativecommons.org/about, accessed 7 June 2011].

(2011c), 'Creative Commons – Culture', *Creative Commons* [https://creativecommons.org/culture, accessed 7 June 2011].

Curtis, Russell L., and Louis Zurcher (1973), 'Stable Resources of Protest Movements: the Multi-organizational Field', *Social Forces* 52: 53–61.

David, Paul A. (1993), 'Intellectual Property Institutions and the Panda's Thumb: Patents, Copyrights, and Trade Secrets in Economic theory and History', in: Mitchel B. Wallerstein, Mary E. Mogee and Robin A. Schoen (eds.), *Global Dimensions of Intellectual Property Rights in Science and Technology*, Washington, DC: National Academies Press, pp. 19–61.

(2000), *A Tragedy of the Public Knowledge 'Commons'? Global Science, Intellectual Property and the Digital Technology Boomerang*, SIEPR Discussion Paper No. 00–02, Stanford, CA: Stanford Institute for Economic Policy Research [http://129.3.20.41/eps/dev/papers/0502/0502010.pdf, accessed 27 April 2011].

Davies, Simon (2003), 'The Proposed Software Directive: A User's Comments', *Journal of Information, Law & Technology* 3(1).

Davis, Lee (2004), 'Intellectual Property Rights, Strategy and Policy', *Economics of Innovation and New Technology* 13(5): 399–415.

Deere, Carolyn (2009), *The Implementation Game: The TRIPS Agreement and the Global Politics of Intellectual Property Reform in Developing Countries*, Oxford and New York: Oxford University Press.

della Porta, Donatella, and Mario Diani (2006), *Social Movements. An Introduction*, 2nd edn, Malden, MA: Blackwell.

della Porta, Donatella, and Lorenzo Mosca (2005), 'Global-Net for Global Movements? A Network of Networks for a Movement of Movements', *Journal of Public Policy* 25(1): 165–90.

Demker, Marie (2011), 'Sailing Along New Cleavages: Understanding the Success of the Swedish Pirate Party in the European Parliament Election 2009', paper presented at *ISA Annual Convention*, Montreal, Canada, 16 March 2011 [http://goo.gl/6jlI2, accessed 17 May 2011].

Desmarais, Annette Aurelle (2007), *La Via Campesina. Globalization and the Power of Peasants*, Halifax, NS: Fernwood Pub.

Deutsche Forschungsgemeinschaft (2009), 'Open Access und Forschungsförderung durch die Deutsche Forschungsgemeinschaft' [www.dfg.de/dfg_magazin/forschungspolitik_standpunkte_perspektiven/open_access/index.html, accessed 6 July 2011].

Diamond v. Diehr (1981), (US Supreme Court) 450 US 175.

Diani, Mario (1992), 'The Concept of Social Movement', *The Sociological Review* 40(1): 1–25.

(2000), 'Simmel to Rokkan and Beyond: Towards a Network Theory of (New) Social Movements', *European Journal of Social Theory* 3(4): 387–406.

(2003), 'Networks and Social Movements: A Research Programme', in: Mario Diani and Doug McAdam (eds.), *Social Movements and Networks*, Oxford University Press, pp. 299–319.

Diani, Mario, and Doug McAdam, eds. (2003), *Social Movements and Networks. Relational Approaches to Collective Action*, Oxford University Press.

Diver, Laurence (2008), 'Would the Current Ambiguities within the Legal Protection of Software be Solved by the Creation of a Sui Generis Property Right for Computer Programs?', *Journal of Intellectual Property Law Practice* 3(2): 125–38.

Dixon, Padraig, and Christine Bauhardt (2002), 'The Economics of Intellectual Property: A Review to Identify Themes for Future Research' [www.dklevine.com/archive/dixon-review.pdf, accessed 19 January 2009].

Dobusch, Leonhard, and Kirsten Gollatz (2012), 'Piraten zwischen transnationaler Bewegung und lokalem Phänomen', in: Christoph Bieber and Claus Leggewie (eds.), *Unter Piraten: Erkundungen in einer neuen politischen Arena*, Bielefeld: Transcript, pp. 25–40.

Dobusch, Leonhard, and Sigrid Quack (2008), *Epistemic Communities and Social Movements: Transnational Dynamics in the Case of Creative Commons*, MPIfG Discussion Paper 08/8, Cologne: Max-Planck-Institut für Gesellschaftsforschung [www.mpifg.de/projects/govxborders/downloads/Dobusch/_Quack_2008_DP_EpistemicComm.pdf, accessed 9 December 2009].

Doctorow, Cory (2003), *Down and Out in the Magic Kingdom*, New York: Tor.

Drahos, Peter (1995), 'Information Feudalism in the Information Society', *The Information Society* 11(3): 209–22.

(1999), 'Biotechnology Patents, Markets and Morality', *European Intellectual Property Review* 21(9): 441–9.

(2002), 'Negotiating Intellectual Property Rights: Between Coercion and Dialogue', in: Peter Drahos and Ruth Mayne (eds.), *Global Intellectual Property Rights. Knowledge, Access, and Development*, Basingstoke: Palgrave, pp. 161–82.

(2005), 'Intellectual Property Rights in the Knowledge Economy', in: David Rooney, Greg Hearn, and Abraham Ninan (eds.), *Handbook on the Knowledge Economy*, Cheltenham, Glos: Edward Elgar Publishing, pp. 139–51.

(2007), 'Four Lessons for Developing Countries from the Trade Negotiations Over Access to Medicines', *Liverpool Law Review* 28(1): 11–39.

Drahos, Peter, and John Braithwaite (2003), *Information Feudalism. Who Owns the Knowledge Economy?*, New York: New Press.

Drezner, Daniel W. (2007), *All Politics is Global*, Princeton University Press.

Drucker, Peter F. (1969), *The Age of Discountinuity. Guideliness to Our Changing Society*, London: Pan Books.

Durkheim, Emile (1933), *The Division of Labor in Society*, New York: Macmillan.

Dutfield, Graham (2001), 'TRIPS-Related Aspects of Traditional Knowledge', *Case Western Reserve Journal of International Law* 33: 233.

Earl, Jennifer et al. (2004), 'The Use of Newspaper Data in the Study of Collective Action', *Annual Review of Sociology* 30(1): 65–80.

Eckl, Julian (2005), 'Die Auseinandersetzungen über EU-"Softwarepatent"-Richtlinie als Testfall für demokratische Beteiligungsmöglichkeiten an der Gestaltung der internationalen politischen

Ökonomie', paper presented at *Tagung der Sektion internationale Politik der DVPW*, Mannheim, 6 October 2005.

EFF (2008), 'RIAA v. The People: Five Years Later', *Electronic Frontier Foundation* [www.eff.org/wp/riaa-v-people-years-later, accessed 1 March 2010].

EICTA et al. (2005), *SME Manifesto on Patents for Computer-Implemented Inventions* [www.softwarechoice.org/download_files/SME_manifesto_0105.pdf, accessed 25 November 2008].

Eimer, Thomas R. (2007), *Zwischen Allmende und Clubgut – Der Einfluss von Free/ Open Source Akteuren in der Europäischen Union*, Hagen: Fernuniversität Hagen.

(2008), 'Decoding Divergence in Software Regulation: Paradigms, Power Structures, and Institutions in the United States and the European Union', *Governance* 21(2): 275–96.

(2011), *Arenen und Monopole Softwarepatente in den USA und in Europa*, Wiesbaden: VS Verlag.

Eimer, Thomas R., and Susanne Lütz (2010), 'Developmental States, Civil Society, and Public Health: Patent Regulation for HIV/AIDS Pharmaceuticals in India and Brazil', *Regulation & Governance* 4(2): 135–53.

Eisinger, Peter K. (1973), 'The Conditions of Protest Behavior in American Cities', *American Political Science Review* 67(1): 11–28.

Eldred v. *Ashcroft* (2003), (US Supreme Court) 537 US 186.

Ensthaler, Jürgen (2009), 'Die Schranken des Urheberrechts', in: *Gewerblicher Rechtsschutz und Urheberrecht*, Berlin, Heidelberg: Springer, pp. 91–8.

(2010), 'Der patentrechtliche Schutz von Computerprogrammen nach der BGH-Entscheidung "Steuerungseinrichtung für Untersuchungsmodalitäten"', *GRUR* 112(1): 1–6.

EP (2001), *European Parliament Resolution on Access to Drugs for HIV/AIDS Victims in the Third World*, Brussels: European Parliament [www.europarl.europa.eu/sides/getDoc.do?type=TA&reference=P5-TA-2001–0154&format=XML&language=EN, accessed 1 November 2010].

(2002), *Hearing on Patentability of Computer Implemented Inventions (COM(2002) 92)*, Brussels: European Parliament [www.europarl.europa.eu/meetdocs/committees/juri/20021107/01a_en.pdf, accessed 10 April 2010].

(2003a), 'European Parliament – Protocol of the Plenary Debate, Tuesday, 23 September 2003 – Patentability of computer-implemented inventions' [www.europarl.europa.eu/sides/getDoc.do?pubRef=-//EP//TEXT+CRE+20030923+ITEM-002+DOC+XML+V0//EN&language=EN, accessed 6 April 2010].

(2003b), *Position of the European Parliament Adopted at First Reading on 24 September 2003 with a View to the Adoption of Directive 2003/.../ EC of the European Parliament and of the Council on the Patentability of Computer-Implemented Inventions*, EP-PE_TC1-COD(2002)0047, Brussels: European Parliament [www.europarl.europa.eu/sides/getDoc.do?pubRef=-//EP//TEXT+CRE+20030923+ITEM-002+DOC+XML+V0//EN&language=EN, accessed 6 April 2010].

(2004), *Rules of Procedure of the European Parliament*, 16th edn, Brussels.

246   References

(2005a), 'European Parliament – Protocol of the Plenary Debate, Tuesday, 5 July 2005 – Patentability of Computer-Implemented Inventions' [www. europarl.europa.eu/sides/getDoc.do?pubRef=-//EP//TEXT+CRE+20050 705+ITEM-006+DOC+XML+V0//EN&language=EN, accessed 6 April 2010].

(2005b), 'European Parliament – Protocol of the Plenary Debate, Tuesday, 6 July 2005 – Patentability of Computer-Implemented Inventions' [www. europarl.europa.eu/sides/getDoc.do?pubRef=-//EP//TEXT+CRE+20050 706+ITEM-007+DOC+XML+V0//EN&language=EN, accessed 18 May 2010].

Ernesto [pseud.] (2009), 'Swedes Demonstrate Against Pirate Bay Verdict', *TorrentFreak* [http://torrentfreak.com/swedes-demonstrate-against-pirate-bay-verdict-090418/, accessed 22 May 2011].

ESC (1998), 'Opinion of the Economic and Social Committee on "Promoting Innovation Through Patents: Green Paper on the Community Patent and the Patent System in Europe"', *Official Journal of the European Communities* 41(C 129): 8–15.

(2003), 'Opinion of the Economic and Social Committee on the Proposal for a Directive of the European Parliament and of the Council on the Patentability of Computer-Implemented Inventions (COM(2002) 92 final – 2002/0047 (COD))', *Official Journal of the European Communities* 46(C 61).

EuroLinux Alliance (1999), 'Eurolinux Meets EU Patent Legislators', *ffii.org* [http://eurolinux.ffii.org/news/euipCAen.html, accessed 5 April 2010].

(2000), 'Petition for a Software Patent Free Europe', *ffii.org* [http://web.archive.org/web/20051227032443/petition.eurolinux.org/index_html?NO_ COOKIE=true, accessed 5 April 2010].

Feser, Edward (2005), 'There is no such Thing as Unjust Initial Acquisition', in: Ellen Frankel Paul, Fred Dycus Miller and Jeffrey Paul (eds.), *Natural Rights Liberalism from Locke to Nozick*, Cambridge University Press, pp. 56–80.

FFII (1999), 'Protokoll der Gründungssitzung' [http://old.ffii.org/assoc/statut/ gruendung/index.de.html, accessed 7 January 2010].

(2004), 'European Software Patent Statistics' [http://eupat.ffii.org/patents/ stats/index.en.html, accessed 31 March 2010].

(2005), 'JURI Committee Leaves Council Text Largely Unchanged' [http:// wiki.ffii.org/Juri050620En, accessed 18 May 2010].

Fisher, Bart S., and Ralph G. Steinhardt (1982), 'Section 301 of the Trade Act of 1974', *Law and Policy in International Business* 14(3): 569–603.

Fisher, William W., III (1999), 'Geistiges Eigentum – ein ausufernder Rechtsbereich: Die Geschichte des Ideenschutzes in den Vereinigten Staaten', in: Hannes Siegrist and David Sugarman (eds.), *Eigentum im internationalen Vergleich*, Göttingen: Vandenhoeck & Ruprecht, pp. 265–91.

(2001), 'Theories of Intellectual Property', in: Stephen R Munzer (ed.), *New Essays in the Legal and Political Theory of Property*, Cambridge University Press, pp. 168–99.

Fleischer, Rasmus, and Palle Torsson (2006), 'Piratbyran's speech at Reboot', Copyriot [http://copyriot.blogspot.com/2006/06/ piratbyrans-speech-at-reboot.html, accessed 20 May 2011].

Flickr (2004), 'Creative Commons', *Flickr Blog* [http://blog.flickr.net/ en/2004/06/29/creative-commons/, accessed 7 June 2011].

Floridi, Luciano (2010), *Information: A Very Short Introduction*, Oxford University Press.

Flynn, Matthew, and Egléubia Andrade de Oliveira (2009), 'Regulatory Capitalism in Emerging Markets: An Institutional Analysis of Brazil's Health Surveillance Agency (ANVISA)', paper presented at 104th Annual Meeting of the ASA held on 8–11 August in San Francisco, California, 2009 [www.allacademic.com/meta/p308497_index.html, accessed 21 November 2012].

Flyvbjerg, Bent (2006), 'Five Misunderstandings About Case-Study Research', *Qualitative Inquiry* 12(2): 219–45.

Ford, Nathan (2004), 'Patents, Access to Medicines and the Role of Non-Governmental Organisations', *Journal of Generic Medicines* 1: 137–45.

Ford, Nathan et al. (2004), 'The Role of Civil Society in Protecting Public Health over Commercial Interests: Lessons from Thailand', *The Lancet* 363(9408): 560–3.

Forman, Lisa (2008), '"Rights" and Wrongs: What Utility for the Right to Health in Reforming Trade Rules on Medicines?', *Health and Human Rights* 10(2): 37–52.

Foucault, Michel (1981), *Sexualität und Wahrheit. Vol. 1. Der Wille zum Wissen*, Frankfurt: Suhrkamp.

(1991), *Die Ordnung des Diskurses*, Frankfurt: Fischer.

French Delegation (2000), *MR/8/00 – Proposal Submitted by the French Delegation at the Diplomatic Conference for the Revision of the EPC 2000 in Munich* [http://documents.epo.org/projects/babylon/eponet.nsf/0/EACEB5602C7 C94B7C1257280005ACC92/$File/mr00008.pdf, accessed 7 April 2010].

French Presidency of the G8 (2011), *G8 Declaration – Renewed Commitment for Freedom and Democracy* [www.g20-g8.com/g8-g20/root/bank/print/1314. htm, accessed 28 May 2011].

G8 (2006), 'St. Petersburg Summit: Chair's Summary' [www.g8.utoronto.ca/ summit/2006stpetersburg/summary.html, accessed 21 January 2010].

(2007), 'Heiligendamm Summit: Chair's Summary' [www.g-8.de/Content/ EN/Artikel/__g8-summit/anlagen/chairs-summary,templateId=raw,prop erty=publicationFile.pdf/chairs-summary.pdf, accessed 29 July 2009].

(2008), 'Hokkaido Toyako Summit: World Economy' [www.g8.utoronto.ca/ summit/2008hokkaido/2008-economy.html, accessed 24 February 2010].

(2009), 'G8 Leaders Declaration: Responsible Leadership for a Sustainable Future' [www.g8italia2009.it/static/G8_Allegato/G8_ Declaration_08_07_09_final,0.pdf, accessed 24 February 2010].

Galvão, Jane (2005), 'Brazil and Access to HIV/AIDS Drugs: A Question of Human Rights and Public Health', *American Journal of Public Health* 95(7): 1110–16.

Gambardella, Alfonso, Paola Giuri and Myriam Mariani (2005), *The Value of European Patents. Evidence From a Survey of European Inventors. Final Report of the PatValEU Project*, Pisa: Laboratory of Economics and Management (LEM), Sant' Anna School of Advanced Studies [www.alfonsogam-bardella.it/patvalfinalreport.pdf, accessed 24 July 2011].

Gamson, William A. (1992), *Talking Politics*, Cambridge University Press.

(1995), 'Constructing Social Protest', in: Hank Johnston and Bert Klandermans (eds.), *Social Movements and Culture*, Minneapolis, MN: University of Minnesota Press, pp. 85–106.

Garfinkel, Simson L. (1994), 'Patently Absurd', *Wired*, July 1994 [www.wired.com/wired/archive/2.07/patents_pr.html, accessed 4 April 2010].

Garfinkel, Simson L., Richard M. Stallman and Mitchell Kapor (1991), 'Why Patents are Bad for Software', *Issues in Science & Technology* 8(1): 50–5.

Geertz, Clifford (1973), 'Thick Description: Toward an Interpretive Theory of Culture', in: *The Interpretation of Cultures: Selected Essays*, New York: Basic Books, pp. 3–30.

Gehlen, Claudia (2006), *Lobbying in Brussels: The EU Directive on the Patentability of Computer-Implemented Inventions (A)*, Insead Case Study 11/2006–5375, Fontainebleau: Insead.

Geist, Michael (2009), 'The ACTA Internet Chapter: Putting the Pieces Together', *Michael Geist* [www.michaelgeist.ca/content/view/4510/125/#copycon, accessed 4 November 2009].

(2012), 'CETA Update, Part Two: ACTA Provisions Are Still Very Much Alive', *Michael Geist* [www.michaelgeist.ca/index2.php?option=com_content&task=view&id=6609&Itemid=125&pop=1&page=0, accessed 25 August 2012].

George, Julie (2009), 'Intellectual Property and Access to Medicines: Developments and Civil Society Initiatives in India', in: Renata Reis, Veriano Terto Jr and Maria Cristina Pimenta (eds.), *Intellectual Property Rights and Access to ARV Medicines. Civil Society Resistance in the Global South*, Rio de Janeiro: ABIA, pp. 110–36.

Gerhards, Jürgen, and Dieter Rucht (1992), 'Mesomobilization: Organizing and Framing in Two Protest Campaigns in West Germany', *American Journal of Sociology* 98(3): 555–96.

Giradeau, Astris (2009), 'Hadopi: le bâton adopté', *Libération*, 23 October 2009 [www.liberation.fr/medias/0109598891-hadopi-le-baton-adopte, accessed 2 March 2010].

Goffman, Erving (1974), *Frame Analysis. An Essay on the Organization of Experience*, New York: Harper.

Gombe, Spring, and James Love (2010), 'New Medicines and Vaccines. Access, Incentives to Investment, and Freedom to Innovate', in: Gaëlle Krikorian and Amy Kapczynski (eds.), *Access to Knowledge in the Age of Intellectual Property*, Cambridge, MA: Zone Books, pp. 531–46.

Goody, Jack, and Ian Watt (1963), 'The Consequences of Literacy', *Comparative Studies in Society and History* 5(3): 304–45.

Gorlin, Jacques (1985), 'A Trade Based Approach for the International Copyright Protection for Computer Software'. Unpublished, on file with author.

Gramsci, Antonio (1992), *Prison Notebooks*, New York: Columbia University Press.

Grassmuck, Volker (2002), *Freie Software. Zwischen Privat- und Gemeineigentum*, Bonn: Bundeszentrale für Politische Bildung.

(2009), 'The World Is Going Flat(-Rate)', *Intellectual Property Watch* [www. ip-watch.org/weblog/2009/05/11/the-world-is-going-flat-rate/, accessed 25 June 2009].

Greenwood, Justin (2003), *Interest Representation in the European Union*, Houndmills: Palgrave Macmillan.

Guellec, Dominique, and Bruno van Pottelsberghe de la Potterie (2007), *The Economics of the European Patent System: IP Policy for Innovation and Competition*, Oxford University Press.

Hajer, Maarten A. (1993), 'Discourse Coalitions and the Institutionalization of Practice: The Case of Acid Rain in Britain', in: Frank Fischer and John Forester (eds.), *The Argumentative Turn in Policy Analysis and Planning*, Durham, NC: Duke University Press, pp. 43–76.

Halbert, Debora (1997), 'Intellectual Property Piracy: The Narrative Construction of Deviance', *International Journal for the Semiotics of Law* 10(1): 55–78.

Hallstrom, Lars K. (2004), 'Eurocratising Enlargement? EU – Elites and NGO – Participation in European Environmental Policy', *Environmental Politics* 13(1): 175.

Hammwöhner, Rainer et al. (2007), 'Qualität der Wikipedia. Eine vergleichende Studie', in: Achim Oßwald, Maximilian Stempfhuber and Christian Wolff (eds.), *Open Innovation. Neue Perspektiven im Kontext von Information und Wissen*, Konstanz: UVK Verlagsgesellschaft, pp. 77–90.

Hardin, Garrett (1968), 'The Tragedy of the Commons', *Science* 162(3859): 1,243–8.

Hart, Robert, Peter Holmes and John Reid (2000), *The Economic Impact of Patentability of Computer Programs. Report to the European Commission (Study Contract ETD/99/B5–3000/E/106)*, London: Intellectual Property Institute [http://europa.eu.int/comm/internal_market/en/indprop/comp/ studyintro.htm, accessed 19 January 2009].

Haunss, Sebastian (2001), 'Was in aller Welt ist "kollektive Identität"? Bemerkungen und Vorschläge zu Identität und kollektivem Handeln', *Gewerkschaftliche Monatshefte* 05/2001: 256–67.

(2004), *Identität in Bewegung. Prozesse kollektiver Identität bei den Autonomen und in der Schwulenbewegung*, Wiesbaden: VS Verlag für Sozialwissenschaften.

(2011), 'Kollektive Identität, soziale Bewegungen und Szenen', *Forschungsjournal Soziale Bewegungen* 24(4): 41–53.

Haunss, Sebastian, and Lars Kohlmorgen (2008), *Codebook for the Analysis of Political Claims in Conflicts on Intellectual Property Rights in Europe* [www.ipgovernance. eu/publications/IPGovCodebook.pdf, accessed 19 January 2009].

(2009), 'Lobbying or Politics? Political Claims-Making in IP Conflicts', in: Sebastian Haunss and Kenneth C. Shadlen (eds.), *Politics of Intellectual Property*, Cheltenham, Glos: Edward Elgar Publishing, pp. 107–28.

(2010), 'Conflicts about Intellectual Property Claims: The Role and Function of Collective Action Networks', *Journal of European Public Policy* 17(2): 242–62.

Haunss, Sebastian, and Kenneth C. Shadlen, eds. (2009), *Politics of Intellectual Property. Contestation over the Ownership, Use, and Control of Knowledge and Information*, Cheltenham, Glos: Edward Elgar Publishing.

Health Action International, Médecins Sans Frontières and Consumer Project on Technology (1999), *Amsterdam Statement to WTO Member States on Access to Medicine* [www.cptech.org/ip/health/amsterdamstatement.html, accessed 19 August 2010].

Health Action International, ed. (1997), *Power, Patents and Pills*, HAI-Europe.

Hegel, Georg W. F. (2001), *Philosophy of Right*, translated by S. W. Dyde, Kitchener, Ontario: Batoche Books. [First published 1820.]

Held, David, and Anthony McGrew (2002), *Globalization/Anti-Globalization*, Cambridge: Polity Press.

Helfer, Laurence R. (2004), 'Regime Shifting: The TRIPs Agreement and New Dynamics of International Intellectual Property Lawmaking', *Yale Journal of International Law* 29(1): 1–83.

Heller, Michael A. (1998), 'The Tragedy of the Anticommons: Property in the Transition from Marx to Markets', *Harvard Law Review* 111(3): 621–88.

Henry v. A.B. Dick Co. (1912), (US Supreme Court) 224 US 1.

Herring, Ronald J. (1990), 'Rethinking the commons', *Agriculture and Human Values* 7: 88–104.

Hess, Charlotte, and Elinor Ostrom (2003), 'Ideas, Artifacts, and Facilities: Information as a Common-Pool Resource', *Law and Contemporary Problems* 66(1&2): 111–46.

Hirsch, Joachim, and Roland Roth (1986), *Das neue Gesicht des Kapitalismus – Vom Fordismus zum Post-Fordismus*, Hamburg: VSA.

Höffner, Eckhard (2010), *Geschichte und Wesen des Urheberrechts*, Munich: Verl. Europ. Wirtschaft.

Holzinger, Katharina (2008), *Transnational Common Goods: Strategic Constellations, Collective Action Problems, and Multi-Level Provision*, New York: Palgrave Macmillan.

Holzinger, Katharina, and Christoph Knill (2005), 'Causes and Conditions of Cross-National Policy Convergence', *Journal of European Public Policy* 12(5): 775–96.

Horns, Axel H. (2010), 'A Unified European Patent System – The Historical Perspective', *IP::JUR* [www.ipjur.com/blog2/index.php?/archives/138-A-Unified-European-Patent-System-The-Historical-Perspective.html, accessed 1 April 2010].

Huang, Ronggui (2010), *RQDA: R-based Qualitative Data Analysis*, R package version 0.1–9 [http://rqda.r-forge.r-project.org/, accessed 23 March 2011].

Hughes, Justin (1988), 'The Philosophy of Intellectual Property', *Georgetown Law Journal* 77: 287–366.

Hunt, Scott A., Robert D. Benford and David A. Snow (1994), 'Identity Fields: Framing Processes and the Social Construction of Movement Identities', in: Joseph R. Gusfield (ed.), *New Social Movements: From Ideology to Identity*, Philadelphia: Temple University Press, p. 368.

Huntington, Samuel P. (1968), *Political Order in Changing Societies*, New Haven: Yale University Press.

Huygen, Annelies et al. (2009), *Ups and downs. Economic and Cultural Effects of File Sharing on Music, Film and Games*, TNO-rapport 34782, Delft: TNO.

Imig, Doug, and Sidney Tarrow, eds. (2001), *Contentious Europeans. Protest and Politics in an Emerging Polity*, Lanham, MD: Rowman & Littlefield.

Ingram, Michael (2005), 'Slyck Interviews The Pirate Bay', *Slyck News* [www.slyck.com/story819_Slyck_Interviews_The_Pirate_Bay, accessed 17 May 2011].

Irish Presidency (2004), 'The Competitiveness Council Priorities Paper' [http://web.archive.org/web/20040513140700/http://www.eu2004.ie/templates/document_file.asp?id=2054, accessed 4 May 2010].

Jaffe, Adam B., and Josh Lerner (2004), *Innovation and Its Discontents: How Our Broken Patent System is Endangering Innovation and Progress, and What to Do About It*, Princeton University Press.

Jasper, James M. (1997), *The Art of Moral Protest. Culture, Biography, and Creativity in Social Movements*, University of Chicago Press.

Jessop, Bob (2001), *Regulation Theory and the Crisis of Capitalism*, Cheltenham, Glos: Edward Elgar.

Johns, Adrian (2002), 'Pop Music Pirate Hunters', *Daedalus* 131(2): 67–77.

Jones, Michael (2004), 'Eldred v. Ashcroft: The Constitutionality of the Copyright Term Extension Act', *Berkeley Technology Law Journal* 19(1): 85.

JURI (2005), *Amendments 40–256 – Draft Recommendation for Second Reading – Patentability of Computer-Implemented Inventions*, AM566052EN.doc, Brussels: EP, Committee on Legal Affairs [www.europarl.europa.eu/meetdocs/2004_2009/documents/pr/565/565497/565497en.pdf, accessed 6 May 2010].

Kapczynski, Amy (2008), 'The Access to Knowledge Mobilization and the New Politics of Intellectual Property', *The Yale Law Journal* 117(5): 804–85.

(2010), 'Access to Knowledge: A Conceptual Genealogy', in: Gaëlle Krikorian and Amy Kapczynski (eds.), *Access to Knowledge in the Age of Intellectual Property*, Cambridge, MA: Zone Books, pp. 17–32.

Katz, Eddan (2010), 'Mapping A2K Advocacy', in: Jeremy Malcolm (ed.), *Access to Knowledge for Consumers. Reports of Campaigns and Research 2008–2010*, Kuala Lumpur: Consumers International, pp. 271–95.

Katz, Eddan, and Gwen Hinze (2009), 'The Impact of the Anti-Counterfeiting Trade Agreement on the Knowledge Economy: The Accountability of the Office of the U.S. Trade Representative for the Creation of IP Enforcement Norms Through Executive Trade Agreements', *The Yale Journal of International Law Online* 31(1): 24–35.

Keck, Margaret E., and Kathryn Sikkink (1998), *Activists Beyond Borders*, Ithaca, NY: Cornell University Press.

Kelle, Udo, Gerald Prein and Katherine Bird (1995), *Computer-Aided Qualitative Data Analysis: Theory, Methods and Practice*, Thousand Oaks, CA: Sage.

Kitschelt, Herbert (1989), *The Logics of Party Formation. Ecological Politics in Belgium and West Germany*, Ithaca, NY: Cornell University Press.

Knoke, David, and Song Yang (2008), *Social Network Analysis*, 2nd edn, Thousand Oaks, CA: Sage.

Koopmans, Ruud (1993), 'The Dynamics of Protest Waves: West Germany, 1965 to 1989', *American Sociological Review* 58(5): 637–58.

(2002), *Codebook for the Analysis of Political Mobilisation and Communication in European Public Spheres* [http://europub.wz-berlin.de/Data/Codebooks%20 questionnaires/D2-1-claims-codebook.pdf, accessed 19 January 2009].

Koopmans, Ruud, and Paul Statham (1999a), 'Ethnic and Civic Conceptions of Nationhood and the Differential Success of the Extreme Right in Germany and Italy', in: Marco Giugni, Doug McAdam and Charles Tilly (eds.), *How Social Movements Matter*, Minneapolis, MN: University of Minnesota Press, pp. 225–51.

(1999b), 'Political Claims Analysis: Integrating Protest Event And Political Discourse Approaches', *Mobilization* 4(2): 203–21.

Koshy, Suresh (1995), 'The Effect of TRIPs on Indian Patent Law: A Pharmaceutical Industry Perspective', *Boston University Journal of Science & Technology Law* 1(4): 9–10.

Krempl, Stefan (2003), 'EU-Rat schiebt Entscheidung zu Softwarepatenten auf', *heise online* [www.heise.de/newsticker/meldung/EU-Rat-schiebt-Ent scheidung-zu-Softwarepatenten-auf-89371.html?view=print, accessed 3 May 2010].

(2009), 'Zehntausende auf Datenschutz-Großdemo in Berlin', *heise online* [www.heise.de/newsticker/meldung/Zehntausende-auf-Datenschutz-Gro ssdemo-in-Berlin-755669.html?view=print, accessed 22 May 2011].

Kriesi, Hanspeter (1995), 'The Political Opportunity Structure of New Social Movements: Its Impact on Their Mobilization', in: J. Craig Jenkins and Bert Klandermans (eds.), *The Politics of Social Protest*, Minneapolis, MN: University of Minnesota Press, pp. 167–98.

(2004), 'Political Context and Opportunity', in: David A. Snow, Sarah A. Soule and Hanspeter Kriesi (eds.), *The Blackwell Companion to Social Movements*, Malden, MA: Blackwell, pp. 67–90.

Kriesi, Hanspeter et al. (1992), 'New Social Movements and Political Opportunities in Western Europe', *European Journal of Political Research* 22(2): 219–44.

Krikorian, Gaëlle (2009), 'The Politics of Patents: Conditions of Implementation of Public Health Policy in Thailand', in: Sebastian Haunss and Kenneth C. Shadlen (eds.), *Politics of Intellectual Property*, Cheltenham, Glos: Edward Elgar Publishing, pp. 29–55.

(2010), 'Access to Knowledge as a Field of Activism', in: Gaëlle Krikorian and Amy Kapczynski (eds.), *Access to Knowledge in the Age of Intellectual Property*, Cambridge, MA: Zone Books, pp. 57–98.

Krikorian, Gaëlle, and Amy Kapczynski, eds. (2010), *Access to Knowledge in the Age of Intellectual Property*, Cambridge, MA: Zone Books.

Krömer, Jan, and Evrim Sen (2006), *No Copy – Die Welt der digitalen Raubkopie*, Leipzig: Tropen.

Kübler, Hans-Dieter (2005), *Mythos Wissensgesellschaft*, Wiesbaden: VS Verlag.

Kumar, Krishan (2005), *From Post-Industrial to Post-Modern Society. New Theories of the Contemporary World*, 2nd edn, Malden, MA: Blackwell.

Laaff, Meike (2010), 'Bundesparteitag der Piraten: Kernis gegen Vollis', *taz.de* [www.taz.de/1/politik/deutschland/artikel/1/kernis-gegen-vollis/, accessed 26 May 2011].

Laclau, Ernesto, and Chantal Mouffe (1985), *Hegemony and Socialist Strategy*, London: Verso Books.

Latrive, Florent, and Laurent Mauriac (2002), 'Tous les candidats dans l'opposition', *Libération*, 12 March 2002.

Laub, Christoph (2006), 'Software Patenting: Legal Standards in Europe and the US in view of Strategic Limitations of the IP Systems', *The Journal of World Intellectual Property* 9(3): 344–72.

Leifeld, Philip (2009), 'Die Untersuchung von Diskursnetzwerken mit dem Discourse Network Analyzer (DNA)', in: Volker Schneider et al. (eds.), *Politiknetzwerke. Modelle, Anwendungen und Visualisierungen*, Opladen: VS Verlag für Sozialwissenschaften, pp. 391–404.

Leifeld, Philip, and Sebastian Haunss (2012), 'Political Discourse Networks and the Conflict over Software Patents in Europe', *European Journal of Political Research* 51(3): 382–409.

Lerner, A. P. (1934), 'The Concept of Monopoly and the Measurement of Monopoly Power', *The Review of Economic Studies* 1(3): 157–75.

Lerner, Josh (2002), *Patent Protection and Innovation Over 150 Years*, National Bureau of Economic Research Working Paper Series No. 8977 [www.nber.org/papers/w8977, accessed 15 May 2011].

Lessig, Lawrence (1999), *Code and Other Laws of Cyberspace*, New York: Basic Books.

(2001), *The Future of Ideas. The Fate of the Commons in a Connected World*, New York: Random House.

(2004), *Free Culture. How Big Media Uses Technology and the Law to Lock Down Culture and Control Creativity*, New York: The Penguin Press.

(2006), *Code. Version 2.0*, New York: Basic Books.

(2008), *Remix. Making Art and Commerce Thrive in the Hybrid Economy*, London: Bloomsbury Academic.

Levy, Steven (2002), 'Lawrence Lessig's Supreme Showdown', *Wired*, 2002 [www.wired.com/wired/archive/10.10/lessig_pr.html, accessed 3 June 2011].

Li, Miaoran (2009), 'The Pirate Party and the Pirate Bay: How the Pirate Bay Influences Sweden and International Copyright Relations', *Pace International Law Review* 21(1): 281–307.

Libbenga, Jan (2006), 'Pirate Bay Resurfaces, while Protesters Walk the Street', *The Register* [www.theregister.co.uk/2006/06/05/pirate_bay_reemerges/print.html, accessed 20 May 2011].

Limpananont, Jiraporn et al. (2009), 'Access to Aids Treatment and Intellectual Property Rights' Protection in Thailand', in: Renata Reis, Veriano Terto Jr and Maria Cristina Pimenta (eds.), *Intellectual Property Rights and Access to ARV Medicines. Civil Society Resistance in the Global South*, Rio de Janeiro: ABIA, pp. 137–63.

LobbyControl (2006), *Lobby Planet. Brüssel das EU-Viertel*, Cologne: LobbyControl.

Locke, John (1690), *Second Treatise of Government*, Project Gutenberg EBook, January 2005.

Love, James, and Tim Hubbard (2009), 'Prizes for Innovation of New Medicines and Vaccines', *Annals of Health Law* 18: 155.

Luhmann, Niklas (1987), *Soziale Systeme. Grundriss einer allgemeinen Theorie*, Frankfurt: Suhrkamp.

Lutterbeck, Bernd, Matthias Bärwolff and Robert A. Gehring, eds. (2008), *Open Source Jahrbuch 2008. Zwischen freier Software und Gesellschaftsmodell*, Berlin: Lehmanns Media.

Lyon, David (1988), *The Information Society. Issues and Illusions*, Worcester: Polity Press.

(1994), *The Electronic Eye: The Rise of Surveillance Society*, Minneapolis, MN: University of Minnesota Press.

Machlup, Fritz (1958), *An Economic Review of the Patent System*, Study No. 15, Washington, DC: Subcommittee on Patents, Trademarks, and Copyrights of the Committee on the Judiciary, US Senate, 85th Congress, 2nd Session, Government Printing Office.

Mara, Kaitlin (2010), 'World Health Assembly Creates New Initiative For R&D Financing', *Intellectual Property Watch* [www.ip-watch.org/weblog/2010/05/21/world-health-assembly-creates-new-initiative-for-rd-financing/print/, accessed 1 December 2010].

Marson, Ingrid (2005), 'Patent Restart Request Ratified', *ZDNet News* [www.zdnet.co.uk/news/regulation/2005/02/17/patent-restart-request-ratified-39188227/print/, accessed 5 May 2010].

Marx, Karl, and Friedrich Engels (1888), *Manifesto of the Communist Party* [www.gutenberg.org/cache/epub/61/pg61.html, accessed 11 March 2011].

Maskus, Keith E. (1998), 'The International Regulation of Intellectual Property', *Weltwirtschaftliches Archiv* 134(2): 186–208.

(2000a), *Intellectual Property Rights in the Global Economy*, Washington, DC: Institute for International Economics.

(2000b), 'Intellectual Property Rights and Economic Development', *Case Western Reserve Journal of International Law* 32(2): 471.

Mattelart, Armand (2003), *The Information Society. An Introduction*, London: Sage.

Matthews, Duncan (2002), *Globalising Intellectual Property: The Trips Agreement*, New York: Routledge.

(2007), 'The Role of International NGOs in the Intellectual Property Policy-Making and Norm-Setting Activities of Multilateral Institutions', *Chicago-Kent Law Review* 82(3): 1,369–86.

Maurer, Stephen M., P. Bernt Hugenholtz and Harlan J. Onsrud (2001), 'Europe's Database Experiment', *Science* 294(5543): 789–90.

May, Christopher (1998), 'Capital, knowledge and ownership: The "information society" and intellectual property', *Information, Communication & Society* 1(3): 246.

(2000), *A Global Political Economy of Intellectual Property Rights. The new enclosure?*, London – New York: Routledge.

(2002), *The Information Society: A Sceptical View*, Cambridge: Polity Press.

(2007), *The World Intellectual Property Organization: Resurgence and the Development Agenda*, London: Routledge.

May, Christopher, and Susan K. Sell (2006), *Intellectual Property Rights: A Critical History*, Boulder, CO: Lynne Rienner.

Mayne, Ruth (2002), 'The Global Campaign on Patents and Access to Medicines: An Oxfam Perspective', in: Peter Drahos and Ruth Mayne (eds.), *Global Intellectual Property Rights. Knowledge, Access, and Development*, Basingstoke: Palgrave, pp. 244–58.

McAdam, Doug (1982), *Political Process and the Development of Black Insurgency 1930–1970*, University of Chicago Press.

——— (1996), 'Conceptual Origins, Current Problems, Future Directions', in: Doug McAdam, John D. McCarthy, and Mayer N. Zald (eds.), *Comparative Perspectives on Social Movements: Political Opportunities, Mobilizing Structures, and Cultural Framings*, Cambridge University Press, pp. 23–40.

——— (2003), 'Beyond Structural Analysis: Toward a More Dynamic Understanding of Social Movements', in: Mario Diani and Doug McAdam (eds.), *Social Movements and Networks*, Oxford University Press, pp. 281–98.

McAdam, Doug, Sidney Tarrow and Charles Tilly (2001), *Dynamics of Contention*, Cambridge University Press.

McCarthy, Arlene (2002), *The Need for a Directive and Issues at Stake. Working Document on the Proposal for a Directive of the European Parliament and of the Council on the Patentability of Computer-Implemented Inventions (COM((2002) 92 – (C5–0082/2002 – 2002/0047(COD))*, PE 316.199/2, Brussels: European Parliament [www.europarl.europa.eu/meetdocs/committees/juri/20020619/471443EN.pdf, accessed 15 April 2010].

——— (2003), *Report on the Proposal for a Directive of the European Parliament and of the Council on the Patentability of Computer-Implemented Inventions (COM(2002) 92 – C5–0082/2002 – 2002/0047(COD))*, PE 327.249, A5–0238/2003, Brussels: European Parliament.

McCarthy, John D., and Mayer N. Zald (1977), 'Resource Mobilization and Social Movements. A Partial Theory', *American Journal of Sociology* 82(6): 1,212–41.

McCoy, David et al. (2009), 'The Bill & Melinda Gates Foundation's grant-making programme for global health', *The Lancet* 373(9675): 1,645–53.

McGreal, Chris (2001), 'Shamed and Humiliated – the Drugs Firms Back Down', *The Guardian*, 19 April 2001 [www.guardian.co.uk/uk/2001/apr/19/highereducation.world/print, accessed 11 October 2010].

Médecins Sans Frontières (2006), *Neither Expeditious, nor a Solution: The WTO August 30th Decision is Unworkable*, Geneva: Médecins Sans Frontières [www.msfaccess.org/fileadmin/user_upload/medinnov_accesspatents/WTOaugustreport.pdf, accessed 19 August 2010].

——— (2007), 'Save the Pharmacy of the Developing World!' [www.msfaccess.org/main/access-patents/introduction-to-access-and-patents/milestones/2007-save-the-pharmacy-of-the-developing-world/, accessed 14 August 2010].

——— (2010), *Untangling the Web of Antiretroviral Price Reductions*, 13th edn (July 2010), Geneva: Médecins Sans Frontières, p. 5 [available at http://utw.msfaccess.org/downloads/11].

Médecins Sans Frontières and Cipla (2001), 'Joint MSF/CIPLA Statement' [http://lists.essential.org/pipermail/ip-health/2001-February/000944.html, accessed 21 October 2010].

Meister, Andre (2011), *Zugangserschwerungsgesetz. Eine Policy-Analyse zum Access-Blocking in Deutschland*, Berlin: Humbold Universität zu Berlin [www.netzpolitik.org/wp-upload/Master-Meister-Zugangserschwerungsg esetz.pdf, accessed 21 May 2011].

Melucci, Alberto (1980), 'The New Social Movements. A Theoretical Approach', *Social Science Information* 19: 199–226.

(1985), 'The Symbolic Challenge of Contemporary Movements', *Social Research* 52(4): 789–816.

(1989), *Nomads of the Present. Social Movements and Individual Needs in Contemporary Society*, London: Hutchinson.

(1995), 'The Process of Collective Identity', in: Hank Johnston and Bert Klandermans (eds.), *Social Movements and Culture*, London: Routledge, pp. 41–64.

(1996), *Challenging Codes. Collective Action in the Information Age*, Cambridge University Press.

Menescal, Andréa Koury (2005), 'Changing WIPO's Ways?', *Journal of World Intellectual Property* 8(6): 761–96.

Mgbeoji, Ikechi (2001), 'Patents and Traditional Knowledge of the Uses of Plants: Is a Communal Patent Regime Part of the Solution to the Scourge of Bio Piracy?', *Indiana Journal of Global Legal Studies* 9(1): 163–86.

(2008), 'Colonial Origins of Intellectual Property Regimes in African States', in: David Armstrong (ed.), *Routledge Handbook of International Law*, Hoboken, NJ: Taylor & Francis, pp. 316–30.

Michel, Jean-Baptiste et al. (2011), 'Quantitative Analysis of Culture Using Millions of Digitized Books', *Science* 331(6014): 176–182.

Miegel, Fredrik, and Tobias Olsson (2008), 'From Pirates to Politicians: The story of the Swedish File Sharers Who Became a Political Party', in: Nico Carpentier et al. (eds.), *Democracy, Journalism and Technology: New Developments in an Enlarged Europe*, Tartu University Press, pp. 203–15.

Mises, Ludwig von (1951), *Socialism*, New Haven, CT: Yale University Press.

Moir, Hazel V. J. (2009), 'Who Benefits? An Empirical Analysis of Australian and US Patent Ownership', in: Sebastian Haunss and Kenneth C. Shadlen (eds.), *Politics of Intellectual Property*, Cheltenham, Glos: Edward Elgar Publishing, pp. 182–210.

Mulgan, Geoff, Omar Salem and Tom Steinberg (2005), *Wide Open. Open Source Methods and Their Future Potential*, London: Demos.

Müller, Florian (2006), *No Lobbyist As Such. The War over Software Patents in the European Union*, Starnberg: SWM Software Marketing.

Munoz Tellez, Viviana (2006), *The Global Campaign on Access to Medicines: Re-Shaping Intellectual Property Rules at the World Trade Organisation*, Briefing Papers of the IP-NGOs project, London: Queen Mary University.

Muzaka, Valbona (2009), 'Developing Countries and the Struggle on the Access to Medicines Front: Victories Won and Lost', *Third World Quarterly* 30(7): 1,343–61.

Nack, Ralph, and Bruno Phélip (2000), 'Report on the Diplomatic Conference for the Revision of the European Patent Convention, Munich, November 20–29, 2000' [https://www.aippi.org/download/reports/ DiplomaticConference.pdf, accessed 7 April 7].

National Institutes of Health (2008), *Revised Policy on Enhancing Public Access to Archived Publications Resulting from NIH-Funded Research*, NOT-OD-08-033.

New, William (2005), 'Agreement Out Of Reach In WIPO Patent Harmonisation Talks', *Intellectual Property Watch* [www.ip-watch.org/weblog/2005/06/03/agreement-out-of-reach-in-wipo-patent-harmonisation-talks/print/, accessed 28 October 2010].

Niedermayer, Oskar (2011), *Parteimitglieder in Deutschland: Version 2011*, Berlin: FU Berlin.

Nisbet, Robert (1970), *Social Change and History: Aspects of the Western Theory of Development*, London: Oxford University Press.

Nokia et al. (2003), 'Re: Proposed Directive on the Patentability of Computer-Implemented Inventions (CIIs)' [http://eupat.ffii.org/news/03/telcos1107/index.en.html, accessed 3 May 2010].

de Nooy, Wouter, Andrej Mrvar and Vladimir Batagelj (2005), *Exploratory Social Network Analysis with Pajek*, Cambridge University Press.

Nordhaus, William D. (1969), *Invention Growth, and Welfare: A Theoretical Treatment of Technological Change*, Cambridge, MA: MIT Press.

Norris, Pippa (2001), *Digital Divide. Civic Engagement, Information Poverty, and the Internet Worldwide*, Cambridge University Press.

Nozick, Robert (1974), *Anarchy, State, and Utopia*, New York: Basic Books.

Nuss, Sabine (2006), *Copyright & Copyriot. Aneignungskonflikte um geistiges Eigentum im informationellen Kapitalismus*, Münster: Westfälisches Dampfboot.

OECD (2008), *Growing Unequal? Income Distribution and Poverty in OECD Countries*, OECD Publishing.

Offe, Claus (1985), 'New Social Movements: Challenging the Boundaries of Institutional politics', *Social Research* 52(4): 817–68.

Okediji, Ruth L. (2003), 'The International Relations of Intellectual Property: Narratives of Developing Country Participation in the Global Intellectual Property System', *Singapore Journal of International & Comparative Law* 7: 315–85.

Olesen, Thomas (2006), '"In the Court of Public Opinion": Transnational Problem Construction in the HIV/AIDS Medicine Access Campaign, 1998–2001', *International Sociology* 21(1): 5–30.

Osborn, June E. (2008), 'The Past, Present, and Future of AIDS', *Journal of the American Medical Association* 300(5): 581–3.

Ostrom, Elinor (1990), *Governing the Commons: The Evolution of Institutions for Collective Action*, Cambridge University Press.

Ostrom, Vincent, and Elinor Ostrom (1977), 'Public Goods and Public Choices', in: E. S. Savas (ed.), *Alternatives for delivering public services: Toward improved performance*, Boulder, CO: Westview Press, pp. 7–49.

Parsons, Talcott (1966), *Societies: Evolutionary and Comparative Perspectives*, Englewood Cliffs, NJ: Prentice-Hall.

Patterson, Lyman Ray (1968), *Copyright in Historical Perspective*, Nashville, TN: Vanderbilt University Press.

Pauwelyn, Joost (2010), 'The Dog that Barked but Didn't Bite: 15 Years of Intellectual Property Disputes at the WTO', *Journal of International Dispute Settlement* 1(2): 389 –429.

PbT Consultants (2001), *The Results of the European Commission Consultation Exercise on the Patentability of Computer Implemented Inventions*, Notts [http://europa.eu.int/comm/internal_market/en/indprop/comp/softana-lyse.pdf, accessed 19 January 2009].

Peterson, Stace (2011), 'YouTube and Creative Commons: Raising the Bar on User Creativity', *YouTube Blog* [http://youtube-global.blogspot. com/2011/06/youtube-and-creative-commons-raising.html, accessed 7 June 2011].

Pfanner, Eric (2009), 'France Approves Wide Crackdown on Net Piracy', *The New York Times*, 23 October 2009 [www.nytimes.com/2009/10/23/ technology/23net.html, accessed 12 July 2011].

Phillips, Jeremy (1982), 'The English Patent as a Reward for Invention: The Importation of an Idea', *The Journal of Legal History* 3(1): 71–9.

Pietras, Jarosław (2004), 'Głosowanie w Sprawie Patentów – Odsłona Druga', *linux.pl* [http://biznes.linux.pl/?id=news&show=1009, accessed 5 May 2010].

Pigou, Arthur C. (1932), *The Economics of Welfare*, 4th edn, London: Macmillan.

Piratenpartei (2010), 'Parteiprogramm', *Piratenwiki* [http://wiki.piratenpartei. de/Parteiprogramm, accessed 26 May 2011].

Piratpartiet (2008), 'Pirate Party Declaration of Principles 3.2' [http://docs. piratpartiet.se/Principles%203.2.pdf, accessed 21 May 2011].

(2010), 'Principprogram version 3.4 [Declaration of Principles 3.4]' [www. piratpartiet.se/principer, accessed 25 May 2011].

Plooij-van Gorsel, Elly (2003), *Opinion of the Committee on Industry, External Trade, Research and Energy for the Committee on Legal Affairs and the Internal Market on the Proposal for a Directive of the European Parliament and of the Council on the Patentability of Computer-Implemented Inventions (COM(2002) 92 – C5–0082/2002 – 2002/0047(COD))*, PE 321.981, Brussels: European Parliament.

Polanvyi, Michael (1944), 'Patent Reform', *The Review of Economic Studies* 11(2): 61–76.

Polletta, Francesca (1998), 'Contending Stories: Narrative in Social Movements', *Qualitative Sociology* 21(4): 419–46.

Popper, Karl (1957), *The Poverty of Historicism*, London: Routledge.

Porat, Marc Uri (1977), *The Information Economy: Definition and Measurement*, Superintendent of Documents, US Government Printing Office, Washington, DC 20402 (Stock No. 003–000–00512–7) [www.eric.ed.gov/ ERICWebPortal/contentdelivery/servlet/ERICServlet?accno=ED142205, accessed February 22 2011].

Pratruangkrai, Petchanet (2009), 'CL "will not be outlawed"', *The Nation*, Bangkok, 6 March 2009 [www.nationmultimedia.com/home/apps/print. php?newsid=30097298, accessed 15 September 2010].

Pugatch, Meir Perez (2004), *The International Political Economy of Intellectual Property Rights*, Cheltenham, Glos: Edward Elgar Publishing.

Raschke, Joachim (1993), *Die Grünen. Wie sie wurden, was sie sind*, Cologne.

Reichman, Jerome H. (2003), 'The TRIPs Agreement Comes of Age: Conflict or Cooperation in the Post-Transitional Phase?', in: Thomas Cottier and Petros C. Mavroidis (eds.), *Intellectual Property: Trade, Competition, and*

Sustainable Development, Ann Arbor, MI: University of Michigan Press, pp. 115–39.

Reis, Renata, Veriano Terto Jr and Maria Cristina Pimenta, eds. (2009), *Intellectual Property Rights and Access to ARV Medicines. Civil Society Resistance in the Global South*, Rio de Janeiro: ABIA.

researchineurope.com (2003), 'An Open Letter to the European Parliament Concerning the Proposed Directive on the Patentability of Computer-Implemented Inventions' [http://www.sussex.ac.uk/units/spru/nprnet/policy/patentdirltr.htm, accessed 15 April 2010].

Reusch, Franz Heinrich (1883), *Der Index der verbotenen Bücher: Ein Beitrag zur Kirchen- und Literaturgeschichte*, Bonn: Verlag von M. Cohen & Sohn.

Ringer, Fritz K. (1980), 'Bildung, Wirtschaft und Gesellschaft in Deutschland 1800–1960', *Geschichte und Gesellschaft. Zeitschrift für historische Sozialwissenschaft* 6(1): 5–35.

Rocard, Michel (2003), *Opinion of the Committee on Culture, Youth, Education, the Media and Sport for the Committee on Legal Affairs and the Internal Market on the Proposal for a Directive of the European Parliament and of the Council on the Patentability of Computer-Implemented Inventions (COM(2002) 92 – C5–0082/2002 – 2002/0047(COD))*, PE 312.545, Brussels: European Parliament.

(2005a), *Draft Recommendation for Second Reading on the Council Common Position for Adopting a Directive of the European Parliament and of the Council on the Patentability of Computer-Implemented Inventions (11979/1/2004 – C6–0058/2005 – 2002/0047(COD))*, PR565497EN.doc, EP, Committee on Legal Affairs [www.europarl.europa.eu/meetdocs/2004_2009/documents/pr/565/565497/565497en.pdf, accessed 6 May 2010].

(2005b), *Amendments 1–17. Draft Recommendation for Second Reading. Patentability of Computer-Implemented Inventions. Compromise Amendment by Michel Rocard*, AM570487EN.doc, Brussels: EP, Committee on Legal Affairs [www.europarl.europa.eu/meetdocs/2004_2009/documents/am/570/570487/570487en.pdf, accessed 18 May 2010].

Rosenau, James N. (2002), 'Governance in a New Global Order', in: David Held and Anthony G. McGrew (eds.), *Governing Globalization. Power, Authority and Global Governance*, Cambridge: Polity Press, pp. 70–86.

Rossini, Carolina, and Kurt Opsahl (2012), 'TPP Creates Legal Incentives For ISPs To Police The Internet. What Is At Risk? Your Rights', *Electronic Frontier Foundation* [https://www.eff.org/deeplinks/2012/08/tpp-creates-liabilities-isps-and-put-your-rights-risk, accessed 27 August 2012].

Rostow, Walt Whitman (1959), 'The Stages of Economic Growth', *The Economic History Review* 12(1): 1–16.

Roth, Roland (1994), *Demokratie von unten. Neue soziale Bewegungen auf dem Wege zur politischen Institution*, Cologne: Bund-Verlag.

Ryan, Michael P. (1998), *Knowledge Diplomacy. Global Competition and the Politics of Intellectual Property*, Washington, DC: Brookings Institution Press.

Sabatier, Paul A., and Cristopher M. Weible (2007), 'The Advocacy Coalition Framework: Innovations and Clarifications', in: Paul A. Sabatier (ed.), *Theories of the Policy Process*, Boulder, CO: Westview Press, pp. 189–220.

Saez, Catherine (2010), 'Drug Access Waiver Debate Looms For June TRIPS Council Meeting', *Intellectual Property Watch* [www.ip-watch.org/weblog/2010/05/31/drug-access-waiver-debate-looms-for-june-trips-council-meeting/print/, accessed 19 August 2010].

Samuelson, Pamela (1994), 'Copyright's Fair Use Doctrine and Digital Data', *Communications of the ACM* 37(1): 21–7.

Samuelson, Paul A. (1954), 'The Pure Theory of Public Expenditure', *The Review of Economics and Statistics* 36(4): 387–9.

Sassen, Saskia, ed. (2002), *Global Networks, Linked Cities*, New York: Routledge.

Saunders, Clare (2007), 'Using Social Network Analysis to Explore Social Movements: A Relational Approach', *Social Movement Studies* 6(3): 227–43.

Saurugger, Sabine (2008), 'Interest Groups and Democracy in the European Union', *West European Politics* 31(6): 1,274–91.

Schaaber, Jörg (2006), *Eine kleine Chronologie. 25 Jahre BUKO Pharma-Kampagne*, Bielefeld: BUKO Pharma-Kampagne.

Schneider, Ingrid (2010), *Das europäische Patentsystem Wandel von Governance durch Parlamente und Zivilgesellschaft*, Frankfurt: Campus-Verl.

Schneider, Volker et al., eds. (2009), *Politiknetzwerke. Modelle, Anwendungen und Visualisierungen*, Opladen: VS Verlag für Sozialwissenschaften.

Schulzki-Haddouti, Christiane (2000), 'Basisvorschlag für Europapatente', *Telepolis* [www.heise.de/tp/r4/artikel/8/8528/1.html, accessed 5 April 2010].

Scotchmer, Suzanne (1991), 'Standing on the Shoulders of Giants: Cumulative Research and the Patent Law', *The Journal of Economic Perspectives* 5(1): 29–41.

Scott, Alan (1996), 'Movements of Modernity: Some Questions of Theory, Method and Interpretation', in: Jon Clark and Mario Diani (eds.), *Alain Touraine*, London: Routledge, pp. 77–91.

Sell, Susan K. (1989), 'Intellectual Property as a Trade Issue: From the Paris Convention to GATT', *Legal Studies Forum* 13(4): 407.

(1995), 'The Origins of a Trade-Based Approach to Intellectual Property Protection', *Science Communication* 17(2): 163–85.

(2002a), 'TRIPS and the Access to Medicines Campaign', *Wisconsin International Law Journal* 20(3): 481–522.

(2002b), 'Intellectual Property Rights', in: David Held and Anthony G. McGrew (eds.), *Governing Globalization. Power, Authority and Global Governance*, Cambridge: Polity Press, pp. 171–88.

(2003), *Private Power, Public Law. The Globalization of Intellectual Property Rights*, Cambridge University Press.

(2008), 'The Global IP Upward Ratchet, Anti-Counterfeiting and Piracy Enforcement Efforts: The State of Play' [www.ip-watch.org/files/SusanSellfinalversion.pdf, accessed 3 July 2008].

(2010a), 'Cat and Mouse: Forum-Shifting in the Battle Over Intellectual Property Enforcement', paper presented at *Transnational Copyright: Organization, Mobilisation and Law*, Villa Vigoni, Lake Como, Italy, 12 June 2010.

(2010b), 'The Rise and Rule of a Trade-Based Strategy: Historical Institutionalism and the International Regulation of Intellectual Property', *Review of International Political Economy* 17(4): 762.

Sell, Susan K., and Christopher May (2001), 'Moments in Law: Contestation and Settlement in the History of Intellectual Property', *Review of International Political Economy* 8(3): 467–500.

Sell, Susan K., and Aseem Prakash (2004), 'Using Ideas Strategically: The Contest Between Business and NGO Networks in Intellectual Property Rights', *International Studies Quarterly* 48(1): 143–75.

Shadlen, Kenneth C. (2009a), 'The Politics of Patents and Drugs in Brazil and Mexico: The Industrial Bases of Health Policies', *Comparative Politics* 42(1): 41–58.

(2009b), 'The Post-TRIPS Politics of Patents in Latin America', in: Sebastian Haunss and Kenneth C. Shadlen (eds.), *Politics of Intellectual Property*, Cheltenham, Glos: Edward Elgar Publishing, pp. 13–28.

Shapiro, Carl (2001), 'Navigating the Patent Thicket: Cross Licenses, Patent Pools, and Standard Setting', *Innovation Policy and the Economy* 1(1): 119–50.

Siegrist, Hannes (2006a), 'Geschichte des geistigen Eigentums und der Urheberrechte. Kulturelle Handlungsrechte in der Moderne', in: Jeanette Hofmann (ed.), *Wissen und Eigentum. Geschichte, Recht und Ökonomie stoffloser Güter*, Bonn: Bundeszentrale für Politische Bildung, pp. 64–80.

(2006b), 'Die Propertisierung von Gesellschaft und Kultur. Konstruktion und Institutionalisierung des Eigentums in der Moderne', *Comparativ. Zeitschrift für Globalgeschichte und Vergleichende Gesellschaftsforschung* 16(5–6): 9–52.

Simitis, Spiros (1984), 'Die informationelle Selbstbestimmung – Grundbedingung einer verfassungskonformen Informationsordnung', *Neue Juristische Wochenschrift* 1984: 398–405.

Singelmann, Joachim (1978), *From Agriculture to Services. The Transformation of Industrial Employment*, Beverly Hills, CA: Sage.

Siwek, Stephen E. (2006), *Copyright Industries in the U.S. Economy: The 2006 Report*, Washington, DC: IIPA [www.iipa.com/pdf/2006_siwek_full.pdf, accessed 4 February 2010].

Smets-Solanes, Jean-Paul, and Benoît Faucon (1999), *Logiciels libres: liberté, égalité, business*, Paris: Edispher.

SNF (2008), *FAQ zu den SNF-Bestimmungen "Open Access & Scientific Publications"* [www.snf.ch/SiteCollectionDocuments/allg_reglement_valorisierung_d.pdf, accessed 6 July 2011].

Snow, David A. (2004), 'Framing Processes, Ideology, and Discursive Fields', in: David A. Snow, Sarah Anne Soule, and Hanspeter Kriesi (eds.), *The Blackwell Companion to Social Movements*, Blackwell Companions to Sociology, Oxford: Blackwell, pp. 380–412.

Snow, David A. et al. (1986), 'Frame Alignment Processes, Micromobilization and Movement Participation', *American Sociological Revue* 51(4): 464–81.

Snow, David A., and Robert D. Benford (1988), 'Ideology, Frame Resonance, and Participant Mobilization', in: Bert Klandermans, Hanspeter Kriesi and Sidney Tarrow (eds.), *From Structure to Action. Comparing Social*

Movement Research Across Cultures, Greenwich, CT: JAI Press, pp. 197–217.

(1992), 'Master Frames and Cycles of Protest', in: Adlon D. Morris and Carol McClurg Mueller (eds.), *Frontiers in Social Movement Theory*, New Haven, CT: Yale University Press, pp. 133–55.

Spencer, Herbert (1893), *Principles of Sociology*, London: William and Norgate.

Stalder, Felix (2011), 'The State of Free Culture, 2011', *Kosmos* Spring-Summer 2011: 50–2.

Stallman, Richard (1999), 'The GNU Operating System and the Free Software Movement', in: Chris DiBona, Sam Ockman and Mark Stone (eds.), *Open Sources: Voices from the Open Source Revolution*, Sebastopol, CA: O'Reilley.

Stehr, Nico (1994a), *Knowledge Societies*, London: Sage.

(1994b), *Arbeit, Eigentum und Wissen. Zur Theorie von Wissensgesellschaften*, Frankfurt: Suhrkamp.

(1999), 'The Future of Social Inequality', *Society* 36(5): 54–9.

(2001), 'Moderne Wissensgesellschaften', *Aus Politik und Zeitgeschichte* B36/2001: 7–14.

(2002), *Knowledge and Economic Conduct*, University of Toronto Press.

(2004), 'Wissensgesellschaften', in: Friedrich Jaeger (ed.), *Handbuch der Kulturwissenschaften*, Stuttgart, Weimar: Metzler, pp. 34–49.

Sztompka, Piotr (1993), *The Sociology of Social Change*, Oxford: Blackwell.

't Hoen, Ellen (2001a), 'German Minister Calls on Industry to Withdraw from SA Case' [www.essentialdrugs.org/edrug/archive/200103/msg00045.php, accessed 1 November 2010].

(2001b), 'The 39 Suing in South Africa (cont)' [www.essentialdrugs.org/edrug/archive/200104/msg00040.php, accessed 27 October 2010].

(2002), 'TRIPS, Pharmaceutical Patents, and Access to Essential Medicines: A Long Way from Seattle to Doha', *Chicago Journal of International Law* 27: 39–67.

(2009), *The Global Politics of Pharmaceutical Monopoly Power. Drug Patents, Access, Innovation and the Application of the WTO Doha Declaration on TRIPS and Public Health*, Diemen: AMB.

TankGirl (2006), 'Larger Parties Bend to Support Filesharing under Political Pressure', *p2pconsortium* [www.p2pconsortium.com/index.php/topic/9496-swedish-net-war-diary/page__st__20__p__79405#entry79405, accessed 21 May 2011].

Tarrow, Sidney (1994), *Power in Movement. Social Movements, Collective Action and Politics*, New York: Cambridge University Press.

Taylor, Verta (1989), 'Social Movement Continuity: The Women's Movement in Abeyance', *American Sociological Review* 54(5): 761–75.

Thambisetty, Sivaramjani (2009), 'Timing, Continuity, and Change in the Patent System', in: Sebastian Haunss and Kenneth C. Shadlen (eds.), *Politics of Intellectual Property*, Cheltenham, Glos: Edward Elgar Publishing, pp. 211–37.

Tilly, Charles (1978), *From Mobilization to Revolution*, Reading, MA: Addison-Wesley.

(1984), *Big Structures, Large Processes, Huge Comparisons*, New York: Russell Sage Foundation.

(1994), 'Social Movements as Historically Specific Clusters of Political Performances', *Berkeley Journal of Sociology* 38: 1–30.

(2004), *Social Movements, 1768–2004*, Boulder, CO: Paradigm.

Titscher, Stefan et al. (2000), *Methods of Text and Discourse Analysis*, London: Sage.

Tönnies, Ferdinand (1926), *Gemeinschaft und Gesellschaft. Grundbegriffe der reinen Soziologie*, 6th and 7th edns, Berlin: R. Curtius.

Touraine, Alain (1968), *Le communisme utopique: le mouvement de mai*, Paris: Éditions du Seuil.

(1972), *Die postindustrielle Gesellschaft*, Frankfurt: Suhrkamp.

(1981), *The Voice and the Eye*, Cambridge University Press.

(1988), *Return of the Actor: Social Theory in Postindustrial Society*, Minneapolis: University of Minnesota Press.

Towse, Ruth, Christian Handke and Paul Stepan (2008), 'The Economics of Copyright Law: A Stocktake of the Literature', *Review of Economic Research on Copyright Issues* 5(1): 1–22.

Troy, Irene, and Raymund Werle (2008), *Uncertainty and the Market for Patents*, MPIfG Working Paper 08/2, Cologne: Max Planck Institute for the Study of Societies [www.mpifg.de/pu/workpap/wp08-2.pdf, accessed 19 January 2009].

Tsai, George (2009), 'Canada's Access to Medicines Regime: Lessons for Compulsory Licensing Schemes under the WTO Doha Declaration', *Virginia Journal of international Law* 49(4): 1,063–97.

Tysver, Daniel A. (2008), 'The History of Software Patents: From Benson and Diehr to State Street and Bilski', *BitLaw* [www.bitlaw.com/software-patent/history.html, accessed 26 January 2009].

UNAIDS (2008), *2008 Report on the Global AIDS Epidemic*, JC1510E, Geneva: UNAIDS [http://data.unaids.org/pub/GlobalReport/2008/JC1510_2008GlobalReport_en.zip].

UNCTAD-ICTSD, ed. (2005), *Resource Book on TRIPS and Development*, Cambridge University Press.

University of the People (2011), 'About Us and How to Get Tuition-Free Online Education' [www.uopeople.org/groups/tuition-free-education, accessed 14 July 2011].

Urry, John (2000), *Sociology Beyond Societies: Mobilities for the Twenty-First Century*, London: Routledge.

US Patent and Trademark Office (2011), *Patenting by Organizations, 2010, Parts A1, B, Granted: 01/01/2010 – 12/31/2010, A Patent Technology Monitoring Team Report* [www.uspto.gov/web/offices/ac/ido/oeip/taf/topo_10.htm, accessed 24 July 2011].

Wallerstein, Immanuel (1991), *Unthinking Social Science. The Limits of Nineteenth-Century Paradigms*, Cambridge: Polity Press.

Webster, Frank (2006), *Theories of the Information Society*, 3rd edn, London: Routledge.

Wikimedia Foundation (2009), 'Wikimedia Community Approves License Migration', *Wikimedia blog* [http://blog.wikimedia.org/2009/05/21/wikimedia-community-approves-license-migration/, accessed 7 June 2011].

Williams, Francis (1999), 'Campaign over Drug Licensing to Grow', *Financial Times*, 29 March 29 1999 [http://lists.essential.org/random-bits/msg00045.html, accessed 19 August 2010].

Wilson, Drew (2010), 'ASCAP Declares War on Free Culture', *ZeroPaid* [www.zeropaid.com/news/89494/ascap-declares-war-on-free-culture/, accessed 8 June 2011].

WIPO (1975), *Report of the World Intellectual Property Organization to the Economic and Social Council of the United Nations at its Fifty-Ninth Session (Analytical Summary for the Year 1974)*, Geneva: WIPO.

(2003a), *Guide on Surveying the Economic Contribution of the Copyright-Based Industries*, Geneva: WIPO.

(2003b), *Intellectual Property – A Power Tool for Economic Growth*, Geneva: WIPO.

World Bank (2012), *World Bank Announces Open Access Policy for Research and Knowledge, Launches Open Knowledge Repository*, Press Release No: 2012/379/EXTOP, World Bank [http://web.worldbank.org/WBSITE/EXTERNAL/NEWS/0,contentMDK:23164491~pagePK:64257043~piPK:437376~theSitePK:4607,00.html, accessed 30 August 2012].

World Health Assembly (1999), *Resolution: Revised Drug Strategy*, World Health Organization [http://apps.who.int/gb/archive/pdf_files/WHA52/ew38.pdf, accessed 17 August 2010].

(2006), *Public Health, Innovation, Essential Health Research and Intellectual Property Rights: Towards a Global Strategy and Plan of Action*, Resolution WHA59.24 of the Fifty-ninth World Health Assembly, Geneva: World Health Organization [www.who.int/phi/Res59_R24-en.pdf, accessed 1 December 2010].

World Health Organization (1998), *Revised Drug Strategy (Draft)*, EB101.R24, World Health Organization.

Wright, Brian Davern (1983), 'The Economics of Invention Incentives: Patents, Prizes, and Research Contracts', *American Economic Review* 73(4): 691–707.

WTO (2001), *Declaration on the TRIPS Agreement and Public Health (Doha Declaration)*, WT/MIN(01)/DEC/2, Doha: World Trade Organization [www.wto.org/english/thewto_e/minist_e/min01_e/mindecl_trips_e.pdf, accessed 19 August 2010].

(2003), 'Decision of the General Council of 30 August 2003: Implementation of Paragraph 6 of the Doha Declaration on the TRIPS Agreement and Public Health' [www.wto.org/english/tratop_e/trips_e/implem_para6_e.htm, accessed 19 August 2010].

(2005), 'Amendment of the TRIPS Agreement' [www.wto.org/english/tratop_e/trips_e/wtl641_e.htm, accessed 19 August 2010].

(2010), 'The WTO in Brief: Part 2' [www.wto.org/english/thewto_e/whatis_e/inbrief_e/inbr02_e.htm, accessed 14 August 2010].

Wullweber, Joscha (2004), *Das grüne Gold der Gene. Globale Konflikte und Biopiraterie*, Münster: Westfälisches Dampfboot.

Yu, Peter K. (2007), 'International Enclosure, the Regime Complex, and Intellectual Property Schizophrenia', *Michigan State Law Review* 2007(1): 1–33.

(2008), 'Access to Medicines, BRICS Alliances, and Collective Action', *American Journal of Law & Medicine* 34: 345.

(2009a), 'A Tale of Two Development Agendas', *Ohio Northern University Law Review* 34: 465–573.

(2009b), 'Building Intellectual Property Coalitions for Development', in: Jeremy de Beer (ed.), *Implementing the World Intellectual Property Organization's Development Agenda*, University of Wilfrid Laurier Press.

Interviews

1. Ellard, David (2006), 'David Ellard, European Commission, interviewed by Sebastian Haunss & Lars Kohlmorgen, Brussels, 5 December 2006, Interview 1, transcript'.
2. Smits, Yolanda (2006), 'Yolanda Smits, International Federation of the Phonographic Industry Europe, interviewed by Sebastian Haunss & Lars Kohlmorgen, Brussels, 5 December 2006, Interview 2, transcript'.
3. Lichtenberger, Eva (2006), 'Eva Lichtenberger, MEP Greens/EFA, interviewed by Sebastian Haunss & Lars Kohlmorgen, Brussels, 5 December 2006, Interview 3, transcript'.
4. Kutterer, Cornelia (2006), 'Cornelia Kutterer, BEUC – Bureau Européen des Unions de Consommateurs, interviewed by Sebastian Haunss & Lars Kohlmorgen, Brussels, 5 December 2006, Interview 4, transcript'.
5. Maebe, Jonas (2006), 'Jonas Maebe, FFII, interviewed by Sebastian Haunss & Lars Kohlmorgen, Brussels, 6 December 2006, Interview 5, transcript'.
6. Zickgraf, Stefan (2006), 'Stefan Zickgraf, UEA-PME, interviewed by Sebastian Haunss & Lars Kohlmorgen, Brussels, 6 December 2006, Interview 6, transcript'.
7. Vandewalle, Laurence (2006), 'Laurence Vandewalle, Greens/EFA, interviewed by Lars Kohlmorgen, Brussels, 6 December 2006, Interview 7, transcript'.
8. Bowles, Sharon (2006), 'Stefan Zickgraf, MEP ALDE, interviewed by Sebastian Haunss & Lars Kohlmorgen, Brussels, 6 December 2006, Interview 8, transcript'.
9. Rocard, Michel (2007), 'Michel Rocard, MEP PSE, interviewed by Sebastian Haunss, Strasbourg, 17 January 2007, Interview 9, transcript'.
10. Kauppi, Piia-Noora (2007), 'Piia-Noora Kauppi, MEP EPP-ED, interviewed by Sebastian Haunss, Strasbourg, 17 January 2007, Interview 10, transcript'.
11. van den Broek, Eline (2007), 'Eline van den Broek, ALDE, interviewed by Sebastian Haunss, Strasbourg, 17 January 2007, Interview 11, transcript'.
12. Harbour, Malcolm (2007), 'Malcolm Harbour, MEP EPP-ED, interviewed by Sebastian Haunss, Strasbourg, 17 January 2007, Interview 12, transcript'.
13. Mann, Erika (2007), 'Erika Mann, MEP PSE, interviewed by Sebastian Haunss, Brussels/Hamburg, 15 February 2007, Interview 13, transcript'.

14. Sommer, Johannes, Guido Hollmann and André Rebentisch (2007), 'Johannes Sommer, Guido Hollmann, André Rebentisch, patentfrei.de, interviewed by Sebastian Haunss & Lars Kohlmorgen, Hamburg, 26 February 2007, Interview 14, transcript'.

15. Henrion, Benjamin (2007), 'Benjamin Henrion, iMatix/FFII, interviewed by Sebastian Haunss & Lars Kohlmorgen, Brussels, 18 April 2007, Interview 15, transcript'.

16. Dietl, Andreas (2007), 'Andreas Dietl, EDRI – European Digital Rights, interviewed by Sebastian Haunss & Lars Kohlmorgen, Brussels, 18 April 2007, Interview 16, transcript'.

17. Mingorance, Francisco (2007), 'Francisco Mingorance, BSA – Business Software Association, interviewed by Sebastian Haunss & Lars Kohlmorgen, Brussels, 20 April 2007, Interview 17, notes'.

18. Thornby, Charlotte (2007), 'Charlotte Thornby, Sun Microsystems, interviewed by Sebastian Haunss & Lars Kohlmorgen, Brussels, 20 April 2007, Interview 18, notes'.

19. Taylor, Fiona, and Tilmann Kupfer (2007), 'Fiona Taylor and Tilmann Kupfer, ETNO – European Telecommunications Network Operators' Association, interviewed by Sebastian Haunss & Lars Kohlmorgen, Brussels, 20 April 2007, Interview 19, transcript'.

20. Körber, Arno (2007), 'Arno Körber, Siemens, interviewed by Lars Kohlmorgen, Munich, 15 June 2007, Interview 20, transcript'.

21. Kolle, Gert (2007), 'Gert Kolle, European Patent Office, interviewed by Lars Kohlmorgen, Munich, 15 June 2007, Interview 21, transcript'.

22. Pilch, Hartmut (2007), 'Hartmut Pilch, FFII, interviewed by Lars Kohlmorgen, Munich, 15 June 2007, Interview 22, transcript'.

23. Lessig, Lawrence (2007), 'Lawrence Lessig, Creative Commons, interviewed by Sigrid Quack & Leonhard Dobusch, Berlin, 30 May 2007, Interview 23, transcript'.

24. Hietanen, Herkko (2007), 'Herkko Hietanen, Creative Commons Finland, interviewed by Leonhard Dobusch, Berlin/Helsinki (via telephone), 8 May 2007, Interview 24, transcript'.

25. Shaver, Lea (2010), 'Lea Shaver, Information Society Project, Yale Law School, interviewed by Sebastian Haunss, New Haven/Konstanz (via telephone), 18 January 2010, Interview 25, transcript'.

26. Latif, Ahmed Abdel (2010), 'Ahmed Abdel Latif, ICTSD – International Centre for Trade and Sustainable Development, interviewed by Sebastian Haunss, New Haven, CT, 12 February 2010, Interview 26, transcript'.

27. Katz, Eddan (2010), 'Eddan Katz, Electronic Frontier Foundation, interviewed by Sebastian Haunss, New Haven, CT, 12 February 2010, Interview 27, transcript'.

28. Wojcicki, Esther (2010), 'Esther Wojcicki, Creative Commons, interviewed by Sebastian Haunss, New Haven, CT, 12 February 2010, Interview 28, transcript'.

29. Love, James (2010), 'James Love, Knowledge Ecology International, interviewed by Sebastian Haunss, New Haven, CT, 13 February 2010, Interview 29, transcript'.

30. Baloch, Irfan, and Esteban Burrone (2010), 'Irfan Baloch and Esteban Burrone, WIPO, interviewed by Sebastian Haunss, Geneva, 20 April 2010, Interview 30, transcript'.

31. von Schoen-Angerer, Tido (2010), 'Tido von Schoen-Angerer, Médecins Sans Frontières, interviewed by Sebastian Haunss, Geneva, 20 April 2010, Interview 31, transcript'.

32. Roffe, Pedro (2010), 'Pedro Roffe, ICTSD – International Centre for Trade and Sustainable Development, interviewed by Sebastian Haunss, Geneva, 21 April 2010, Interview 32, transcript'.

33. Munoz Tellez, Viviana (2010), 'Viviana Munoz Tellez, South Centre, interviewed by Sebastian Haunss, Geneva, 21 April 2010, Interview 33, transcript'.

34. New, William (2010), 'William New, Intellectual Property Watch, interviewed by Sebastian Haunss, Geneva, 21 April 2010, Interview 34, transcript'.

Appendix 1: Documents used for the frame analysis in Chapter 5

International organization documents

Brundtland, Gro Harlem (1999), Speech of the WHO Director-General Dr Gro Harlem Brundtland, in: Germán Velásquez and Pascale Boulet (eds.), *Globalization and Access to Drugs: Implications of the WTO/TRIPS Agreement*, Geneva: World Health Organization, pp. 67–73.

World Health Assembly (1999), *Resolution: Revised Drug Strategy*, World Health Organization [http://apps.who.int/gb/archive/pdf_files/WHA52/ew38.pdf, accessed 17 August 2010].

World Health Organization (1998), *Revised Drug Strategy (Draft)*, World Health Organization, EB101.R24.

WTO (2001), *Declaration on the TRIPS Agreement and Public Health (Doha Declaration)*, Doha: World Trade Organization, WT/MIN(01)/DEC/2 [www.wto.org/english/thewto_e/minist_e/min01_e/mindecl_trips_e.pdf, accessed 19 August 2010].

WTO (2003), 'Decision of the General Council of 30 August 2003: Implementation of Paragraph 6 of the Doha Declaration on the TRIPS Agreement and Public Health' [www.wto.org/english/tratop_e/trips_e/implem_para6_e.htm, accessed 19 August 2010].

National government documents

Africa Group (2001), 'Africa Group Statement on TRIPS, Access to Medicines and Public Health' at the TRIPS Council, issued 20 June 2001 [www.cptech.org/ip/wto/tc/africagroup.html, accessed 5 November 2010].

COM (1998), European Commission (DG1), Note for the Attention of the 113 Committee (Deputies), 5 October 1998. Subject: WTO TRIPS/World Health Organization – Revised Drug Strategy. Meeting of the Ad Hoc Working Group, 13–16 October 1998, Brussels: European Commission, 1/D/3/BW D (98) [http://keionline.org/ node/924, accessed 4 November 2010].

Lamy, Pascal (2004), 'The TRIPs Agreement 10 Years On', Speech of EU Trade Commissioner Pascal Lamy at the International Conference on the 10th Anniversary of the WTO TRIPs Agreement, Brussels, 23 June 2004, [http://europa.eu/ rapid/pressReleasesAction.do?reference=SPEECH/04/327& format=PDF&aged=1 &language=EN&guiLanguage=en, accessed 11 April 2010].

Mandelson, Peter (2007), EC Commissioner Peter Mandelson. Letter to Thai Minister of Commerce Krirk-krai Jirapaet, 10 July 2007 [www.wcl. american.edu/pijip/documents/mandelson07102007.pdf, accessed 15 July 2011].

Prodi, Romano (2003), Speech by Romano Prodi, President of the European Commission, at the Round Table on Access to Medicines, Brussels, 28 April 2003 – Charlemagne Building, SPEECH/03/215, Brussels [http:// europa.eu/rapid/pressReleasesAction.do?reference=SPEECH/03/215& format=HTML&aged=1&language=EN&guiLanguage=en, accessed 4 November 2010].

USTR (2001), US Statement at the TRIPS Council Meeting on 20 June 2001 [http://lists.essential.org/pipermail/pharm-policy/2001-June/001175.html, accessed 5 November 2010].

USTR (2007), *2007 Special 301 Report*, Washington DC: Office of the United States Trade Representative [www.ustr.gov/sites/default/files/asset_ upload_file230_11122.pdf, accessed 15 July 2011].

USTR (2010), Statement of the USTR at the WTO Council for TRIPS Annual Review of the Paragraph 6 System on Wednesday, 27 October 2010, Agenda item F, Annual Review of the Paragraph 6 System, Topic 5 [http://lists. keionline.org/pipermail/a2k_lists.keionline.org/2010-November/000261. html, accessed 4 November 2010].

Industry documents

Adelman, Ken (2007), 'Troubles from Thailand', *Washington Times*, 26 April 2007, Washington DC.

Bale, Harvey E. (1999), 'Globalization: Pharmaceuticals and Vaccines', in: Germán Velásquez and Pascale Boulet (eds.), *Globalization and Access to Drugs: Implications of the WTO/TRIPS Agreement*, Geneva: World Health Organization, pp. 93–7.

Earnshaw, David (1999), 'Access to Medicines: An Urgent Need for Solutions', *WHO Drug Information*, 13(4), 220–2.

Perry, Greg (1999), 'Globalization of Pharmaceuticals – Effects of Trade Agreements on Intellectual Property and Public Health', in: Germán Velásquez and Pascale Boulet (eds.), *Globalization and Access to Drugs: Implications of the WTO/TRIPS Agreement*, Geneva: World Health Organization, pp. 99–105.

PhRMA (2007), 'Compulsory Licensing Trend Dangerous' [www.phrma.org/ node/669, accessed 3 November 2010].

NGO documents

Correa, Carlos (1999), 'Trade Agreements on Intellectual Property and Public Health in Developing Countries', in: Germán Velásquez and Pascale Boulet (eds.), *Globalization and Access to Drugs: Implications of the WTO/ TRIPS Agreement*, Geneva: World Health Organization, pp. 87–8.

Health Action International, Médecins Sans Frontières and Consumer Project on Technology (1999), 'Amsterdam Statement to WTO Member States on Access to Medicine' [www.cptech.org/ip/health/amsterdamstatement. html, accessed 19 August 2010].

Health GAP (2001), 'Medical Apartheid. Patents, Public Health and Access to Medicines, New York: Health GAP' [http://web.archive.org/web/20030820083035 / http://www.globaltreatmentaccess.org/TRIPS. pdf, accessed 29 October 2010].

Ling, Chee Yoke (2006), 'Health Before Patents – At Any Cost', Penang, Malaysia: Third World Network, South North Development Monitor (SUNS) #6154 [www.twnside.org.sg/title2/intellectual_property/health. reports/Healthbeforepatentsatnaycost.1DEc.doc, accessed 5 November 2010].

Mirza, Zafar (1999), 'Globalization and Pharmaceuticals: Implications for Public Health Policy Perspectives', in: Germán Velásquez and Pascale Boulet (eds.), Globalization and Access to Drugs: Implications of the WTO/TRIPS Agreement, Geneva: World Health Organization, pp. 89–92.

Médecins Sans Frontières, Health Action International and Consumer Project on Technology (1999), 'Open Letter to the WTO Member Countries on TRIPS and Access to Health Care Technology' [www. msfaccess.org/resources/key-publications/key-publication-detail/index. html%3ftx_ttnews%5Btt_news%5D=1421&cHash=49b728b24b&no _cache=1&print=1, accessed 11 August 2010].

MSF (2001), Access News no 5, July 2001 [www.msfaccess.org/fileadmin/user_upload/access-news/AccessNews-05.pdf, accessed 15 July 2011].

MSF (2010), Access News no 19, July 2010 [www.msfaccess.org/fileadmin/user_upload/diseases/hiv-aids/FINAL_AccessNews_lo-res.pdf, accessed 15 July 2011].

Oxfam (2006), 'Patents Versus Patients. Five Years After the Doha Declaration', Oxford: Oxfam International, Oxfam Briefing Paper 95 [www.oxfam.org. uk/resources/policy/health/downloads/bp95_patents_gr.pdf, accessed 15 July 2011].

Student Global AIDS Campaign, Health GAP, American Medical Students Association Essential Action, Global AIDS Alliance, Universities Allied for Essential Medicines, Stop HIV/AIDS in India Initiative et al. (2007), 'Abbott Labs Must Stop Attacks on Thai People With AIDS' [www.cptech. org/ip/health/c/thailand/ngos04242007.doc, accessed 3 November 2010].

Third World Network and Oxfam (2001), 'Patents and Medicines: The WTO Must Act Now!' [www.twnside.org.sg/title/joint4.htm, accessed 5 November 2010].

Treatment Action Campaign (2001), 'Treatment Action Campaign Statement: What has Happened to the Bristol-Myers Squibb $1/Day Offer?' [www. cptech.org/ip/ health/sa/tac05082001.html, accessed 5 November 2010].

Index

Lionel Bently, Jennifer Davis and Jane C. Ginsburg
Copyright and Piracy: An Interdisciplinary Critique
978 0 521 19343 6

Megan Richardson and Julian Thomas
Framing Intellectual Property: Legal Constructions of Creativity and Appropriation 1840–1940
978 0 521 76756 9

Dev Gangjee
Relocating the Law of Geographical Indications
978 0 521 19202 6

Andrew Kenyon, Megan Richardson and Ng-Loy Wee-Loon
The Law of Reputation and Brands in the Asia Pacific Region
978 1 107 01772 6

Annabelle Lever
New Frontiers in the Philosophy of Intellectual Property
978 1 107 00931 8

Sigrid Sterckx and Julian Cockbain
Exclusions from Patentability: How the European Patent Office is Eroding Boundaries
978 1 107 00694 2

Sebastian Haunss
Conflicts in the Knowledge Society: The Contentious Politics of Intellectual Property
978 1 107 03642 0